THE CAMBRIDGE COMPANION TO
GÜNTER GRASS

Günter Grass is Germany's best-known and internationally most successful living author, from his first novel *The Tin Drum* to his recent controversial autobiography. He is known for his tireless social and political engagement with the issues that have shaped postwar Germany: the difficult legacy of the Nazi past, the Cold War and the arms race, environmentalism, unification and racism. He was awarded the Nobel Prize for Literature in 1999. This *Companion* offers the widest coverage of Grass's oeuvre across the range of media in which he works, including literature, television and visual arts. Throughout, there is particular emphasis on Grass's literary style, the creative personality which inhabits all his work, and the impact on his reputation of revelations about his early involvement with Nazism. The volume sets out, in a fresh and lively fashion, the fundamentals that students and readers need in order to understand Grass and his individual works.

A complete list of books in the series is at the back of the book.

THE CAMBRIDGE COMPANION TO
GÜNTER GRASS

EDITED BY
STUART TABERNER

CAMBRIDGE
UNIVERSITY PRESS

CAMBRIDGE UNIVERSITY PRESS
Cambridge, New York, Melbourne, Madrid, Cape Town, Singapore, São Paulo, Delhi

Cambridge University Press
The Edinburgh Building, Cambridge CB2 8RU, UK

Published in the United States of America by Cambridge University Press, New York

www.cambridge.org
Information on this title: www.cambridge.org/9780521700191

First published 2009

Printed in the United Kingdom at the University Press, Cambridge

A catalogue record for this publication is available from the British Library

Library of Congress Cataloging-in-Publication Data
The Cambridge companion to Günter Grass / edited by Stuart Taberner.
p. cm.
Includes index.
ISBN 978-0-521-87670-4 (hardback) – ISBN 978-0-521-70019-1 (pbk.)
1. Grass, Günter, 1927– I. Taberner, Stuart. II. Title.

PT2613.R338Z587 2009
838′.91409–dc22

2009012563

ISBN 978-0-521-87670-4 hardback
ISBN 978-0-521-70019-1 paperback

CONTENTS

v

CONTENTS

ILLUSTRATIONS

GÜNTER GRASS'S PROSE WORKS

A number of Grass's prose works are discussed in detail in two or more chapters:

The Tin Drum [1959] (chapters 3, 4, 5, 14)
Cat and Mouse [1961] (chapters 3, 5, 14)
Dog Years [1963] (chapters 3, 5)
Local Anaesthetic [1969] (chapters 3, 5)
The Flounder [1977] (chapters 3, 6)
The Rat [1986] (chapters 8, 14)
The Call of the Toad [1992] (chapters 9, 14)
Too Far Afield [1995] (chapters 3, 9)
Crabwalk [2002] (chapters 3, 5)

Other prose works are discussed in the chapters listed:

From the Diary of a Snail [1972] (chapter 7)
The Meeting at Telgte [1979] (chapter 7)
Headbirths or The Germans Are Dying Out [1980] (chapter 8)
Show Your Tongue [1988] (chapter 8)
Dead Wood: An Epitaph [1990] (chapter 8)
My Century [1999] (chapter 9)
Peeling the Onion [2006] (chapter 10)

CONTRIBUTORS

PETER ARNDS is Professor of Comparative Literature and Literary Translation at Trinity College Dublin and has recently also taught at Kabul University, Afghanistan. His numerous publications on German and comparative literature include books on Wilhelm Raabe, Charles Dickens and Günter Grass. Apart from the many scholarly articles he has published he has contributed to the culture and society pages of the *Frankfurter Allgemeine Zeitung* and is the author of several pieces of prose and poetry. Presently, he is President of the *Society of Contemporary American Literature in German* and is working on a book-length project on the novel of 'mythical realism'.

DAVID BARNETT is Senior Lecturer and Head of Drama at the University of Sussex. His research is concerned with politics, representation and aesthetics in contemporary drama, directing and theatre and focuses on metadrama, political and postdramatic theatre, primarily in the German and English-language traditions. He has written extensively on Heiner Müller and Rainer Werner Fassbinder, and has published articles and essays on Elfriede Jelinek, Werner Schwab, Heiner Goebbels, Howard Barker, Michael Frayn, Brian Friel, Heinar Kipphardt, René Pollesch, Albert Ostermaier, Rainald Goetz, Joseph Goebbels, Urs Widmer, Rolf Hochhuth, Franz Xaver Kroetz, Oliver Czeslik, Falk Richter and Kattrin Röggla. His book *Rainer Werner Fassbinder and the German Theatre* appeared in 2005.

REBECCA BRAUN currently holds a Leverhulme Early Career Fellowship at the School of Cultures, Languages and Area Studies, University of Liverpool. She has published widely on Günter Grass: the monograph *Constructing Authorship in the Work of Günter Grass* (2008), the edited volume (with Frank Brunssen) *Changing the Nation: Günter Grass in International Perspective* (2008), and various articles, including 'The Art of Self-Construction: Günter Grass's Use of Orwell and Camus in *Headbirths or The Germans Are Dying Out*' (2004) and '"Mich in Variationen erzählen": Günter Grass and the Ethics of Autobiography' (2008). A monograph on German authors and the media from 1960 to the present is in preparation.

STEPHEN BROCKMANN is Professor of German at Carnegie Mellon University in Pittsburgh, Pennsylvania. He is the author of *Literature and German Reunification* (1999*), German Literary Culture at the Zero Hour* (2004), and *Nuremberg: The Imaginary Capital* (2006). From 2002–2007 he was the managing editor of the *Brecht Yearbook*. In the autumn term of 2007 he was Visiting Leverhulme Professor at the University of Leeds.

HELEN FINCH is a Lecturer in German at the University of Liverpool. She has published articles on W. G. Sebald and Günter Grass, and is currently working on a monograph comparing the works of W. G. Sebald with those of Peter Handke and Botho Strauß.

FRANK FINLAY is Professor of German at the University of Leeds and currently President of the Conference of University Teachers of German in Great Britain and Ireland. His publications include books and articles on literature, culture and aesthetics in postwar Germany and Austria, with a recent focus on writing since the *Wende*. He is a member of the editorial team nearing completion of the 27-volume *Kölner Ausgabe der Werke Heinrich Bölls* and is joint Director of the Leeds–Swansea Colloquia on Contemporary German-language Literature.

KATHARINA HALL is Lecturer in German at the University of Swansea. She has published widely on contemporary German literature, history and culture, including articles on the work of W. G. Sebald, Bernhard Schlink and Zafer Şenocak. Her monograph, *Günter Grass's 'Danzig Quintet': Explorations in the Memory and History of the Nazi Era from Die Blechtrommel to Im Krebsgang*, and an edited volume, *Esther Dischereit*, appeared in 2007. She is currently the principal investigator on the major research project 'Detecting the Past: Representations of National Socialism in English- and German-language crime fiction, television and film', and is co-editor, with David Basker, of the volume *German Crime Fiction*.

ROGER HILLMAN is Reader in Film Studies and German Studies at the Australian National University, Canberra. Research interests span European cinema, film in relation to music and to history, and Turkish-German authors and directors. Recent publications include *Unsettling Scores: German Film, Music, Ideology* (2005); (co-ed.) *Reading Images, Viewing Texts: Crossdisciplinary Perspectives* (2006); (co-authored) *Transkulturalität: Türkisch-deutsche Konstellationen in Literatur und Film* (2007).

KAREN LEEDER is Professor of Modern German Literature at the University of Oxford and Fellow of New College. She has published widely on modern German literature, especially poetry, and has translated work by a number of German writers into English: most recently: *After Brecht: A Celebration* (2006). An edited volume, *Schaltstelle. Neue deutsche Lyrik im Dialog* appeared in 2007 as did a special edition of *German Life and Letters*: *Flaschenpost: German Poetry and the Long Twentieth Century*. A collection of essays, *The New German Poetry* is due out in 2008 and a volume on poetic lateness is in preparation.

PATRICK O'NEILL is Professor of German at Queen's University at Kingston, Canada. Among his books are *Günter Grass: A Bibliography, 1955–1975* (1976), an edition of *Critical Essays on Günter Grass* (1987), *Günter Grass Revisited* (1999) as well as other books and articles on German, English, and comparative literature and on aspects of narratology and translation studies.

STUART PARKES is Emeritus Professor of German at the University of Sunderland. He has published widely on contemporary German literature, especially Martin Walser. He is the author of *Writers and Politics in West Germany* (1986) and *Understanding Contemporary Germany* (1997), as well as co-editor of a series of seven volumes on contemporary literature.

JULIAN PREECE is Professor of German at Swansea University and author of *The Life and Work of Günter Grass: Literature, History, Politics* (2001, 2nd edn 2004) and *The Rediscovered Writings of Veza Canetti: Out of the Shadows of a Husband* (2007). Also editor and ghost-writer of *Nine Lives: Ethnic Conflict in the Polish–Ukrainian Borderlands* by Waldemar Lotnik (1999) and editor of the *Cambridge Companion to Kafka* (2002). He represents Western Europe on the Advisory Board of the Günter Grass Foundation Bremen and edits (with Frank Finlay) the Leeds–Swansea Series in Contemporary German Literature.

RICHARD E. SCHADE is a Professor of German Studies at the University of Cincinnati. He came to his focus on Grass through research on early modern literary culture, Luther to Lessing, and has published widely on Grimmelshausen and the icono-graphic imagination. He has been the Managing Editor of the *Lessing Yearbook* since 1986. Additionally, he serves as Honorary Consul of Germany, a presidential appointment.

MONIKA SHAFI is the Elias Ahuja Professor of German and the current Director of Women's Studies at the University of Delaware, USA. She is the author of *Utopische Entwürfe in der Literatur von Frauen* (1989), *Gertrud Kolmar: Eine Einführung in das Werk* (1995), *Balancing Acts: Intercultural Encounters in Contemporary German and Austrian Literature* (2001) as well as articles on nineteenth and twentieth century German literature. Most recently, her edition, *Approaches to Teaching Grass's The Tin Drum* was published by the Modern Language Association of America (2008).

STUART TABERNER is Professor of Contemporary German Literature, Culture and Society at the University of Leeds. His most recent monograph *German Literature of the 1990s and Beyond* appeared in 2005 and he is editor of a number of collections, including *Recasting German Identity* (2002, with Frank Finlay), *German Literature in the Age of Globalisation* (2004); *German Culture, Politics and Literature into the Twenty-First Century: Beyond Normalization* (2006, with Paul Cooke) and *Contemporary German Fiction: Writing in the Berlin Republic* (2007).

ACKNOWLEDGMENTS

Without the support of the British Academy, which graciously funded a workshop in Leeds in July 2007 at which many of the contributors were present, this book would have been a less coherent and less ambitious enterprise.

I am especially grateful, of course, to all the contributors to the volume for their hard work and tolerance of my editing. As always, I am indebted to my colleagues at Leeds, and particularly to Professor Frank Finlay and Professor Paul Cooke. Friends as well as colleagues, Frank and Paul have always been willing to discuss, offer advice and provide inspiration. Finally, I would like to express my gratitude to Ali for her forbearance while I was busy at my computer with this book – we now have a new, shared project, and I promise to turn all my energies to that enterprise!

CHRONOLOGY

1927   Born on 16 October in Langfuhr in Danzig (now the Polish city of Gdańsk) to Wilhelm and Helene Grass.

1933   Hitler comes to power. Grass begins primary school.

1935   The Nuremberg laws formalise the Nazis' anti-Semitic measures.

1937   Grass begins secondary school.

1938   German troops move into Austria as the country is incorporated into Hitler's Reich (*Anschluß*). In September, following the Munich conference, the British and French allow Hitler to annex the Sudetenland (the German-speaking region of Czechoslovakia). On 9 November, the Night of the Broken Glass takes place (*Kristallnacht*) during which Jewish premises are burned down.

1939   Hitler invades Poland on 1 September. The first shots are fired in Danzig. On 3 September Britain and France declare war against Germany.

1940   France is invaded and defeated. Much of western Europe has already fallen, or will be defeated soon. British troops are forced to evacuate at Dunkirk.

1941   Hitler invades the Soviet Union, formerly allied with Germany during the joint invasion of Poland in 1939.

1942   Grass leaves school.

1943   Grass joins the Luftwaffe (airforce) auxiliary.

1944   Grass carries out wartime work service (*Arbeitsdienst*) and is subsequently called up into the army. In 2006, he revealed that he had been a member of the 10th SS Panzer Division Frundsberg.

1945	Grass is wounded at Cottbus and subsequently captured by the Americans in hospital in Marienbad (Mariánské Lázně). He is briefly interned as a prisoner-of-war.
1946	Grass works in a mine near Hildesheim where he is introduced to social-democratic politics and attends a rally by the Social Democratic leader Kurt Schuhmacher. He is reunited with his parents and his sister.
1947	Grass starts an apprenticeship as a stone mason in Düsseldorf. The first meeting of what would become the Group 47 is organised by Hans Werner Richter.
1948	The Deutschmark (German mark) is introduced as a new currency into the three western occupation zones in Germany. This solidifies the growing division between the western zones and the Soviet zone. Grass enrols at the Düsseldorf Academy of Art.
1949	The Federal Republic of Germany (West Germany) is founded in May. The German Democratic Republic (East Germany) is founded in the Soviet zone in October.
1951	Grass hitch-hikes around Italy.
1952	Grass meets Anna Schwarz in Switzerland. They are married in 1954.
1953	Grass moves to West Berlin and begins study at the Academy of Fine Arts. He witnesses the uprising in East Berlin against the communist authorities.
1954	Grass's mother dies.
1955	Grass wins third prize in a poetry competition organised by the radio station Süddeutscher Rundfunk. He is invited to attend the Group 47 and reads there. He signs a contract for his work with Luchterhand publishers and has his first art exhibition in Stuttgart.
1956	Grass publishes the poetry collection *The Advantages of Wind-Chickens*. He moves to Paris.
1957	Grass's first play (*Flood*) is performed in Frankfurt. His sons Franz and Raoul are born.
1958	Grass reads from *The Tin Drum* at the Group 47 and is awarded its prize.

1959   *The Tin Drum* is published. The prize awarded by the City of Bremen is subsequently retracted on account of the novel's 'immorality'.

1961   The Berlin Wall is erected, prompting Grass's first public intervention in an open letter to Anna Seghers, the chairwoman of the East German Writers' Union. *Cat and Mouse* is published in October. Grass's daughter Laura is born.

1963   *Dog Years* is published. Grass is elected a member of the Academy of Arts.

1965   Grass's son Bruno is born. Grass speaks at 52 public meetings in support of the Social Democrats during the election campaign. Willy Brandt's SPD loses the election.

1966   Grass's play *The Plebeians Rehearse the Uprising* is staged for the first time. Hansjürgen Pohland's film version of *Cat and Mouse* is released. The Grand Coalition between the CDU (Christian Democrat Union) and the SPD is formed, sparking widespread protests amongst students who believe that there is now no effective parliamentary opposition.

1967   Grass travels to Israel. His collection of poetry *Cross-Examined* is published.

1968   Student protests intensify and Grass is caught up in the debate about the extent to which such extra-parliamentary protest is legitimate. The collection of short stories *Stories, Stories* is published under the pseudonym Artur Knoff (the name of a brother of his mother, who was killed in the First World War).

1969   Grass speaks 94 times in support of the SPD in the election campaign. His *Local Anaesthetic* is published. Willy Brandt becomes Chancellor.

1970   Grass goes to Warsaw with Willy Brandt, where Brandt famously falls to his knees in a gesture of apology to the Polish population and also the murdered Jews of the city.

1972   *From the Diary of a Snail* is published. Grass is separated from his wife Anna and begins a relationship with Veronika Schröter.

1974   Grass leaves the Catholic Church.

1975   Grass travels to India.

1976   Helmut Schmidt becomes Chancellor.

1977   Wave of terrorist kidnappings and murders by the Red Army Faction (*Rote Armee Fraktion*).

1979   Grass publishes *The Meeting at Telgte*. He marries Ute Grunert. Volker Schlöndorff's adaptation of *The Tin Drum* wins the Golden Palm prize at the Cannes film festival and an Oscar for best foreign film. Grass's daughter Nele is born (her mother is Ingrid Krüger).

1980   *Headbirths or The Germans are Dying Out* is published.

1983   Grass becomes President of the Academy of Arts.

1984   The collection of speeches *Learn to Resist* is published.

1986   Grass travels to Calcutta. *The Rat* appears.

1987   Grass's collected works in ten volumes is published, edited by Volker Neuhaus. Helmut Kohl becomes Chancellor.

1988   The multi-media work *Show Your Tongue* is published.

1989   The Berlin Wall is opened on 9 November. Grass speaks out against Kohl's plans for the unification of Germany.

1990   Grass continues to speak out against the prospect of a rapid unification of the two German states. Unification takes place on 3 October. *Dead Wood* appears in October.

1991   Grass's collection of graphic art, *Four Decades. A Report from the Workshop* appears.

1992   Grass publishes *The Call of the Toad*.

1993   *Novemberland* is published.

1995   The novel *Too Far Afield* is published.

1997   Martin Buchhorn's film adaptation of *The Rat* appears.

1998   Gerhard Schröder becomes Chancellor.

1999   Grass's *My Century* is published. He is awarded the Nobel Prize for Literature in September.

2001   *Five Decades. A Report from the Workshop* is published.

2002   *Crabwalk* appears.

2003   The illustrated book of poetry *Last Dances* appears.

2006   Grass reveals in an interview with the *Frankfurter Allgemeine Zeitung* on 12 August that he had served with the Waffen SS from late 1944 to May 1945. The publication of his auto-biographical work *Peeling the Onion* is brought forward.

2007   The collection of poems, *Everyone's Fool*, a response to the media and political furore surrounding Grass's Waffen SS revelation, is published.

2008   The autobiographical prose work *The Box* is published, taking up where *Peeling the Onion* leaves off in 1959.

STUART TABERNER

Introduction

Just as the idea for this volume was being developed for the *Cambridge Companion* series in the summer of 2006 the dramatic news broke that Günter Grass, the internationally renowned, Nobel prize-winning author who was to be its subject, had admitted for the first time in public that he had been a member, aged seventeen, of the Waffen SS, the elite German army organisation notorious for its fanatical obedience to Hitler and its prominent role in Nazi atrocities. In Germany, Grass's critics rushed to denounce what they saw as his hypocrisy (after all, he had long been lecturing his compatriots on the need to confront their past openly), with conservative journalist and newspaper editor Joachim Fest memorably commenting that he would not buy a used car from 'this man', while his supporters leaped to his defence, claiming that his revelation, overdue though it might be, by no means invalidated more than half a century of vigorous campaigning for the embedding of democratic values in the post-fascist Federal Republic, Grass's unrelenting concern with the Nazi period in his literary works as far back as the publication of *The Tin Drum* in 1959, or his untiring agitation for freedom and human rights across the globe. Internationally, Grass's fellow authors mostly stood up for an esteemed colleague, pointing not only to his record of political activism and social engagement on causes ranging from environmentalism and the Third World to racism and social exclusion but also to the breadth of his achievements as a writer, poet, dramatist, artist and essayist.

In truth, it is likely that Grass's disclosure, printed in an interview on 12 August 2006 with the author in the *Frankfurter Allgemeine Zeitung* in advance of the publication of his autobiographical work *Peeling the Onion*, will have little lasting or substantial impact on the way in which his work is read or, indeed, on the way in which the author's lifetime of social, political and cultural intervention as a public intellectual is evaluated. (It is worth noting that not all the contributors to the present volume agree with this prognosis for the impact of Grass's admission on interpretations of his work.) It was already well known that he had been seduced by Nazism as a boy and had wholeheartedly wished for Hitler to emerge victorious. In fact, at least since the early 1960s, Grass had transformed reflection on his own 'biographical failure' into a staple of his essays, speeches and literary texts. More probable is that the 'Grass affair' of 2006 will feature in academic discussion of the culture and society of the post-unification Federal Republic as a moment when conservatives challenged an iconic representative of the country's 'culture of contrition'[1] in the hope of undermining the centrality of repeatedly restated remorse to its presentation of its national identity. Alternatively, it may come to be seen as a moment when it became possible, just as the wartime generation was passing away, and reflecting the way Germans were now speaking differently about the Nazi era, to admit degrees of complicity without inviting immediate condemnation.

Nevertheless, the 'Grass affair' does give us pause for thought in assembling a volume such as this. Above all, we are prompted to reflect, perhaps more than might be customary in a book dedicated to the discussion of the artistic achievements of a contemporary author and written primarily for university undergraduates and graduate students, on the considerable differences of opinion that Grass provokes, and in fact had already always provoked even before his startling revelation. Or, more accurately, we may be prompted to consider the differences in the *parameters* within which literary scholars in particular frame their enquiries and the *criteria* according to which they assess the life and work of the author. Indeed, in the case of a renowned writer such as Grass, who has been exhaustively and authoritatively discussed in secondary literature, it may be that the impetus to explore the different perspectives from which critics approach his work is in any event a welcome development. If the readers to whom this book is addressed find that they recognise the frames of reference which its contributors bring to bear on their topics, they may be more able to generate their own insights or counter-arguments, identifying what the approach used in a given chapter is most suited to bring out – and what it may have missed or overlooked.

This volume, then, does not set out to present a series of essays which are uniform in either approach or in their assessment of Grass's accomplishments – indeed, my previous paragraph presupposes diversity rather than homogeneity. Although the volume as a whole aims to address the breadth of his activities as an artist, writer, poet, dramatist and polemicist, its fifteen chapters exemplify different ways of framing an examination of Günter Grass's life and work and thus offer, to their readers, a choice of perspectives and thereby the possibility of real engagement with the ongoing and ever-mutating project of exploring what Grass *is*.

First and foremost, scholars have tended to relate Grass's artistic activities to his biography. Indeed, this is an approach that the author frequently invites, insofar as he makes specific reference to his own experiences of both National Socialism and the decades which followed the German defeat of 1945 and the establishment of the Federal Republic in 1949 (the autobiographical *Peeling the Onion* does this explictly, of course, as does *My Century*, from 1999, a year-by-year fictionalisation of the period from 1900 in which the author's own life is frequently caught up following his birth in 1927). Thus, many of the chapters in this volume relate Grass's artistic works to his life. This includes his time as a child in Danzig, the Baltic port split off from Germany by the League of Nations after the First World War, before Hitler's invasion of Poland in September 1939, his adolescent enthusiasm for the Nazis, brief service in the German army (as we now know, in the Waffen SS), and his capture by the Americans in hospital in May 1945 in Marienbad (now Mariánské Lázně in the Czech Republic) and detention in the prisoner-of-war camp in Bad Aibling. With regard to the immediate postwar period, reference is frequently made to Grass's apprenticeship as a sculptor and painter at the Düsseldorf Academy of Art and The Academy of Fine Arts in West Berlin, his growing political awareness, travels to Italy, France and Spain, and to his instantaneous and wholly unanticipated fame following the publication of his first novel, *The Tin Drum*, in 1959. Relating to his life since the early 1960s, key biographical strands are identified such as his political campaigning on behalf of the Social Democratic Party (SPD), and particularly its leader Willy Brandt, his disillusionment with party politics in West Germany, interest in environmental issues and the Third World, including travel in India in the mid-1970s and late 1980s, and his outspoken opposition to German unification in 1990 and many interventions in debates in Germany and beyond through to the present day.

This approach, which sees the 'truth value' of Grass's activities as a graphic artist, poet, dramatist, essayist and writer as guaranteed by his 'authentic' life-experience, generally brings with it a positive assessment of his work and foregrounds the importance of Grass as a person. Thus the emphasis is on his energetic and engaged spirit, his commitment to liberal causes, and to democratic principles, and his willingness to 'speak out' (or, to adapt the name of his 1988 mixed-media text *Zunge zeigen*, 'show his tongue') and, to paraphrase the title of his 1991 collection of essays *Gegen die verstreichende Zeit*, to write 'against the passing of time'.

Naturally, this approach has been challenged. On the one hand, to relate an artist's work so directly to his or her life – even, or perhaps especially, at the invitation of the author in question – appears to some scholars, including some in this collection, unduly to limit the range of interpretations that can be derived from aesthetic works to those which are 'authorised' by the artist or reducible to his or her 'real life'. Art, it is argued, is always more than a lens through which we may glimpse the 'truth' of the artist's life or glimpse his or her 'intentions'. Moreover, such a 'biographical reading' might be considered to be overly generous, accepting the 'truth' of what the artist presents as 'lived experience' and endowing perspectives derived from an 'authentic' life-story with a certain, unassailable legitimacy. In *Peeling the Onion*, Grass's fictional self declares that he is writing the book 'because I want to have the last word'.[2] Some may feel that it is important to challenge this desire to frame the public reception of his life and work, all the more so following the revelation that his previous presentation of his biography had been incomplete.

A second approach to Grass, and one which is adopted by several chapters in this volume, is to focus on his work as an artist, dramatist, poet and writer and to evaluate individual texts or artefacts as *aesthetic constructs*. Here, the relationship between Grass's artistic production and his biography assumes a lesser role. Instead, the emphasis is on the range of his endeavours, his varying proficiency in the different media in which he creates (e.g., drawing, drama, poetry, or fiction), and the internal aesthetic structure of individual works and the extent of their success, or otherwise, as works of art. Grass's literary fiction may be examined, therefore, but the focus is just as likely to be on key poems such as 'Kleckerburg' from the 1967 collection *Cross-Examined*, or collections of poems, on individual sketches, etchings, or lithographs, or collections of these, or on dramatic works from an early 'absurd' or 'poetic' phase (the 1950s) or a second, 'political' phase (the 1960s). A case might be made, for example, to counter the oft repeated claim that Grass's only outstanding literary text is *The Tin Drum*, or to argue for his competence as an artist or as a poet when others judge him to be a writer of fiction above all and only a secondary talent in relation to drawing, verse or drama. Alternatively, the emphasis might be on the various German traditions and artists which have shaped Grass's work – German Baroque art and literature, Dürer, the picaresque novel, especially Grimmelshausen's *Simplicius Simplicissimus* (1669), or Fontane, Brecht and Thomas Mann, to name but a few – on his place within the contemporary German literary landscape, or on his dialogue with international influences and non-German authors, for example, 'magical realism' and writers such as Gabriel García Márquez, John Irving or Salman Rushdie, and the manner in which he has come to be seen as part of a 'global literature'.

Very often the focus might be on the different phases in Grass's career. In relation to his literary output, for example, a first phase might be characterised by Grass's interest in the 1950s and 1960s, in the German past and West German politics and by his development of a unique aesthetic style. This would encompass his early indebtedness to expressionism and existentialism (also very marked in his first efforts as a graphic artist), his subsequent development as a Baroque storyteller in the so-called Danzig Trilogy (*The Tin Drum*, 1959; *Cat and Mouse*, 1961; and *Dog Years*, 1963), and his excursion into shorter prose fiction relating to contemporary political campaigns in *Local Anaesthetic* (1969) and *From the Diary of a Snail* (1972). A subsequent phase might be characterised by the extension of his concerns beyond Germany to the effects of world overpopulation, global poverty, the danger of nuclear catastrophe (particularly after the Chernobyl reactor explosion in 1986) and the environment in *Headbirths or The Germans Are Dying Out* (1980), *The Rat* (1986), *Show Your Tongue* (1988), and *Dead Wood: An Epitaph* (1990), with sideways glances at two 'odd' texts, *The Flounder* (1977), dealing, amongst other things, with the 'battle' between the sexes, and *The Meeting at Telgte* (1979), a novella which debates the effectiveness of writing as a form of political intervention using a gathering of writers during the Thirty Years War as a thinly veiled allusion to the postwar West German Group 47. Following this, an argument might be made that Grass enters yet another phase with his 'unification' and 'post-unification' novels *The Call of the Toad* (1992) and *Too Far Afield* (1995), and, most recently, his intervention in debates on 'Germans as victims', *Crabwalk* (2002), and the wartime experience of 'ordinary' Germans in *Peeling the Onion* (2006).

This approach promises a more intensive engagement with the 'aesthetic logic' of individual works, their relationship to one another, and the relationship between, indeed the interconnectedness of, the different media in which Grass works. The emphasis might be on character development, perhaps across a number of works, on the importance of milieu (Danzig, for example), on plot development or thematic concerns – again, often across multiple texts, drawings or artefacts – or on the role of narrators and complex narrative structures (in *Dog Years*, for example, there are three books each with its own narrator). Alternatively, there may be an emphasis on Grass's appearances in his own texts as character, author and public figure (e.g., in *Local Anaesthetic* and *From the Diary of a Snail*, or in *Crabwalk*), or, particularly in relation to his poetry, his drama and his drawings, the varied influences on his work and his position (usually) as an 'outsider' on the German (and international) scene. More broadly, there may be a concern with the way in which Grass's work has been adapted, most obviously in film versions of his literary texts but also by other writers or artists incorporating his innovations into their own aesthetic production.

For some scholars, however, this approach, for all that it usefully focuses attention on issues of aesthetic value, Grass's abilities in different genres and different media, and the thematic and stylistic coherence of his production across these media and over time, may underplay the 'biographical integrity' of his work and thereby its profound engagement with German history, and indeed world history. A focus on aesthetic questions, in fact, may underpin judgments about individual texts as works of art which ignore their social impact, 'representative' nature (e.g. that they 'speak to' readers who recognise aspects of their own biographical experience in Grass's), or their historical significance (e.g. that they were the first to address particular issues or were written as an immediate response to a current debate or political event).

A third approach, implicit in the criticisms levelled against the two approaches outlined above (but not without its own drawbacks, as we shall see), highlights the interconnectedness of Grass's artistic endeavours and his social and political engagement as a 'public intellectual'. Biography is important here to the extent that Grass is held to deploy a narratively constructed version of his own experiences for public consumption in his aesthetic works and his interventions as an essayist, speech-maker and political campaigner. In this approach, however, the 'truth value' of the life-story he presents – whether it is 'authentic' or not – is less important than the use he makes of it to create and sustain his 'public persona', legitimise his interventions, and lend authority and credence to his political positions. Equally, aesthetic matters are important to the extent that particular aesthetic strategies are held to promote Grass's views in this way or that, to frame debates on key social or political principles, or to steer the reader in certain directions. For example, in relation to *Crabwalk* (2002), scholars have argued that the inclusion of the perspectives of three generations of one family re-stages the contest to interpret and memorialise the Nazi past between those who experienced the war directly, those born during the war or just after (i.e. those who would later become the student protesters of '68), and a subsequent cohort less inclined to judge than their '68er' parents and perhaps more susceptible to sentimentalised narratives of 'German victimhood'.

The focus in this approach is very often on the relationship between Grass's narrative fiction – his graphic art, poetry and, to a lesser degree, his drama are largely set to one side – and his essays and speeches. Frequent reference is made to the campaign speeches he made in the 1960s in support of the SPD and to key essays and speeches since that period, for example, on civic values, contemporary issues such as the deployment of American nuclear weapons in West Germany in the 1980s, or the Third World, or against German unification both before and after 1990. In each case, literary texts are read as expounding, or expanding, the ideas that are to be found in Grass's public interventions. *Too Far Afield* (1995), for example, is typically understood as an elaboration of a series of essays the author wrote protesting against the impending 'catastrophe' of unification – given their forebears' responsibility for the Holocaust, he claimed, Germans should never again live in a powerful, unified state – and against the 'colonisation' of East Germany after the incorporation of the former German Democratic Republic (GDR) had taken place in October 1990.

This interest in Grass as a public figure and on the link between his artistic production and his social engagement typically extends to a consideration of his construction as a 'media figure' – a status that he has deliberately exploited, mobilising his public persona 'Fame', as he puts it in *From the Diary of a Snail*[3] and elsewhere – and to Grass's relationship with other writer-intellectuals, particularly those of his own generation such as Martin Walser and Hans Magnus Enzensberger or (from East Germany) Christa Wolf, and his dialogue with them both on major issues of public concern and on the role of the politically engaged writer itself. It also regularly extends to the reception of his work by journalists, social commentators, academics and even Federal Chancellors. Thus the *Verriss* (damning review) of *Too Far Afield* by Marcel Reich-Ranicki, possibly Germany's most influential critic, in the pages of the weekly magazine *Der Spiegel* has been much discussed (not least because of the magazine's cover of 21 August 1995 which featured Reich-Ranicki tearing up Grass's book, a clever play on the word *Zerriss*, meaning to rip to pieces) as a politically motivated attack on Germany's most prominent writer-intellectual. Indeed, *Too Far Afield* was frequently condemned at the time as too pro-GDR, as 'soft' on the repressive state and its security services (the *Stasi*), and as anti-western. For scholars, the public reception of both Grass the public intellectual and Grass's artistic, literary, poetic and dramatic works is a key source for their enquiries into the defining debates of (West) Germany's social and political culture.

Scholars who adopt this approach characteristically (and unsurprisingly) reveal something of their own political engagement with Grass's public persona and artistic work, and indeed of their own background. In the United Kingdom and the United States, an older generation of critics tends to be broadly sympathetic towards Grass's campaigning for greater democracy and greater enlightenment in relation to Germany's Nazi past, admiring his role as 'conscience of the nation' and perhaps envious of the prominence that writer-intellectuals can achieve in Germany. In the Federal Republic, opinions are more divided, between respect for his attempts to encourage Germans to address the Nazi past and frustration at what seems to some to be a naïve reading, even arrogantly so, of the public mood – this was particularly the case in the run up to unification when Grass set himself against the wishes of the majority, as expressed in elections at that time, for a swift incorporation of the GDR into the Federal Republic. Many women scholars (but not only women), alternatively, might be more interested in Grass's presentation of gender politics (for example, in *The Flounder*, from 1977, which ostensibly deals with the struggle between men's destructive urges and women's maternal accomplishments but which many have read as an anti-feminist tract). A younger generation of critics, similarly, might be keen to examine what it sees as Grass's blindspots in relation to masculine identity, different forms of sexuality, or perhaps representations of ethnic minorities.

Such 'political' readings of Grass, of course, run the risk of reducing his artistic endeavours to the content of his essays – much as the emphasis on biography, as we saw earlier, risks framing his output as an artist, writer, poet and dramatist as a simple reflection of his life-story. Grass's essays, moreover, were written as direct interventions in current political issues; his aesthetic texts, it is argued, are surely intended to be more complex and indeed more ambivalent (art is supposed to provoke discussion rather than make a particular case). To attempt to analyse his work in this way appears to some colleagues to do it an injustice – and to miss the point.

All three of the approaches described above are in conversation in this book, reflecting the choices made by the contributors in their assessment of the strengths and weaknesses of different ways of 'reading Grass'. And, of course, many of the chapters collated here combine elements of more than one of these ways of looking at Grass's life and work along with elements of other possible perspectives.

By way of conclusion, it may be appropriate to say a few words about the contributors to this *Cambridge Companion*. The volume builds on more than forty years of commentary on Günter Grass: amongst English-language critics, honourable mentions must be made of Ann L. Mason's *The Skeptical Muse: A Study of Günter Grass's Conception of The Artist* (1974) and John Reddick's *The Danzig Trilogy of Günter Grass* (1975), which did much to galvanise Grass criticism in the United States and United Kingdom; in Germany, the labours of Volker Neuhaus may claim a similar distinction – and contains chapters by many prominent Grass experts writing today on this versatile and complex German artist. In addition, it introduces the work of a younger generation of critical readers of Grass's texts, namely Rebecca Braun, Helen Finch and Katharina Hall, who are helping to keep Grass scholarship fresh and inspiring. It is the ambition of this volume that the conversation between the different chapters contained within it may inspire the next generation of Grass critics – the readers of this book – to make their own contribution to the discussion.

Notes

1. Karl Wilds, 'Identity Creation and the Culture of Contrition: Recasting "Normality" in The Berlin Republic', *German Politics*, 9:1 (2000), 83–102.
2. Günter Grass, *Peeling the Onion* (London: Harvill Secker, 2007), p. 8.
3. Günter Grass, *From the Diary of a Snail*, trans. by Ralph Manheim (New York: Harcourt, 1976), p. 75.

I

JULIAN PREECE

Biography as politics

Günter Grass's memoir of his first thirty years, *Peeling the Onion* (2006), which he published a year short of his eightieth birthday, refocused attention on the autobiographical themes of his first three books, *The Tin Drum* (1959), *Cat and Mouse* (1961), and *Dog Years* (1963), which cover much of the same period and made him famous. Grass suddenly becomes a very autobiographical author when these are put together with his next set of prose fiction, which runs *From the Diary of a Snail* (1972) through to *The Flounder* (1977) and *The Rat* (1986), in which the authorial first person, or 'author function' to cite Rebecca Braun's useful new term (see her chapter in this volume), orchestrates the polyphonic narratives. And in *Local Anaesthetic* (1969), *The Call of the Toad* (1992), and *Too Far Afield* (1995), the central characters are roughly Grass's age at the time of publication (early forties in 1969, around seventy in the 1990s) and have a number of biographical features in common with him – both Starusch and Fonty have guilty wartime secrets, for instance.

Yet it is not until the mid-1990s that autobiographical modes predominate in his literary writing, which follows a trend evident in his public statements from the beginning of the previous decade. The collection of one hundred stories which make up *My Century* (1999), for example, alternate between memoir and fiction in ways which may be seen as emblematic for his entire oeuvre. The result is the story of his historical and cultural identity from the events which have shaped it, whether or not he experienced them first hand. There are distinctions to be made: *Peeling the Onion* is fictive autobiography, whereas most of the other books are forms of autobiographical fiction.

In his early fiction Grass attached some of his own experiences to a series of central characters: Oskar in *The Tin Drum*, Pilenz and Mahlke in *Cat and Mouse*, Liebenau in *Dog Years*, and Starusch alias Störtebeker, who appears in secondary roles in his first two novels before taking the lead in *Local Anaesthetic*. Harry Liebenau turns out to have most in common with

Grass, which is at first surprising because the author of the 'Love Letters' to Tulla Pokriefke, which constitute *Dog Years'* middle section, is the least colourful of the five. Once the war is over, Liebenau becomes a frustrated but opportunistic radio producer who looks back in silent shame at his undistinguished past as a teenage *Mitläufer*, or fellow-traveller. At the same time he makes a living by accusing others, such as the Danzig actor turned SA-man, Walter Matern. Before the war Matern helped beat up his erst-while best friend, the half-Jewish Eddi Amsel, but devotes himself after 1945 to avenging crimes committed by others while keeping quiet about his own. At the same time, he is convinced that his former victim is perse-cuting him. Matern and Amsel were both born in 1917, which makes them a crucial decade older than Grass. Matern is an autobiographical possibility of the type Grass imagined in the narrative essay *Headbirths or The Germans are Dying Out* (1980), in which he sketched out his likely path through the Hitler years had he been born ten years earlier. By the same token Amsel can be seen as a wishful self-projection as artist-victim.

Grass would have been less histrionic than Matern, but a compromised Nazi also-ran, who published his first poems in official outlets and who supported the Nazi cause with enthusiasm: 'The Danzig SS-Home Guard could have counted on my service in the late summer of '39, or at least on the support of my pen.'[1] Anyone surprised to discover that the teenage Grass had been a member of an SS-division will find that his pre-dated life in this autobiographical fantasy sounds rather like that of a non-commissioned SS-officer on the Eastern Front. In the same book he also imagines the biography of the firebrand right-wing politician and Prime Minister of Bavaria, Franz Josef Strauss, who was the bête noire of the West German Left, had it been merged with his own and had Strauss decided to become a writer rather than a politician. In other words, he recognised some of the demon Strauss in himself.

Oskar Matzerath (b.1924), whose disgust at the adult world is so great that he decides to halt his growth on his third birthday, has time to see and do a little more too. But one consequence of his three-year-old shape is that he cannot be held accountable for his misdeeds, such as his betrayals of both his 'putative' fathers, first the Polish Catholic Jan Bronski to the Germans in September 1939, then the German Protestant Alfred Matzerath to the Russians in January 1945. Oskar also took Goebbels' shilling when he joined Bebra's military theatre troupe between 1943 and 1944 to perform before the soldiers in occupied France. He stood by when the nuns on the Normandy beach were shot by German machine gunners on the eve of the Allied invasion. Of course, Oskar does not follow the conventional career path through the various youth and paramilitary organisations which the

Nazi state prescribed for his contemporaries. In some respects this makes him for Grass a wishful retrospective self-projection. He has that supreme freedom from responsibility which artists in different ages have sometimes claimed for themselves (as long as he eludes the euthanasia programme for abnormally shaped individuals). He pursues his own interests, searching for the meaning of life or gratifying his sexual desires, instead of showing a consistently moral interest in the historical events going on around him. At the end he engineers his arrest for a crime that he did not commit because his ill-defined guilt needs a focus. On his thirtieth birthday, after serving two years in prison, he is found to be innocent and released back into the world, where he will have to learn to live with the contradiction of being guilty in the wider sense but innocent of any particular charge. In so many ways so very unusual, Oskar is in this respect both an authorial alter ego and a German Everyman.

Joachim Mahlke (b.1926) was drafted (into a tank division, like Grass) a year before Pilenz and the other boys he hung around with on the half-sunken Polish minesweeper in the summers of 1940 and 1941. This gives him time to win the Knight's Cross by destroying forty Soviet tanks on the retreat from the east, which he does in order to overcome adolescent inhibitions rather than from ideological zeal or commitment to the Fatherland. He then comes to comprehend what his deeds entailed and to recognise the self-serving tales of heroics he had heard at school for the propaganda they were. Pilenz, who recounts Mahlke's story, is caught between not being old enough to have anything of great significance on his conscience (except that he betrayed his friend in his hour of need by not helping him when he deserted from the army) and knowing that he could have taken such an opportunity had one presented itself to him. His behaviour towards Mahlke is an everyday moral failure, all the more horrifying because it was unforced. He expresses his dilemma succinctly when he says about the schoolteacher who was deported to Stutthof concentration camp: 'I hope I didn't testify against him.'[2] With the passage of time and the complete turnaround in circumstances after 1945, the grown-up Pilenz cannot be sure.

For Matern, his one-time schoolfriend, betrayer, and finally narrative employee on the *Dog Years* project, Amsel is simply the 'Other', less an alter ego than the embodiment of all things that Matern is not and which consequently frighten him. Both friends are highly unrealistic, stylised figures, but Amsel, scarecrow-maker, ballet director and capitalist impresario, is a function of Matern's pathological resentment complex. This is why beating him up and leaving him for dead does not get rid of him. It explains how Amsel survives to become a leading figure in the West German postwar Economic Miracle. Amsel is both Jewish and not Jewish. His father made himself into a 'German' by modelling his behaviour on what the Austrian philosopher Otto Weininger had defined as German in the notorious anti-Semitic chapter of *Sex and Character* (1903). Amsel junior is then made into a 'Jew' by his contemporaries who are informed about his father's origins by their parents.

Grass explores the Amsel syndrome further through the humanitarian Hermann Ott 'called Doubt' in *From the Diary of a Snail* who is persecuted as if he were Jewish because he shows compassion and is interested in the arts. The use of this figure was questioned by the German writer W.G. Sebald in an article in the journal *Der Deutschunterricht* in 1983 because concentrating on an unrepresentative 'good German' falsified what happened in the Third Reich. Ott is presented, however, as a figment who never existed. He is an allegory of the sceptical Social Democratic and anti-Nazi spirit which finally triumphs in the other narrative strand of that book which is set in the electoral present of 1969. Ott is more complicated than that, however. Grass combines elements of the biography of the well-known Jewish literary critic Marcel Reich-Ranicki, and particularly of his survival experience in Warsaw during the Nazi Occupation – which he acknowledges in the book – with elements of his own wartime past, which he did not reveal until *Peeling the Onion*. He thus amalgamates Jewish identity with German. Like Ott with Anton Stomma, Reich-Ranicki ingratiated himself with his captor-protector by telling him stories from the German classics (according to Reich-Ranicki's 1999 autobiography *Mein Leben*); like Grass, Ott's locus of survival is a bicycle shop.

Ott spends most of the war years in a cellar, surrounded by bicycle parts. On the retreat from the Red Army in the winter of 1945 Grass briefly found himself with half a dozen fellow SS soldiers in a recently deserted premises in a village in eastern Germany. Looking round them they realised what its civilian function had been until just a few hours previously and the hurried flight of its owners. Having no obvious means of escape, their corporal orders each to grab a bicycle and pedal for his life. Grass is forced to own up to not knowing how to cycle and is ordered to stay put and provide cover. He is convinced that this inability will result in his getting killed. Before he has time to fire a shot in their defence, however, his comrades are mown down in the street. He then flees through the shop's back entrance. His not knowing how to ride a bike thus saved his life. He told the story in public for the first time in 2006 but it had been a staple part of his personal repertoire and private narrative identity for many years before that.

It may seem here to some readers that Grass is equating his German experience of survival and suffering with that of the Jews. But finding productive strategies for interacting with the 'Other' and overcoming binary oppositions is a preoccupation in much of his writing – from the supposed antithesis between Goethe and Rasputin in *The Tin Drum*, masculinity and femininity in *The Flounder*, the 'German' and the 'Jewish' in *Dog Years*, or German and French identity in *Too Far Afield*. Following the fictional biographies in his novels, non-Jewish Germans must incorporate Jewish experience into their own in order to undermine cultural difference, which is always artificial and sometimes destructive. This is precisely what Matern fails to do by the end of *Dog Years*. Grass's personal answer to a problem which fuelled so much of Hitler's hatred is simple, original, and wholly utopian. He expresses it in *The Call of the Toad*, where the future for Gdańsk is a symbiosis of Poles, Germans, Cassubians and the newly arrived Bengalis who have landed on the Baltic coast in the train of the rickshaw champion Mister Chatterjee. In this utopia all races will contribute to a new hybrid society in which differences in identity based on language, skin colour, history or religion will be abolished. Chatterjee is a literary hommage to Grass's beleaguered British-Indian friend Salman Rushdie who had celebrated hybrid identities in novels such as *Midnight's Children* (1980) and *The Satanic Verses* (1988), and incurred the wrath of Islamic fundamentalists for doing so.

Like Rushdie, Grass is of mixed background, part German, part Slav. Members of his family fought in both sides in the First World War: his Uncle Franz, the model for Jan Bronski in *The Tin Drum*, was executed by the Germans for his role in defending Danzig's Polish Post Office at the beginning of the Second World War. Oskar does not know whether his father is the German Matzerath or the Polish/Cassubian Bronski. Fonty in *Too Far Afield* is similarly split between Germany and France, as are Amsel and Ott between Jewish and non-Jewish Germans. In Grass's fiction German and Slav, like German and Jew, and German and French, turn out to be false opposites.

The single most significant moment in Grass's life, which stretched over at least six months and which he will never fully assimilate, was the defeat of Nazi Germany and the ensuing realisation that he had willingly served a criminal, genocidal regime, believing just about every line of its creed which was fed to him. The realisation of his error came about through the American Re-Education programme, a visit his captors forced him to make to the recently dismantled concentration camp at Dachau, and hearing the Nazi Youth Leader Baldur von Schirach's confession at the Nuremberg Trials. The age seventeen is always key for his fictional characters because of the great involuntary change, which reacted with every fibre of his own being over the summer of 1945. In an interview in 1974 he implied that, rather like Oskar, who claimed that he was born with his mental development already behind him, he had no further growing to do after 1945. Reflecting on encroaching middle age, he said:

> I will soon be forty-seven and do not have any particular problems with ageing, which is perhaps on account of my own development, as I was seventeen, eighteen at the end of the war, and obviously in some respects more than others, I reached adulthood fairly early, which means getting older is no longer so decisive for me.[3]

This is a remarkable conceit. Between seventeen and forty-seven life is marked usually by a series of milestones, none of which Grass feels count very much for him.

The main point in public or official perception about being a German male born in 1927 is that you were too young to have become implicated in war crimes and were thus 'unburdened' by your record in the Third Reich. Yet you had experienced the last years of the war as an adolescent who was aware of what was happening around him and you had inculcated Nazi ways of thinking because you had been socialised in the *Jungvolk* (pre-Hitler Youth organisation), the *Hitlerjugend* (Hitler Youth), the *Arbeitsdienst* (compulsory work service) and finally the military, whether that meant the regular army (*Wehrmacht*) or special forces, such as the SS. In Grass's fiction being an adolescent witness is never an entirely passive role anyway. Remaining inactive in the face of injustice can be a form of action, as Pilenz and in particular Liebenau know too well. Had Grass been just two years older, let alone ten as he conjectured in *Headbirths*, then by 1945 his past could have looked very different. He could have been called up in the autumn of 1942 instead of 1944; it is likely his SS division would have been involved in reprisals against civilians, such as the shooting of partisans, or in supplying the human material to the extermination camps in Poland. He would have had every opportunity to be a party to atrocities. He explained to Françoise Giroud in 1987:

> I was a member of the *Hitlerjugend*, at the end – aged only sixteen – there was time for me to become a soldier, and when I was seventeen the war was over. It took a little while for me for the shock to hit me, for me to realise the full extent of the crime that from this point would weigh on all of us. On my generation as well, even though we were lucky enough to be too young to be pulled directly into the criminal events. But I have never claimed that was to my credit, it was just luck. If I had been three or four years older, it could all have looked very different.[4]

This is the knowledge about his past which has haunted him and informed his fiction. It has also determined his understanding of ideological belief systems and his suspicion of 'faith' in a doctrine, whether sacred or secular. Believing entails suspension of the critical faculties. It means not asking questions because a higher authority, in this case the state, takes decisions on the individual's behalf. Grass challenged the traditional German saying that 'calm is the citizen's first duty', which had been first uttered by the commandant of Berlin after the Prussians' defeat at the battle of Jena and Auerstedt in 1806 and which he remembered being taught at school in the 1930s. On the contrary, he argued in his essay 'Über die erste Bürgerpflicht' (On the Citizen's First Duty) of 1967, that it was the citizen's first duty to make a noise, get involved, become informed, and express a view.

Grass's experiences drove him also to make significant public interventions at two turning points in recent German history. The first was the SPD leader Willy Brandt's candidature for the Chancellorship in the 1960s, crowned with success at the third attempt in 1969, which is narrated in *From the Diary of a Snail*. The second was the reunification of the two German states in 1989–1990. Grass initially opposed this on the principle that because the Holocaust had been committed in the name of Germany, no such nation state should be revived. He quickly went over to criticise what amounted to a West German takeover of the communist East, for reasons, he would argue, subsequent developments vindicated. Respect for the lives and achievements of East Germans is the red thread through the speeches and articles he wrote in the early 1990s. This leads directly into his great novel of unification, *Too Far Afield*, which teems with imaginary life stories. For Grass, there has to be a congruence between personal and national history: the unified German state will only be successful if its citizens can project their own experiences on to it and thus feel at ease within it. For this to happen the state has to make compromises too.

Grass began to recount episodes from his life in his speeches once he had established himself as a public figure. The voters in the 1965 federal elections got to know little about the life of the thirty-seven-year-old writer who was touring the country urging them to make use of their democratic freedoms to make a change of what he told them would be historical proportions. He showed no such reticence when it came to discussing the biography of the SPD leader, however, arguing passionately that electing Brandt would begin to correct the mistakes of the Weimar Republic when democracy failed to take hold in Germany. Brandt had demonstrated through his own actions as an anti-Nazi resister how Germans as a whole should and could have behaved. As Chancellor, Brandt would take account of the recent past when making political decisions on behalf of the Federal Republic. Thus in his person he would help determine the shape, character, and identity of their state. This made his biography more than a moral exemplum to the population. For a writer who deals in images it follows that Brandt's most significant action as Chancellor should be his symbolic gesture of kneeling in front of the memorial to the victims of the Warsaw Ghetto, which he made in December 1970 on the first state visit to Poland undertaken by a German head of government since the war.

The first time Grass makes programmatic use of his own life story in an interview is to talk about generation, which is in some respects a more important category than social class in the Federal Republic, in the election month of September 1965:

> Those people born around the same year as me – we were too young to become Nazis and are too old to say the whole period has nothing to do with us.
> . . .
> Our generation is in fact burdened with the task of communicating between the worn-out fifty to sixty year olds and today's twenty-somethings.[5]

Grass's generational role has evolved over the years, but passing on advice that grows out of his being of his generation has remained a priority. In 1965 he wanted to mediate between the two opposing camps, that is, the older generation with its direct experience of the war and the student protesters of the late 1960s, which were getting set for a conflict which would explode with the Baader–Meinhof terrorist campaigns in the 1970s.

Of course, Grass is always guarded about his past in interviews, just as he is schematic about his biography in his speeches. It is characteristic that he should have been at his most candid to the French journalist Nicole Casanova in 1978 when he revealed what he would not say in German for another twenty years: that his mother had been raped by Red Army soldiers when they conquered Danzig. A chapter of the book-length interview was excerpted in *Der Spiegel*; the book itself was hardly unknown in Germany. Yet no mention of this revelation was made until Michael Jürgs's unofficial biography a quarter of a century later. In this way an exemplary biography evolves with the public body, in Grass's case the Federal Republic of Germany, with which it interacts. In 2002 Germans wanted to reflect on the suffering of their wartime generations and were ready to absorb a piece of information which, in previous decades, certain embittered expellees from the lost German territories in the East, such as Danzig/Gdańsk, would have instrumentalised in their attempt to question the postwar German-Polish border.

In November 1966 Grass presented a version of his life in a political speech for the first time. It is directed at an anonymous younger person, perhaps an imaginary self-reincarnation, who 'feels himself tempted to vote for the NPD', the newly founded, Nazi-revivalist German National Party, which enjoyed some electoral success at state level in the second half of the

1960s. Here for a public purpose Grass tells the story that he will repeat in essence so many times over the coming decades:

> I was born in the year 1927 in Danzig. At the age of ten I was a member of the *Jungvolk*, at the age of fourteen I was made a member of the *Hitlerjugend*. As a fifteen-year-old I was called an air-force helper. At sixteen I was a tank-gunner. And at eighteen I was released from captivity as an American prisoner of war. At this point, and not before, I was a grown-up. At this point, or rather, no, slowly as time went by, it became clear to me what they had done to my youth, beneath all the blaring fanfares and drivel about the 'lands of the East'. At this point, and as the years went by to an ever more terrifying extent, I comprehended what unfathomable crimes had been committed in the name of the future of my generation. As a nineteen-year-old I began to sense the nature of the guilt which our people had heaped on itself, and what burden and what responsibility my generation and that which followed it would have to bear on its shoulders. I began to work, to learn, and my suspicion of a middle-class world which was pretending once again that it was quite harmless became sharper. Today, twenty years later, I know that much has been done, that our provisional divided state, the Federal Republic, whatever its faults, nevertheless offers security within a parliamentary democratic framework. But I also know how vulnerable this state is.[6]

Six months later on an historic first visit to Israel, he gave a more condensed account of the same details and over the next four decades whenever he addresses the war and its legacy it is always with reference to his life.[7] In view of the furore which greeted *Peeling the Onion*, the first detail to stand out in the above cited passage is that he does not say he was in the Wehrmacht (he had never said so): the Waffen SS trained its own tank-gunners. He used phrases such as 'I was drafted', 'I joined the military', 'I became a soldier'. Was it his fault if his readers, in their forgetfulness of the circumstances, assumed that he must mean the regular forces? Perhaps. But in the contexts in which he deployed his highly selective biographical data it is of little significance. In 1966 he was still angry about what happened to him, which is evident in the phrase after the second 'at this point' ('Jetzt erst'): an understanding that Nazi rhetoric overlay crimes which made him guilty too and placed a burden of responsibility on him. His constructions are passive: all these things were done to him by adults (which recalls Oskar's relationship with the world around him). Over the years there will be differences of nuance, but words like 'guilt' (*Schuld*), 'crime' (*Verbrechen*), 'responsibility' (*Verantwortung*) recur, as does the resolve to act and see the positive in an imperfect democratic system.

If in the early years Grass created his own opportunities to speak, by the 1980s he was invited for contributions on significant anniversaries of events from 1933–1945. Now what he said effectively had an official status, though he sometimes despaired of the course the Federal Republic was taking, especially after the SPD ceased to be in power in 1982. Fifty years after Hitler's seizure of power on 30 January 1933, he sought to exploit the memory of that event by encouraging 'resistance' to the NATO re-armament programme, which preoccupied much of the Left for the middle part of what Grass called 'Orwell's Decade'.[8] On the fortieth anniversary of the German defeat he is more personal and begins with a recollection of his situation in May 1945 and his experience of the Hitler years as a whole. He then sketches postwar West German history to show how the Federal Republic had to absorb the lessons of the national defeat and accept the consequences, which he himself had already done on his own account.[9] 'I am German culture', Thomas Mann is supposed to have said; 'the Federal Republic should become like me', is what Grass implied for many years. On the fiftieth anniversary of the start of the war, he began with a recollection of what he had been doing on 1 September 1939 in his home city where the first shots of the war were fired. He then reflects on the loss of his *Heimat* and the necessity of accepting that loss.[10]

His Frankfurt Poetics Lecture, 'Writing after Auschwitz', from February 1990, counted necessarily as an indirect comment on the galloping process of reunification, which had steadily gathered momentum since the unex-pected collapse of the Berlin Wall in November the previous year. Grass begins with another sketch of his own situation in May 1945.[11] Again there were national conclusions to be drawn from his personal story. The subject of the lecture (in which writers are invited to discuss what makes them write in the way they do) is about un-learning and re-learning, accepting that the Holocaust took place, that Germans were responsible for it, and about behaving (and writing) differently *as Germans* in the light of that know-ledge. He repeats that he had not at first believed the reports about the concentration camps which he heard as an American POW, taking the stories as anti-German propaganda. He even at first assumed that the evidence at Dachau was faked. His reactions were typical of compatriots of all ages at this time, thus his lesson has general validity.

Grass's first expression of his early experiences in literary form is a poem, which was included in the collection *Ausgefragt* (Cross-examined) in 1969. It is one of his most famous, but in a poem his personality is harder to pin down:

> Born when? Go on, tell us?
> . . .
> That was at the time of the Rentenmark.
> Here, near the Mottlau, which is a tributary,

where Forster bellowed and Hirsch Fajngold said nothing,
here, where I wore out my first pair of shoes
and when I could talk,
I learnt to stutter: sand, dripping wet,
for building castles, until my children's Grail Tower
looked quite Gothic and was washed away.
. . .

Christened inoculated confirmed sent to school
I used to play with shrapnel
And I grew up between
the Holy Ghost and the picture of Hitler
I can still hear the ships' foghorns
half-swallowed sentences, screams into the wind
some church bells, gunfire
and the sound of the Baltic: blubb, piff, pschsch . . .[12]

Through all the words, the conflicts, the verbal and visual fragments in his memory, the contradictory impulses, the stray objects which trigger recollections, the ruins and random surviving scraps of evidence, the sound which the sea makes, which is the same in German as in Polish, is the most constant feature. The poem points once again to the artifical construction of social and cultural identity which can have no more permanence than a sand castle. A poem does not have to have a purpose, as a speech does, but he shows here how the expellees, organised in their still powerful lobby groups, construct a different identity from the same material.

In the 1990s the number of memories and anecdotes increases. In his public exchange of letters with the Japanese novelist Kenzaburō Ōe, he airs the story of the Jehovah's Witness who refused to hold his gun during military training despite pressure first from the officers then his peers.[13] In a speech on comprehensive education he reflected expansively on his teachers, his interrupted schooling, and the role of educators in his work.[14] Autobiographies tend to get written towards the end of the subject's life and these stories lead towards *My Century* and *Peeling the Onion*. As the number of his compatriots who could also remember the period of his childhood dwindled, his responsibility to pass on the fruits of his experience grew. His continued pre-eminence is an indication that the self-understanding of the Federal Republic continues to be based on a reaction to the Hitler years. This is not always to everyone's liking, which accounts for the virulence of the attacks on him in the press, especially in 1995, when *Too Far Afield* appeared to paint a less than happy picture of the reunification years which had just passed, and in 2006, when journalists affected to be shocked by the news that he had been called up to the SS as a sixteen-year-old.

It cannot be a coincidence that two of his best books since *The Tin Drum* generated such negative attention.

It is striking how consistent Grass is with his chosen anecdotes over his complete career. Not all of them happened in the ways that he says, as *Peeling the Onion* makes us remember, and some seem to have a poetic truth which sounds too good to be literarily true, but, while over the years he may elaborate and add details, there are no contradictions. Nearly all the material he draws on both for his fiction and his speeches dates from 1933 to 1945, where the centre of moral gravity of such major novels as *The Flounder* and *Too Far Afield* is also fixed. Beyond an inability to lead an emotionally untroubled life in the aftermath of 1945 on account of what has happened (all his literary characters fail to 'come to terms' with their past), only Oskar's postwar stint as a monumental mason is autobiographically authentic. There are only two anecdotes from the decade after 1945 which seem important. The first is June 1953 when from the western sector of the divided former German capital he witnessed the supression of the workers' uprising in East Berlin and then saw how both sides distorted the events and their causes in order to further their own Cold War agendas. This is the subject of a play (*The Plebeians Rehearse the Uprising*), a chapter in *My Century*, and is mentioned in other statements. It is the origin of his critique of Cold War politics, which reached its crescendo in the 1980s. The other is the currency reform of 1948. These two exemplary episodes from his postwar life are from the period before he was famous, the point at which what he did and what happened to him became more or less public property. The year 1945 is one caesura, and 1959 the other.

Grass has often been fiercely at odds with the governments of the Federal Republic, even after 1969, but its identity is close to his. There are two hiccoughs in this interpretation of recent German history as progress towards increasing democracy through the lens of the life of Günter Grass. An intimate of such left-wing luminaries as Klaus Wagenbach and Ulrike Meinhof, Grass argued with Brandt against forming a Grand Coalition with the Christian Democrats in December 1966 (even though such a step had been implicit in their programme since the decisive Bad Godesberg conference in 1958) because it would result in the Left abandoning not only the SPD but all electoral politics. Grass was right. The result was polarisation, conflict and political failure in the 1970s. The Left did not rediscover parliamentary democracy for nearly fifteen years and the founding of *Die Grünen* (The Greens) who were not prepared to share government until 1998. In the early 1980s at the height of the new arms race it was Grass himself who was out of step when he called on young men to boycott the army and echoed the radical Left in calling for 'resistance' because of the earlier failure to resist Hitler. Here one could say that he was on the wrong side of history. Through his writings and persona since 1990 he has been a nagging reminder of a past that cannot yet be discarded, which has annoyed those who have wanted to move on.

Writers can only enjoy such significance at times of change or crisis or in nations struggling to reassess or assert their identity. During periods of stability in societies more or less at ease with themselves the opportunities to play such symbolically important public roles do not arise. After West Germany had successfully weathered its first decade there was a need for such a figure and he needed to be untainted by his past associations. Grass began in 1961 with a letter of protest against the building of the Berlin Wall, worked for the epochal change of 1969, and came into his own once again in 1989–1990, having rather lost his way in the intervening period. There are many reasons that he became a public figure, but how he managed to retain his position and status for what is now nearly five decades is harder to account for. He was not a very obvious campaigner for the SPD. It was something useful to do with the fame that he had acquired; it was a way to stay in the limelight, to be at the centre of attention, to reach people who did not read his books and to provoke a reaction from them. Politics in West Berlin, where he moved from Paris in 1960, was everywhere and writers were expected to take sides. The loose consortium of West German writers which emerged in the postwar period known as the *Gruppe 47* (Group 47) played an indirect but powerfully political role. Grass did not invent literary 'engagement' but he defined a particular form of it. The scale of his achievement is nevertheless unprecedented and unparalleled.

Notes

1. Günter Grass, *Headbirths or The Germans are Dying Out*, trans. by Ralph Manheim (New York: Fawcett Crest, 1983), pp. 18–19.
2. Günter Grass, *Cat and Mouse*, trans. by Ralph Manheim (Harmondsworth: Penguin, 1966), p. 38.
3. 'Die Verzweiflung arbeitet ohne Netz', interview with Heinz Ludwig Arnold, in Volker Neuhaus (ed.), *Werkausgabe in zehn Bänden*, vol. 10, *Gespräche* (Neuwied: Luchterhand, 1987), pp. 136–71, at p. 144. My translation.
4. Françoise Giroud/Günter Grass, *Wenn wir von Europa sprechen. Ein Dialog* (Frankfurt: Luchterhand, 1989), trans. by Sabine Mann and Ilse Strasmann, p. 172. My translation from the German.
5. 'Manche Freundschaft zerbrach am Ruhm', interview with Günter Grass, in Volker Neuhaus (ed.), *Werkausgabe in zehn Bänden*, vol. 10, *Gespräche* (Neuwied: Luchterhand, 1987), pp. 16–34, at p. 28. My translation.
6. Günter Grass, 'Rede an einen jungen Wähler, der sich versucht fühlt, die NPD zu wählen', in Daniela Hermes (ed.), *Werkausgabe*, vol. 14, *Essays und Reden I* (Göttingen: Steidl, 1997), pp. 182–7, at p. 183. My translation.

7. Günter Grass, 'Rede von der Gewöhnung' (1967), *ibid.*, vol. 14, pp. 220–33, at p. 226.
8. Günter Grass, 'Vom Recht auf Widerstand' (1983), *ibid.*, vol. 16, *Essays und Reden III*, pp. 63–70.
9. Günter Grass, 'Geschenkte Freiheit' (1985), *ibid.*, pp. 140–55.
10. Günter Grass, 'Scham und Schande' (1989), *ibid.*, pp. 217–20.
11. Günter Grass, 'Schreiben nach Auschwitz' (1990), *ibid.*, pp. 235–56.
12. From 'Kleckerburg' (1969), in Volker Neuhaus and Daniela Hermes (eds.), *Werkausgabe*, vol. 1, *Gedichte und Kurzprosa* (Göttingen: Steidl, 1997), pp. 196–9. My translation.
13. Günter Grass, Kenzaburō Ōe, *Gestern vor fünfzig Jahren. Ein Deutsch-japanischer Briefwechsel* (Göttingen: Steidl, 1995), p. 94.
14. Günter Grass, 'Der lernende Lehrer' (1999), in *Werkausgabe* (ed. not named), vol. 20, *Essays und Reden IV 1997–2007*, Göttingen: Steidl, 2007, 40–58.

2

FRANK FINLAY

Günter Grass's political rhetoric

My concern in this chapter is with the rhetoric of Günter Grass's political speeches. I use the term 'political' broadly to characterise orations on matters of public and social interest, particularly where they intersect with moral and ethical concerns. To judge by sheer quantity alone, Grass's speeches and the political activity they represent are an important adjunct to his fictional and poetic work, a view he has endorsed on many occasions while always insisting on their entirely distinct mediations of reality. As a further measure of the importance Grass attaches to politics, he has been willing to sideline his 'creative' writing for lengthy periods, for example in the mid-to-late 1960s and early 1970s, when his electoral campaigning for the Social Democratic Party caused a hiatus in his literary output. Moreover, Grass's speeches are worthy of attention as they document political interventions on a plethora of issues over almost five decades, while the controversies they often provoke have sometimes conditioned the reception of his creative work, as other contributions to this volume demonstrate.

In finding a political platform, Grass, as is widely recognised, was initially assisted by the fame afforded by the meteoric success of *The Tin Drum* (1959), not least as it extended – unusually for a German writer – to the international stage. With the possible exception of his older, fellow German Nobel laureate, Heinrich Böll, he has commanded a public role like no other writer. Moreover, Grass's breakthrough coincided with a pivotal era in postwar West German society and politics, as well as with a new, more expansive phase in the development of the German media which were ever eager to solicit the views of the country's best-known authors.

For the purposes of the present chapter, Grass's political rhetoric has been an important vehicle in his discursive construction both in the media and via his own words and actions as the very model of a 'committed' public intellectual. This has been facilitated by his speeches to the extent that the majority are 'occasional', that is, delivered by invitation within a 'staged' or formalised context, which guarantees them an immediate impact via newspaper syndication and media broadcast. As I shall show at the end of this chapter, the template which Grass has helped to establish was particularly intensively scrutinised at the time of German unification with its viability questioned in what, post-1990, has come to be known as the Berlin Republic.

Speeches 1997–2007

The recently published twentieth volume of the new *Werkausgabe. Essays und Reden IV* (Collected Works. Essays and Speeches IV) covering the decade since 1997 is in many ways typical of Grass's 'non-literary' output.[1] The very brief survey which now follows provides a flavour of the breadth of his concerns during a time when he was otherwise busily working on substantial literary texts, such as *My Century* (1999), *Crabwalk* (2002) and the controversial autobiography *Peeling the Onion* (2006). It is noteworthy that of the volume's thirty-five individual titles, thirty-one are speeches, and while some ruminate on literary matters, including the relationship between literature and history, the dearth of literary representations of German wartime suffering, and warm words in honour of fellow writers such as Adolf Muschg, Christa Wolf, Walter Höllerer, Paul Celan and Ernst Toller, the majority are of a directly 'political' nature.

Grass has long been an outspoken critic of the United States and its record on human rights. In the 1970s and 1980s he had lambasted US intervention in Chile and Nicaragua and aligned himself, along with many other German intellectuals, with the German Peace Movement in protests against the stationing of NATO missiles on German soil, which had raised the spectre of a war at the heart of Europe – with Germany in the front line. Grass made the sophisticated argument that the policy, of which Helmut Schmidt, the SPD Chancellor, had been a prime architect, was a breach of the constitutional principle which permitted only a defensive German military deployment, arguing all the way to the Constitutional Court, where his case was dismissed.

Grass has more recently condemned the 'hybris of hegemony' underlying the US's export of a globalising neo-liberal capitalism (*ERIV*, p. 182). This is greatly at odds with his preferred alternative vision, which had emerged in Willy Brandt's famous commission and report into resolving the disparities between the countries of the less developed 'South' and the industrialised nations of the 'North' (*ERIV*, p. 183). Grass was to witness the multifaceted problems caused by globalisation at first hand on many overseas trips, for example in Calcutta, as documented in *Show your Tongue* (1988). Anxieties about the global impact of industrialised capital, overpopulation and starvation dovetailed with a longstanding concern regarding threats to the environment (deforestation, pollution) and featured also in fictional works such as *The Flounder* (1977) and *The Rat* (1986).

Grass reserves a good deal of recent ire for the foreign policy of American President George W. Bush. In a speech entitled 'Between the Wars' (*ERIV*, pp. 169–71), he charges the US with abusing its untrammelled military might as the world's sole remaining superpower. Thus Bush's post-9/11 'War on Terror', he argues, led to criminal acts of pre-emptive aggression in Afghanistan and, in particular, in Iraq, involving breaches of international law, the undermining of the United Nations, and crass duplicity concerning Saddam Hussein's supposed weapons of mass destruction. However, Grass's pacifism is not knee-jerk. It could be overridden by universalist principles, for example, when he supported the Gulf War of 1991. Similarly, along with many prominent left-leaning German intellectuals such as Peter Schneider, Hans Magnus Enzensberger and Daniel Cohn-Bendit, he advocated NATO's intervention in the Balkan Conflict in the late 1990s (and therefore German involvement in a war for the first time since 1945) to prevent the butchery of Kosovar Albanians by Serbian forces, with, for Grass, its modern-day echoes of the genocide perpetrated by the National Socialists.

Grass's recent speeches demonstrate a concern for many other universal human rights issues, for example in relation to oppressed minorities. In 1997 he established a foundation to improve the lot of the Roma and Sinti (formerly known by the perjorative term 'gypsies') while pointing up their oft overlooked persecution at the hands of the Nazis. Of a piece with such interventions was his condemnation of the tightening of the asylum and immigration laws, which he held partly responsible for fomenting racial intolerance and hatred of the kind manifest in a spate of right-wing attacks against foreigners, some of them fatal, in the early years following unification. Grass reiterated many of these points in a speech to the European Commission in 2000 on behalf of those 'Without Voice' (*ERIV*, pp. 91–97).

In this context another oration is worthy of closer attention, particularly for its provocative rhetorical style and the scandal it duly provoked. Shortly after his seventieth birthday had been fêted in the national media, Grass was invited by Yaşar Kemal, a prominent Turkish-Kurdish author, to deliver the laudation on his award of the Peace Prize of the German book-publishing industry in October 1997 (*ERIV*, pp. 11–22). As with all of Grass's 'occasional' speeches, the immediate context is significant. The award of the Peace Prize (*Friedenspreis*) is one of the most high-profile set-piece events in the German cultural calendar, held on the eve of the Frankfurt Book Fair against the historically symbolic backdrop of the Paulskirche (Church of St. Paul), where a democratisation of Germany had been debated following the revolutions of 1848 – fatefully to little avail. The ceremony is broadcast on television, the award and acceptance speeches widely syndicated in the press, thereby guaranteeing the attention of political and cultural elites, with any controversy likely to appear on the radar of the international media. This was perhaps most notoriously demonstrated one year later when fellow writer Martin Walser unleashed a prolonged debate concerning practices of remembering and commemorating the Holocaust.

Grass begins in measured tones, evoking the democratic spirit of the Paulskirche. He then adumbrates his attack with a brief history lesson. He reminds his audience that the Paulskirche democrats of 1848 were vanquished by Bismarck, the same politician whose support for the Ottoman Empire as a bulwark against Russia had served both countries as a fateful template for their later alliance in the First World War. Having created this historical frame of reference, Grass then turns to a well-informed appreciation of Kemal's literary oeuvre, and of its critique of racial hatred and xenophobia. He skilfully conflates both themes and gives them a peculiar twist in a brief and angry peroration: he condemns present foreign policy on Turkey, declaring 'I am ashamed of my country' because German weapons are enabling the Turks to conduct a 'war of annihilation' against the Kurdish minority. This he then links causally to the latent xenophobia inherent in German nationality laws and the treatment of asylum seekers (*ERIV*, pp. 20–21). The response and uproar in government circles which Grass provoked was prompt, predictable and vituperative, particularly amongst conservative politicians. Such condemnation then elicited supportive statements from fellow intellectuals, ensuring that the hullabaloo remained in the news over a protracted period of time, which, in turn, garnered international attention.

Of particular importance for our discussion is to note the rhetorical strategies Grass deploys with the prime intent of sparking a controversy. Thus the insinuation that Germany's treatment of foreigners is out of step with the democratic traditions embodied in the Paulskirche was sure to touch a raw nerve. As a polemic, his statements are clearly motivated by anger at a specific state of affairs. Grass is aggressive and passionate and eschews logical argumentation, making no attempt to deal with counterclaims. For example, he conveniently skates over the allegedly xenophobic Germany's comparatively favourable record over many years in accepting refugees from a variety of conflicts. Moreover, another rhetorical strategy is deployed when he refers to the Turkish actions against the Kurds as a *Vernichtungskrieg*, that is, a war of annihilation. This is a term frequently used to denote the barbarism of German forces during the invasion of the Soviet Union in 1941. There is a deliberate association of current acts, then, with the crimes of the National Socialists. This verbal hand grenade is designed to goad Grass's targets into a counter-attack, preferably one which would do them little credit, so leaving him safely occupying the moral high-ground. Furthermore, mention of Bismarck imputes an historical teleology and continuity with the period of German imperialism, its aggressive foreign policy which triggered the First World War, and the aberrant *Sonderweg* ('Special Path') which culminated in Hitler and genocide.

Perhaps predictably, Grass is outspoken on the issue of German unification. For example he alights on German–Polish relations in 'On Building Bridges' of July 2001 (*ERIV*, pp. 123–30), in keeping with this native of Danzig's lifelong interest in Poland, which had manifested itself, for example, in the 1980s in support for the Solidarity Movement's opposition to Communist rule. Elsewhere he reminds us that he was an early advocate of a German Confederation in place of a single state (*ERIV*, p. 147), a post-national vision he had initially detailed in 1967 in a speech entitled 'The Communicating Plurality', first published in the high-profile newspaper *Süddeutsche Zeitung*.[2] Here Grass argued that a single German nation cannot exist in the same way as the French, owing to the particular geopolitical realities and, in a rather generalised statement, the 'consequences of a lost war' (*ERBK*, p. 232). For Grass the 'only chance' in upholding a purported cultural unity (he promoted the concept of *Kulturnation*, that is, one based primarily on the shared language and culture of its members, particularly in his 1980 publication *Headbirths*) lay in making a virtue of Germany's long history and traditions of federalism in a confederation of the two German states. Recognition in peace treaties of the finality of the borders occupied by the former East and West Germany would leave the postwar political and military balance undisturbed (*ERBK*, p. 232). Viewed with hindsight what is perhaps most striking about this vision is that in the heady days of 1989/1990, a Conservative Chancellor, Helmut Kohl, was to pay inadvertent homage to it in his hastily formulated 'Ten-Point-Plan' which briefly envisaged a German Confederation before events gathered a momentum beyond the expectations of most politicians and commentators.[3]

In 2002, Grass was guest of honour at a symposium on German unification in Seoul, in the partitioned state of South Korea. Long after his own vision had been swept away by events his address, entitled portentously 'A Lasting Duty', reiterates many of his objections to the unification process, which he dubs the 'annexation' (*Anschluß*) of the East by the West (*ERIV*, p. 203). Again we note the polemical semantic transfer of a term conventionally used in the context of the Third Reich (to refer to Hitler's takeover of Austria in 1938). Grass berates the West German government for the steamroller imposition of a unified currency and the alleged 'plunder' of East German assets by the Trust Agency, which oversaw the privatisation of its state industries. He also charges the Western authorities with a fundamental lack of respect for East German citizens who had suffered forty years of totalitarian rule. Finally, he identifies a concerted attempt by the West German cultural elite to defame all East German writers and intellectuals as collaborators in the regime, with the sole purpose of consigning their works to the dust heap of history (*ERIV*, pp. 154f). This is an allusion to the bitter literary and cultural 'wars' which raged in the early 1990s, in the crossfire of which Grass was also caught and which coalesced around charges of the various degrees of failure of the writers as artists and public intellectuals in both East and West.

Tensions rose when Grass and other left-leaning figures (e.g. Jürgen Habermas, Walter Jens, and East German writers Christa Wolf and Christoph Hein) introduced the Holocaust – in the rhetorical metonym 'Auschwitz' – into the debate. In his high-profile Frankfurt Lecture on Poetics, *Writing after Auschwitz*, in February 1990, to cite but one example, Grass contends that National Socialism, as the apotheosis of an aggressive state nationalism, had perpetrated crimes of such magnitude that Germans had forfeited the right to a united nation-state in perpetuity.[4] This stance drew a well-documented volley of condemnation and opprobrium from nationalist enthusiasts. Moreover, to refuse unification because of an insistence on guilt and atonement was tantamount to moral escapism and ignored that reconciliation in a unified state was the prerequisite for reconciliation with the past and a normalising end to the 'Special Path' of German history.

Having summarised the range of Grass's political concerns as they emerge in speeches of the last decade, placed them in the context of his wider career and identified some characteristic rhetorical strategies, I would now like to examine the extent to which recent and far older orations give us insight into the motivations and aims underpinning Grass's political activities. I will focus on how Grass seeks to discursively construct and justify himself as a politically committed literary intellectual.

'Taking Sides'

In April 1998, Grass was awarded the prestigious Fritz Bauer Prize by the 'Humanistische Union', Germany's oldest human and civil rights organisation on the grounds that, in the words of the ceremonial speech of dedication, he had consistently 'broken out of the ivory tower and intervened in politics'. The Prize had been inaugurated in 1968 in honour of, and named after, the organisation's founder, a campaigning lawyer who was persecuted by the National Socialists and went into exile in Sweden, where he met Willy Brandt. On returning to West Germany in 1949, Bauer had fought tirelessly to bring perpetrators of the Holocaust to justice, most notably as Advocate General of the federal state of Hesse where the Frankfurt 'Auschwitz Trials' took place between 1963 and 1965. Grass's acceptance speech, 'Between the Stools' was first published in the review section of *Die Zeit* (19/1998) under the headline 'Was heißt heute Engagement?' (what is political engagement today?), arguably chosen by the editor to set it in a wider context of debate on the political 'commitment' of intellectuals.

Grass exploits the customary expectations of the acceptance speech genre to account for his own political activities. His taciturn portrait of Bauer paints the latter primarily as a 'loner', compelled to work in a post-fascist legal system which had been morally compromised, as with other areas of public life, by the political amnesty, social and professional reintegration of former Nazis. The remaining two-thirds of the speech are an expressly unapologetic defence by Grass of his position. Grass claims Bauer as a kindred spirit when he bemoans his own isolation; he is a 'one-man political party', unsupported by fellow intellectuals, forever caught as a writer between various camps. The earlier acknowledgment of Bauer's battles for justice within a morally evasive and vacillating 'establishment' imputes a common cause and also evokes an heroic period for the old West Germany – and by implication Grass's singular role in it – which ushered in a decade of radical change and further democratisation. Mention of the Frankfurt Trials puts Grass squarely in the ranks of those who sought a more open and honest engagement with the legacy of National Socialism. The early 1960s also saw government ministers threaten the rule of law in heavy-handed breaches of civil liberties, which raised anxieties about a recrudescent police state, subsequently exacerbated by fears concerning ill-conceived legislation on Emergency Powers. The general climate was not helped when 'oppositional' literary works were vilified by government ministers in the language of National Socialist propaganda, with the prominent but wholly informal association of writers Group 47 notoriously pilloried as a secret reincarnation of the Reichsschrifttumskammer, the body which had regulated literature in Nazi Germany. The collaboration of all the major political parties in a Grand Coalition (1966–1969) under Chancellor Kiesinger, a former Nazi, with only the tiny Liberal FDP as the party of opposition, mobilised an 'Extra-parliamentary Opposition' (APO) whose strong base with students and younger intellectuals was galvanised by an international counter-cultural movement ready to take to the barricades to protest, for example, against American 'imperialism' in Vietnam. For the APO, Social Democrats and their leftist intellectual supporters had 'sold out' and the consistently implacable anti-communist Grass became something of a hate figure.

Grass's well-documented association with the Social Democratic Party (SPD), which was often fraught and varied in intensity over time, has endured albeit in much reduced form to the present day, with the writer campaigning on the party's behalf at the most recent federal elections in 2005. It was at its most intense when Willy Brandt was party leader, shadowing the latter's rise to power in 1969, his re-election in 1971, and his untimely resignation from the Chancellorship in 1974. In Brandt, Grass saw personified a principled resistance to the Nazi regime, as well as a social democracy which took its legitimacy from an understanding of the special responsibility which the legacy of fascism required of Germany. Moreover, Brandt's pragmatic commitment to peace and reconciliation within the parameters and geopolitical borders of the postwar settlement, to be achieved by incremental negotiation, appeared to offer a realistic way forward. In a movingly personal speech on the tenth anniversary of Brandt's death in October 2002 (*ERIV*, pp. 160–68), Grass pinpoints an additional, more personal reason for answering the SPD's call to arms; the vitriolic campaign of defamation and denunciation to which Brandt, sneeringly denigrated as a socialist emigré and illegitimate, had been subjected by conservative politicians during the federal elections of 1961. Grass's words are worth quoting in full, as they summarise neatly the distinction he makes between his literary career and political activity as a concerned citizen. It was the attempted assassination of Brandt's character which compelled him 'as a writer to follow my civic duty and to speak out loudly and clearly' on the slandered politician's behalf; 'I screwed the top back on my ink pot, left my high desk and took sides' (*ERIV*, p. 162).

A number of scholars have provided the background and plotted the trajectory of Grass's 'taking sides' for the SPD from its lowly beginnings in a contribution to a book of a rather lukewarm supportive statements edited by Martin Walser in 1961, via Brandt's breakthrough and consolidation of power. Grass was one of a number of intellectuals who were presented in the media as part of Brandt's inner circle, with the high water-mark reached during the *Ostpolitik* of the early 1970s, a diplomatic and policy initiative to normalise East–West relations when the mutual use of force for settling old scores and territorial claims was renounced in a series of treaties with the satellite states of the Soviet Union. Grass was frequently both companion and proselytiser, being present, with fellow writer Siegfried Lenz, at arguably the most moving spectacle of reconciliation: Brandt's visit to Poland where he genuflected before the monument to the Jews murdered by Germans during the Warsaw Ghetto uprising of 1943, an episode which makes up a chapter devoted to 1970 in *My Century* (1999). One year later, Brandt was awarded the Nobel Peace Prize. Following the private turmoil of a collapsing marriage, the precipitate resignation of his political mentor in 1974, and disenchantment with the arch-pragmatism of his successor, Helmut Schmidt, Grass scaled back his work for the SPD significantly to concentrate on his creative fiction. His joining the party after the demise of the Social–Liberal Coalition of 1983 was merely a public gesture of solidarity, which was to prove short-lived when he quit in protest against its policy on asylum seekers and curbing of civil liberties in 1992.

The 'literary' in Grass's rhetoric

I should now like to consider the five different speeches Grass composed and presented in his first foray into electioneering in the campaign for the SPD of 1965. As one would expect in terms of content, there are many points of repetition and they are easily summarised and perhaps best regarded as variations on one basic theme: the promotion and justification of a change of government and the election of an SPD government with Willy Brandt at its head. Grass's catalogue of issues includes the urgent need to reform the very fabric of West German society via a massive infusion of resources to outmoded education, transport and health systems, including one particular hobby-horse, the controversial overhaul of legislation on abortion. To the modern reader with memories of Grass's oppositional stance to unification in mind, his statements on the German Question reveal a striking degree of consistency with the stance he later adopted after the seismic 'turning point' of 1989/90.

Why should this particular set of speeches merit our attention? They are, after all, seemingly ephemeral documents of a bygone political age, geared purely to the capture of votes. They reward re-reading for a number of reasons; the orations emanate from a time when Grass was, for possibly the last time, relatively unknown as a political activist and, in seeking to both win over a sceptical public from beyond the SPD's core support and justify his own 'taking sides', they presented him with a particular set of rhetorical challenges which, as I shall now demonstrate, he was able to master via the deployment of a number of *literary* techniques.

What is immediately striking from a rhetorical point of view is the way Grass situates himself for his immediate audience. As a non card-carrying SPD supporter he had no need to be 'on message' in terms of the party's manifesto commitments. Nor did censorious party apparatchiks have any control over his tour or the content of his speeches. This allows him to trumpet his independent credentials, emphasising that he is speaking in his own right, before pointing up his total inexperience, even stage fright, at finding himself in the role of a political orator. In the light of eye-witness accounts testifying to Grass's electrifying stage presence, this is, at best, disingenuous and calculated to win his audience's sympathy. Such self-reflexion enables him to discursively construct a deliberately eccentric position, putting him on the side of the audience while simultaneously binding them into a communicative, even dialogic relationship.

Grass's self-positioning and self-presentation as a public intellectual are also aimed at communication with a secondary audience out of direct earshot: his fellow intellectuals. And it is in this regard that Grass's political rhetoric is arguably at its most literary. Thus in order to justify his partisan stance, he deploys intertextual and interdiscursive references to the strong republican tradition of the literary writer as political tribune in the US and France, as well as to examples of 'democratic' German writers in the nineteenth century and the Weimar Republic. To this extent the speeches read as an implicit exhortation to his fellow writers to get off the ideological fence and campaign for democratic renewal. When such support proved unforthcoming, a clearly irritated Grass attacked some of his colleagues in a rather graceless speech when accepting the prestigious Büchner Prize imme-diately after the 1965 elections (*ERBK*, pp. 136–52).

In 'We have a Choice' we are told that the speech was conceived during a sojourn on the Atlantic coast of Maryland, USA. Why he asks, rhetorically, did he not spend his time inventing stories, rather than reflect on conditions in West Germany? Grass's answer draws on a conventional literary trope which his intended intellectual audience would recognise: from the vantage point of a foreign country, the poet, out of deeply felt concerns is compelled to cast aside his true vocation to express a political opinion. Grass uses the phrase 'I couldn't get our . . . fatherland out of my mind', quite possibly an allusion to a verse from Heinrich Heine's famous poem 'Lorelei' of 1843, echoed in Heine's *Nachtgedanken* (Night Thoughts), the last of twenty-four 'political poems' (*Zeitgedichte*) which form the final section of his *Neue Gedichte* and which is one the most famous poems in the German canon, especially its opening verses: 'When I think of Germany at night/I can no longer sleep'. Here the poet's nocturnal sorrow and concern expressed from his Parisian exile for the condition of his homeland intertwine movingly with worries about his mother's health and the separation caused by the prevailing anti-democratic conditions. Grass is allying himself with one of Germany's few politically progressive poets and provides legitimacy for thinking *differently* about Germany.

The intertextuality is far more overt when Grass invokes the example of the American poet and writer, Walt Whitman. With his first-hand insight, as a volunteer hospital worker, to the carnage and divisions of the American Civil War, Whitman is famous for lionising in poems the great reforming President Abraham Lincoln ('Captain, my Captain!'), and extolling the virtues of democracy in his poetry collection, *Leaves of Grass*. Lines from Whitman's poem 'For You, O Democracy' are quoted in another of the campaign speeches, the famous *Hymn of Praise to Willy*, Grass's own paean to a political hero. The intended inference is that Grass's political friendship and expression of support for Brandt is to be viewed in the best traditions of the alliance between politicians and writers. Mention of Whitman is also meant to place Grass in the ranks of those few intellectuals who had publicly supported the democratic institutions of the Weimar Republic, most notably Thomas Mann, who himself had quoted Whitman in his speech defending the Weimar Republic and espousing democratic principles 'About the German Republic' (1922).

Almost forty years later, in 'Between the Stools', Grass reasserted that his politics derived squarely from his 'sense of citizenship' (*Bürgersinn*) and that took its conviction from the historical example of the demise of the Weimar Republic, which had been brought down by extremism on the political left and right (*ERIV*, p. 37). Whether or not Grass struck the right balance in his attribution of blame, there can be no doubt that he advocated with a deeply held conviction the identification of writers as citizens with the Federal Republic and its political processes as the sole course of action to prevent a Weimar-style collapse of democracy, implausible though the latter may now seem with the benefit of hindsight.

A similar intertextual strategy is deployed in Grass's other stump speeches. *What is the Fatherland of the Germans?*, for example, alludes to Ernst Moritz Arndt's famous poem, which is quoted in full at the very outset. Arndt was a writer and poet of the 'national awakening' following Germany's defeat and occupation by Napoleonic forces. It was in writers such as Arndt that generations of nationalists and conservative historians saw the inspiration of Germany's eventual unshackling from a heinous French yoke in the Wars of Liberation (1813–1815), interpreting it as the 'first collective action of the German nation, its first violent rite of passage in an ordeal by fire'.[5] Grass was forced in school, as very likely were many of his audience, to learn Arndt's verses – much beloved by the National Socialists – by rote. Here he invokes this nationalist discourse to initially surprise and command attention before reclaiming it for progressive forces and asserting the continued validity of the 'German Question'. He thus casts himself as a true patriot, a position he then extends in a conceptual leap to his hero, Brandt, by quoting the latter's speech to the German parliament two weeks after the East German Rising of 17 June 1953 in which he exhorted the ruling parties to pursue unity via negotiations (*ERBK*, p. 106).

The unmistakeably allusive title of *J'accuse!* serves to ally Grass with another writer-as-public-intellectual, this time from the French republican tradition, namely Émile Zola and his seminal polemic against the anti-Semitic injustice meted out to the army officer Alfred Dreyfus who, in 1894, was wrongly exiled on trumped up charges of espionage. Zola was at the vanguard of a campaign of fellow writers and intellectuals, which succeeded in overturning the decision and which has become a template for the public intervention of the intellectual to uphold the rule of law. Grass expresses his faith in the transformational power of reason and the values of the Enlightenment. Similar points emerge in 'The Emperor's New Clothes' (*ERBK*, pp. 110–25) with its intertextual link to Hans Christian Andersen's potent parable for the importance of truth-telling and taboo-breaking. Here Grass reiterates his abjuration of the ivory tower, invoking Thomas Mann, and Enlightenment figures such as Klopstock, Lessing and Christian Wolff. Grass claims that the SPD's tradition of reform is based on reason and Enlightenment, enabling the party to renew itself and to acquire the 'new clothes' of sensible policies with broad-based appeal to expose the ruling Conservative 'Emperor', Ludwig Erhard, and the bankruptcy of his policies. Given that elections, too, Grass contends are 'appeals to reason' – the phrase punctuates the speech as a leitmotif – he argues that a vote for the SPD is a vote for reason and is, therefore, in the best Enlightenment traditions (*ERBK*, p. 125).

Grass's legacy as a literary intellectual

In 'taking sides' in the 1960s, Grass put himself at odds with a traditional self-understanding of German intellectuals who regarded political partisanship as compromising their independence, with the 'life of the mind' (*Geist*) to be kept entirely separate from the 'life of power' (*Macht*). In discussions of the German literary landscape between the inception of the Federal Republic in 1949 and 1960, it is conventional to point up the literary intellectual's so-called 'total suspicion of ideology'. In keeping with a long German tradition of a dichotomous relationship between *Geist* and *Macht*, the experience of National Socialism had shown the dangers of an alliance between intellectual and political power, as personified by, say, the philosopher Martin Heidegger and the lawyer Carl Schmitt, while the image of communism which emerged following the demise of Stalin in 1953, as well as the relationship between writers and political authorities in the GDR did much to discredit the partisanship of intellectuals on the left. Leaving aside the obvious caveat that assuming no ideology is *per se* ideological, it was widely thought that any espousal of a specific party political cause would compromise the intellectual's position, undermine his or her authority and question and limit or invalidate his or her credibility as a social critic. This, of course, is not the same as holding back on political comment. Thus the cohort of literary intellectuals which advanced to prominence around 1960 (e.g. Grass, Siegfried Lenz, Uwe Johnson, Martin Walser, Walter Jens, sometimes described as the Hitler Youth or Flak Helper Generation) and older figures, such as Heinrich Böll, did indeed assume increasingly public roles to speak out from a non-partisan platform, on a range of political and moral questions to the extent that they were hailed as the 'conscience of the nation', an epithet most regarded as problematic. However, while many were broadly supportive of the SPD as a vehicle for social and political change in the period prior to the Grand Coalition, most were keen to keep a guarded distance, while others grew increasingly disenchanted with the many compromises that were required to make the party electable. Hence Grass's activism in electoral politics is rightly regarded as unprecedented.

In engaging in public debates that went well beyond his competence as a writer of fiction and notwithstanding the regular broadsides of invective he received, Grass's political rhetoric has played some part in shaping the political culture of postwar Germany. The willingness to arrogate to a literary artist the role of a public intellectual has, however, been on the wane in Germany since the early 1980s, when a new era of Conservative rule established many of the political nostra which became embedded during the unification process of the early 1990s. A more positive interpretation might be that democracy and the rule of law have become so safely embedded in the German body politic by this time that the intellectual's putative role as political watchdog, played out so vociferously in the 1960s and 1970s is no longer required (as Hans Magnus Enzensberger opined on the death of Heinrich Böll in 1985). What is unquestionable is that the discourse on the interaction between the world of letters and the world of politics has been dominated since unification by the view that the status of the writer as public intellectual has undergone a fundamental 'paradigm shift' following the end of the Cold War. Grass's claim to his customary socio-political role – what Stephen Brockmann has memorably called the 'voice of the literary intellectual as spokesman for the German collective superego'[6] – was disavowed, with his rejection of unification rendering him (and his ilk) allegedly unable to draw consequences or perspectives from the new situation in Germany, Europe and the world. This failure owed much to a lingering utopian socialist vision, resulting in a wholesale challenge to the intellectuals' socio-political relevance. Symptomatic of this were newspaper articles and books which variously hailed the 'Twilight of the [Western, leftist] Intellectual' with Grass (together with Habermas and Jens) named as stereotypes.[7]

Conclusion

Our discussion in the first section of this chapter shows that even in old age, Grass has hardly been cowed by the shift in the prevailing political wind of the past two decades. Indeed, with his fame and status arguably reaching its apotheosis with the award of the literary Nobel Prize in 1999, his privileged access to the public arena has been strengthened, while his high-profile acceptance speech, entitled 'To be Continued . . .' was a defiant reaffirmation of his commitment to Enlightenment principles (*ERIV*, pp. 64–79). Moreover, the attempt at a balanced and more nuanced portrayal of German wartime suffering in the critical and popular success of *Crabwalk* (2002) did much to rehabilitate a literary reputation which had from the 1980s undergone a severe mauling. Grass would even appear to have survived the self-inflicted assault on his integrity and, with it, his moral right to speak out, which followed the revelations in 2006 of his adolescent flirtation with the Waffen SS – if the plaudits accompanying the celebration of his eightieth birthday in 2007 and his continued interventions in public debate are anything to go by.

There is, however, an audible world-weariness in some of Grass's commentary on attempts to undermine his public role. Replying to Pierre Bourdieu's question as to why so few intellectuals use 'the symbolic capital their reputation affords them to speak out, and to make heard the voices of those who cannot speak for themselves', Grass nostalgically recalls an era when he was taken seriously and when the broadcast media provided a forum for intelligent debate which has subsequently been yielded to the dominance of trivialising talk-shows.[8] In 'Between the Stools' he even stylises himself, with Habermas and Jens, as the last of a dying breed with a 'permanent duty' to speak out in the service of stimulating a 'living democracy'; 'the last of the Mohicans. Three elderly musketeers . . . three dinosaurs, who can't but help it' (*ERIV*, p. 36).

This stands in marked contrast to the habitus of younger writers from both the old East and West of Germany whose publishing careers fall broadly in the last twenty years. They have tended to eschew the role of the 'representative' intellectual and retreated from public engagement with matters of wider political or social concern. Moreover, whenever younger writers have sought a public platform, they have generally confined themselves to very specific issues or, more commonly, to areas of their immediate expertise, for example, in advocating a rich diversity of writing styles or suitable subjects for literary treatment. For them a public intellectual as personified by Günter Grass and as manifest, not least in his political rhetoric, is indeed 'a fossil from a dead era'[9], one of the 'last of the Mohicans'. Whether this is to the longer-term benefit of political culture in the Berlin Republic remains to be seen.

Notes

1. Günter Grass, *Essays und Reden IV. 1997–2007* (Göttingen: Steidl, 2008). Subsequent references appear in the text as *ERIV* with the page number in brackets. All translations are mine.
2. Günter Grass, *Essays, Reden, Briefe, Kommentare. Werkausgabe in zehn Bänden*, vol. 10, ed. Daniela Hermes (Darmstadt and Neuwied: Luchterhand, 1987), pp. 222–35. Subsequent references appear in the text as *ERBK* with the page number in brackets.
3. See Thomas W. Kniesche, 'Grenzen und Grenzüberschreitungen: Die Problematik der deutschen Einheit bei Günter Grass', *German Studies Review*, 16:1 (Feb. 1993), pp. 61–7, at p. 63.
4. Günter Grass, *Schreiben nach Auschwitz* (Frankfurt am Main: Luchterhand, 1990), p. 43. For a translation of this and other writings on the national question see Günter Grass, *Two States – One Nation* (New York: Harcourt, 1990).
5. Joachim Whaley, 'The German Lands before 1815', in John Breuilly (ed.), *Nineteenth Century Germany. Politics, Culture and Society 1780–1918*, (London: Arnold, 2001), pp. 15–39, at p. 34.
6. Stephen Brockmann, *Literature and German Unification* (Cambridge: Cambridge University Press, 1999), p. 57.
7. Jochen Vogt, 'Have the Intellectuals Failed? On the Sociopolitical Claims and the Influence of Literary Intellectuals in West Germany', *New German Critique*, 58 (1993), 3–23, at pp. 3–4.
8. Günter Grass and Pierre Bourdieu, 'The "Progressive" Restoration. A Franco-German Dialogue', *New Left Review*, 14 (2002), 62–77, at p. 69.
9. Wolfgang Emmerich, 'German Writers as Intellectuals: Strategies and Aporias of Engagement in East and West from 1945 until Today', *New German Critique*, 88 (2003), 37–54, at p. 53.

3

PATRICK O'NEILL

The exploratory fictions of Günter Grass

One of the most striking characteristics of Günter Grass's fictional universe is the remarkable complexity and inventiveness of the narrative strategies deployed throughout half a century of literary composition. His first poems and plays enjoyed modest success; his first novel, however, *The Tin Drum*, caused an immediate sensation on the German literary scene in 1959, rapidly going on to conquer the English-speaking world also. Within the next four years Grass produced two further narratives, *Cat and Mouse* and *Dog Years*, that caused almost as much furore both in Germany and abroad. All three, soon dubbed the 'Danzig Trilogy', were instant bestsellers both in German and in translation; all three were immediately greeted as literary masterpieces and works of comic genius by some readers; and all three were violently condemned by other readers (and non-readers) on grounds ranging from blasphemy and obscenity to treason.

Over the succeeding decades, Grass's steady stream of highly imaginative and flauntedly idiosyncratic narratives has continued to evoke a similarly polarised reaction from his German readers. His works have regularly sold by the hundreds of thousands, regularly aroused the keen admiration of readers primarily interested in literary discourse and its possibilities, and have equally regularly been condemned, frequently with amazing venom, by readers no longer appalled on religious or moral grounds but all the more bitterly offended on the grounds of Grass's outspoken political and historical opinions. And Grass, as high-profile public figure, has expressed outspoken and entirely unvarnished opinions on a panoramic range of topics, from the details of local, regional, and national German elections to the geopolitical manoeuvrings of superpowers, the legacy of Auschwitz, the battle of the sexes, the threat of nuclear winter, the destruction of the environment, third-world poverty, and the rights of oppressed groups everywhere. Already highly visible (and audible) in German political campaigns during the sixties, he has delivered literally hundreds of well-publicised political speeches over the intervening four decades and is the author of a good twenty volumes of political commentaries.

He is also, of course, a well-known poet with a dozen volumes of highly original poetry to his credit; he has written stage plays, radio plays, and ballet scripts; his collected literary essays fill several volumes; and he is a respected graphic artist and sculptor whose work has been exhibited internationally since the mid-1950s. Most of all, however, Grass is a narrative artist of enormous virtuosity, imagination, humour, and originality – and while his utterances as politician and public figure may frequently be both straightforward and aggressively uncomplicated, his statements as writer of fiction rarely are. His narratives, almost always exploratory and interrogative in tone, are invariably characterised by the destabilising complexity of the voice that presents them – a complexity routinely ignored by critics who choose for one reason or another to read multifaceted literary texts as if they were simple – even simple-minded – political tracts. Grass's greatest strengths as a writer of fiction have always been his unflagging inventiveness, his extraordinary technical skill, and his consistently irreverent sense of humour. While it may be true that his lengthier novels are not entirely without their occasional *longueurs*, few even of his most hostile critics would deny that when he is at his best, his writing is nothing short of exhilarating – and fortunately he is at his best a great deal of the time. He has also, and likewise fortunately, been very well served by his English translators, especially Ralph Manheim, who translated all the major narratives from *The Tin Drum* to *The Call of the Toad* (1992).

The narrator of *The Tin Drum* remains one of Grass's most intriguing (and disturbingly comic) literary figures. 'Granted, I am the inmate of a mental hospital',[1] Oskar Matzerath opens his account, implicitly challenging the reader from the very first words to decide what can and cannot be taken at face value in it. At the early age of three, already an expert practitioner of the tin drum of the book's title, Oskar (by his own account) decides to have nothing more to do with the world of grown-ups, especially those who threaten to take his drum away. To accomplish this end the three-year-old, after mature consideration, flings himself headlong down the cellar stairs, suffering no ill effects other than the desired one of curtailing his growth: for the next eighteen years, until his son (who is probably in fact his brother) knocks him (or perhaps he doesn't) into the open grave of his recently deceased father (who may in fact not be his father at all), Oskar retains the stature of a three-year-old. A midget who refuses adamantly ever to be parted from his drum, Oskar has (he says) the supplementary gift of a miraculous voice that enables him to smash glass at will with a well-directed scream.

The major reason why *The Tin Drum* emerged so decisively as a key text of postwar German writing is clearly the entirely inappropriate relationship of Oskar's eccentric narrative style and the half-century of modern German history over which his highly unlikely story is made to unfold. Born in 1924, Oskar completes his narrative in 1954, the intervening decades having seen the incubation, triumph, and publicly acknowledged defeat of Nazism in Germany. Oskar opens his account in 1899, in fact, for 'no one ought to tell the story of his life who hasn't the patience to say a word or two about at least half of his grandparents before plunging into his own existence' (*TD*, p. 17). Not all his readers, Oskar clearly implies, would have either the patience or the desire to put their memory to such a test – or 'if they did' it is just possible that the resulting account might be just as strange a blend of fact and fiction as Oskar's own ostentatiously unbelievable version of how things really were in the Central Europe of his day. Oskar's account, indeed, achieves its satirical thrust precisely because of its relentless and often highly comic obliquity, because of the elaborate care with which fact is disguised as fiction and fiction presented as unassailable fact.

Oskar, like Grass, grows up in Danzig, hotbed of German–Polish tensions over many years. These tensions are presented typically obliquely in Oskar's claim to have not just one but two fathers (the German Matzerath, the Polish Bronski) who vie for his mother's affections. Seen from the perspective of a three-year-old, the entire First World War merits only a reference to the changing design of postage stamps, and the depression of 1923 passes by in a subordinate clause. The rise to power of the Nazi party is likewise relegated to the inconsequential background: Oskar prefers to talk instead about his suddenly increased contact with the theatre as an institution around 1933. Meanwhile, little by little, Matzerath the greengrocer is piecing together his new uniform. 'If I remember right', as Oskar offhandedly phrases it, 'he began with the cap ... For a time he wore a white shirt and black tie with the cap, or else a leather jacket with black armband. Then he bought his first brown shirt and only a week later he wanted the shit-brown riding breeches and high boots' (*TD*, p. 116).

The way in which the lower-middle-class society of which Oskar is part pieces together its acceptance of Nazism just as Matzerath puts together his uniform, starting with the cap signifying allegiance to an abstract political ideal and ending with the boots that will soon be kicking in the windows of Jewish shop-fronts, is brilliantly choreographed. Throughout the first book of the novel, Oskar's comically distorted refraction of German society from 1899 to 1938 strips away the façade of respectability and reticence veiling the rise of Nazism. The novel's satirical thrust, for all the obliqueness of its application, is quite clear: Nazism was not at all some kind of demonic hero-frenzy of the German psyche, some kind of almost supernatural eruption of evil incarnate (such as Thomas Mann had evoked in his *Doctor Faustus* a decade before), horrifying indeed, but in its excess fascinating and even grandiose. Rather it was the coordinated channelling on a monstrous scale of the petty viciousness and frustration and hypocrisy of very ordinary people, leading very ordinary lives until presented with a clearly defined and universally agreed upon focus for their concerted discontent and resentment.

The problem with Oskar's story, however, is that it *is* precisely Oskar's story, not only the story *of* Oskar but also and very emphatically the story *by* Oskar. The cumulative guilt of the nightmare years of German history is refracted and rearranged most overtly in Oskar's grotesquely distorted narrative of his own personal guilt. For Oskar, it emerges by the end of the novel, has in fact been committed to his mental hospital as criminally insane, convicted of the murder of a young woman he had also previously attempted to rape. But her death is by no means the first death in which Oskar, by his own account, is involved. Indeed Oskar achieves the unique distinction of being no less than a triple parricide, for he claims at various points to be responsible for the death of all 'three' of his parents. On each occasion, however, the reader is given enough additional information to be able to conclude that Oskar's claims are preposterous.

In the end, *The Tin Drum*, by relentlessly urging its readers throughout to acknowledge in spite of themselves the total unreliability of its narrator, implicitly invites them to confront the question of how reliable any narrative, whether ostensibly fictional or ostensibly historical, can ever be. The readiness with which Oskar admits to or even eagerly claims guilt for events which are clearly not his personal responsibility very overtly implies the possible existence of other events for which certain readers in the Germany of 1959 were perhaps equally unwilling to accept responsibility. The narrative, in a word, draws the reader's attention to what is omitted by allowing Oskar to exaggerate grotesquely what is not omitted.

While Oskar's story is played out against the backdrop of half a century of German history, the action of Grass's next narrative, *Cat and Mouse* (1961), is much more tightly focused. The narrator is a social worker in his thirties named Pilenz, and the story he tells is of the rise and fall of his best friend, Joachim Mahlke, between 1939 and 1944, when they were both growing boys in wartime Danzig. The resulting narrative – in which what is not told is once again at least as important as what is told – is one of the richest and most fascinating of modern German literature.

The story of Mahlke on its most accessible level is an account of the psychological problems of a troubled teenager and their fatal outcome. As a sickly fourteen-year-old, Joachim Mahlke can neither swim nor dive. The following summer, however, suddenly spurred on by his friends' tall tales of heroic exploits on the half-submerged wreck of a minesweeper in the harbour, Mahlke quickly learns to do both and soon outstrips all-comers, especially in diving, where he now performs extraordinary feats of daring and endurance. Soon the uncontested centre of attention among his peers, his exploits become increasingly impressive – and increasingly outlandish, whether salvaging a long-submerged can of frogs' legs that he calmly eats on the spot before a gagging audience, displaying a fanatic and ostentatious public devotion to the Virgin Mary, or performing heroic feats of competitive schoolboy masturbation.

During the summer of 1942 the seventeen-year-old Mahlke, on impulse, steals a visiting officer's Knight's Cross, hands it in at his school soon after, and is promptly expelled. Called up for military service, he triumphantly wins his own Knight's Cross by 1944, returns to his school in confident expectation of a hero's welcome – and is peremptorily refused permission to address an institution he has so recently dishonoured. Devastated, he goes absent without leave and, with Pilenz's help, returns to the wreck and a favourite former hiding place, located above the water line but reachable only by a difficult dive. Carrying basic provisions, Mahlke dives once more – and never again resurfaces.

Or so Pilenz says, at any rate, for the more we examine Pilenz's description of his role in Mahlke's story, the more complex, evasive, and suspect that role becomes. When Mahlke dives for the last time, for example, he is carrying two cans of meat that Pilenz, a friend in need, has managed to find for him. What he is *not* carrying, however, is the can opener that Pilenz has indeed remembered to bring – but has quite deliberately not given to Mahlke. Only after the latter has been under water for some time does Pilenz begin to hammer on the deck to 'remind' him of the can opener. When there is no response, he eventually rows back to shore – but only after flinging the can opener as far out to sea as he can throw. The psychological complexity of Pilenz's motivation in this climactic scene (and in his subsequent narration of it) has been in gradual preparation throughout the narrative.

Pilenz's narrative begins with the group of schoolboys lying in the school sports field, 'one day, after Mahlke had learned to swim'.[2] Pilenz has a throbbing toothache that he abruptly forgets when the caretaker's cat, attracted by the jerky movements of Mahlke's newly developed and embarrassingly prominent Adam's apple, suddenly springs at Mahlke's throat. No sooner has Pilenz related the incident, however, than he doubly qualifies it in a manner strongly reminiscent of Oskar. Perhaps the cat had not exactly sprung – perhaps 'one of us caught the cat and held it up to Mahlke's neck; or I, with or without my toothache, seized the cat and showed it Mahlke's mouse' (*CM*, p. 8). The incident gives the narrative its title and is entirely emblematic of the cat-and-mouse relationship that develops between Mahlke and the group – and most particularly between Mahlke and Pilenz.

Pilenz's relationship to Mahlke, in short, is characterised from the beginning by an intense ambivalence, examples of which may be found on almost every page of the narrative. Admiration, even hero-worship, is certainly a major factor, for Mahlke succeeds in doing almost everything he attempts better than anybody else, and certainly far better than Pilenz, including winning the dubious affections of the malevolent nymphet Tulla Pokriefke. A tentative suggestion that Pilenz and Mahlke were in fact close friends who sat at the same desk in school is casually advanced, then immediately retracted – though only partially. A central factor, however, is that Pilenz definitely sees himself as an insider, one of the gang, while Mahlke was always an outsider. And no one was ever sure, according to Pilenz, whether Mahlke's extraordinary feats were those of a hero or a clown.

Guilt, however indefinite, is ambiguously central to Pilenz's narrative – as it was to Oskar's. Pilenz's account has to do not only with the destruction of Joachim Mahlke but also with his own need to reconstruct and recontextualise the degree of his own personal involvement and responsibility. His attempt at self-therapy and self-absolution, however, is clearly less than wholly successful. While Pilenz presents what he calls Mahlke's 'monstrous' Adam's apple as both mouse (in attracting ridicule) and cat (in chasing Mahlke through life, forcing him to deeds of exaggerated compensation), Pilenz himself functions likewise as both cat and mouse with regard to Mahlke. As cat, Pilenz is the most obvious representative of the diseased society that finally destroys Mahlke; as mouse, he is obsessed by Mahlke, whose presence was evidently what gave his own life form and meaning, however ambivalently, at the time – just as Mahlke's absence is what appears to give his life any remaining meaning it may have now. Pilenz's motivation as narrator is intriguingly complex: his need to repress a possibly incriminating past is balanced by a need to emphasise, even to exaggerate his own role in it, while his compulsion to confess is balanced by an equally powerful compulsion to manipulate the story told.

The centrepiece of the Danzig Trilogy, *Cat and Mouse* is marked by a formal restraint and economy of expression that is strikingly different from the baroque luxuriance of either its predecessor *The Tin Drum* or its immediate successor *Dog Years*. Its characters are quite realistically portrayed, with little of the grotesquerie and none of the fantastic trappings of either of those novels. While not without its moments of high comedy and farce, it is ultimately the story of a double failure: Mahlke's to adjust, Pilenz's to forget. It is also the story of a highly dubious friendship, an emblematic tale of betrayal and victimisation, told from the perspective of an appropriately (but not always entirely convincingly) rueful aggressor. Grass returns to this productive constellation in *Dog Years*, a new set of variations on betrayal and victimisation, related this time, however, primarily from the perspective of the victim.

The long and highly complex narrative of *Dog Years* (1963) is presented in three books, each with a different narrative voice. The first consists of an account by one Brauxel of the prewar Danzig boyhood years of fat, Jewish, victimised Eddi Amsel and his best friend and greatest victimiser Walter Matern. The second, covering the war years, consists of a lengthy series of 'love letters'[3] ostensibly written by Harry Liebenau to his cousin Tulla Pokriefke, whom we already know as the object of Pilenz's unrequited desires in *Cat and Mouse*. The continuing story of Matern's obsession with Amsel is now strongly coloured by Liebenau's own obsession with Tulla – whose favourite amusement, in turn, is the infliction of unprovoked violence on those who can't defend themselves. A vicious attack on Amsel by a Nazi gang led by Matern is paralleled by an equally savage attack by Tulla on fat, inoffensive Jenny Brunies. Meanwhile, Liebenau's father owns a black German shepherd that is presented to Hitler on an official visit to Danzig, becomes the *Führer*'s favourite dog, and gives the novel its title. The third book, carrying the story to 1957, has as its narrator Walter Matern, who has now conveniently seen the error of his former ways and embarked on a private mission of denazification, sweeping through the newly established West Germany as an avenging fury, savagely punishing former Nazis by throttling their budgerigars, burning their stamp collections, and conscientiously sleeping with their wives, girlfriends, and daughters. Tiring eventually of such personally wearing political convictions, he flees to the newly founded East Germany, the novel ending with an extended mock-apocalyptic confrontation between an increasingly embittered Matern and the now hugely successful businessman Amsel, also known as Brauxel.

As will emerge even from this extremely condensed summary, the most immediately accessible level of *Dog Years* is once again that of overt if highly obliquely expressed social criticism. Its central themes are once again guilt, betrayal and latent savagery. The dogs of the title effectively link the treacherous and vacillating Matern, the pathologically vicious Tulla, the indecisively colluding Liebenau, and the very face of Nazism itself. It is typical of the polyvalence of *Dog Years*, however, that its dogs are characterised not only by savagery but also by the proverbial loyalty of man's best friend, echoing the conflict in Matern's relationship with Amsel, which itself echoes that of Pilenz and Mahlke. Matern's advanced ability to close his eyes to what he has decided not to see is an overt reflection of what is presented as the complacent and convenient amnesia of the new West

Germany, all too solidly constructed on fields of corpses that fatally taint the burgeoning Economic Miracle of the postwar years.

While Matern indignantly rejects any suggestion of complicity or guilt concerning the steadily receding years of the Third Reich, Liebenau is deeply troubled by the thought of his own connivance in almost unimaginable evil. Liebenau, like Günter Grass, was born in 1927 and becomes a writer who attempts in his work to explore and understand the recent German past. Related to the aggressor Matern in his witting or unwitting collusion in crimes past, he is related to the victim Amsel in his attempt to reconstruct those events through the medium of art. For Amsel, in his multiple transformations – some realistic, some fantastic – is the most ostentatiously polyvalent figure in *Dog Years*, parodically embodying the artist who is at once participant in, and detached observer of, the historical reality to be at once reconstructed and deconstructed. If that ironic detachment is crucially necessary for the artist, it is also inevitably ambivalent and at least potentially culpable. Amsel's artistic endeavours range from the prewar mass production of animated scarecrows to the postwar production of aesthetically rewarding ballets (starring a now slender and rejuvenated Jenny Brunies) – not to mention the coordination of all three of the intersecting narratives constituting *Dog Years*, all three of them constructed, as gradually emerges, at Amsel's instigation.

The Tin Drum has one narrator and one centre of attention, Oskar; *Cat and Mouse* has one narrator, Pilenz, and two centres of attention, Mahlke and Pilenz; in *Dog Years* a central concern is the trilaterally interdependent narratorial relationship of Brauxel/Amsel, Matern, and Liebenau – whose accounts may also be read as three separate facets of a single narrative voice, an implied narrator with three mutually relativising voices. Grass was to exploit the discursive possibilities of such a flauntedly divided voice in many of his subsequent major works.

Dog Years is characterised by radical polyvalence. As in *The Tin Drum*, the grotesque plays a central role, and the intermingling of closely observed realistic elements and extravagantly fantastic elements can be seen as the fundamental stylistic principle. All three books of *Dog Years* begin more or less realistically, end more or less fantastically. Everyday reality and narrative reality blur, each calling the other into question. The exuberance of the plot is matched by an extraordinary linguistic exuberance. A bravura example is provided by the evocation of the real and symbolic blackness of the eponymous dog, ranging from 'umbrella-black, blackboard-black, priest-black, widow-black' via 'SS-black, Falange-black, blackbird-black, Othello-black, Ruhr-black' to a final sequence of 'violet-black, tomato-black, lemon-black, flour-black, milk-black, snow-black' (*DY*, p. 513), a linguistic tour-de-force deconstructing all allegedly black-and-white memories of the troubling past. Another example is provided by the extensive and merciless parody of the tortured style of the philosopher and Nazi sympathiser Martin Heidegger, especially in the episode where Matern attempts to persuade himself and anybody who will listen that a pile of obviously human bones outside Stutthof concentration camp has at best only a purely theoretical interest (*DY*, pp. 304–16). Stylistically the most extravagant by far of the narratives constituting the Danzig trilogy, *Dog Years* (which Grass has several times said he thinks a better novel than *The Tin Drum*) delights in its own self-conscious verbal and structural artifice. It is certainly a narrative of social criticism, as were both *The Tin Drum* and *Cat and Mouse*. To an even greater extent than either of these, however, it is also and centrally a narrative about narrative itself and its concealments, its subterfuges, its slippages – and its creative possibilities.

The Danzig Trilogy was followed by a considerably more subdued group of works, centred on the novel *Local Anaesthetic* (1969), whose thematic focus is the tension between action and impotence in the political arena of the late 1960s. The first-person narrator, Eberhard Starusch, a disillusioned forty-year-old teacher in a Berlin secondary school, discusses (or imagines discussing) the issue at obsessive length with his overweeningly rational-minded dentist while simultaneously undergoing protracted and painful dental treatment, bitterly recalling his failed relationship with the daughter of a high-ranking Nazi general, and agonising about his top student's plan to publicly burn his beloved dachshund in protest against the American use of napalm in Vietnam. As Starusch's fantasies of revenge on his former lover become increasingly murderous, his student abruptly abandons political action and youthful idealism in favour of a respectable middle-class career path. Much less flamboyant in tone than the Danzig Trilogy, *Local Anaesthetic* nonetheless introduces new possibilities of narrative complexity, as the almost complete unreliability of Starusch's self-pitying and self-deluding account is gradually and intriguingly allowed to become obvious, radically challenging in the process our ability as readers to distinguish between reality and fantasy, fact and fiction, truth and lies.

During the 1970s and 1980s the novelist Grass temporarily turned from German to wider issues of social concern, and to further possibilities of narrative presentation. The international bestseller *The Flounder* (1977) focuses once again on the relationship of the writer of fiction and the fiction of history. Set largely in Danzig once more, the enormous novel, balancing high comedy and deep seriousness, portrays the continuing battle of the sexes through four millennia, from the Stone Age to the 1970s. *The Flounder*, ostentatiously questioning its own status as narrative by including both an anthology of Grass's own poetry and a substantial collection of culinary recipes, is structured on the failed relationship between a nameless narrator and his wife, the latter querulously portrayed as incorrigibly grasping, unreasonable, and insatiable. The flounder of the title is the magic fish of the Grimm brothers' frankly misogynistic tale 'The Fisherman and his Wife', and Grass's narrator also plays the role of the uxorially challenged fisherman in various manifestations through the ages, while the flounder is made to play that of a perennial triumphalist male *Weltgeist*. The centuries-old dominance of male values is explored in a series of interrelated narratives, even as those values are simultaneously challenged by the voices of their historical victims.

For, as the novel opens, the magic flounder has been caught once again, this time by a militant group of 1970s feminists who are simultaneously avatars of the victimised women of the historical stories and who bring the male chauvinist fish before a Women's Tribunal to answer for the appalling mess that men, on his advice, have managed to make of the world. The latter theme is taken up in a different key in *The Rat* (1986), which combines fantasy, science fiction, and understated humour in focusing on the apocalyptic potential of modern industrial and technological development. The quizzical founding fiction of *The Rat* is that the narrator receives a 'gift rat' for Christmas that metamorphoses into a (female) voice of doom foretelling the inevitable and apocalyptic end of human affairs, while the narrator, a latter-day (male) Scheherazade – legendary Persian queen and the storyteller of *The Book of One Thousand and One Nights* – spins and juggles tale after tale of the past, present, and future in a desperate attempt to talk down and drown out the rat's mercilessly monolithic prophecy of disaster. If the talking fish of *The Flounder* is a parodic embodiment of Hegelian optimism in history, the talking rat is a similarly parodic embodiment of Spenglerian pessimism. In both novels, the ostensible narrative voice is only one component of a self-interrogative double-voiced discourse throughout – *The Flounder* balancing age-old male and female perspectives, *The Rat* balancing millennial hope and fear, and each of them constituting a multifaceted narrative exploration of radically competing positions.

During the 1990s Grass returned once again to his imaginative wellsprings in the highly fraught interrelationship of the German past, present and future. *Too Far Afield* (1995) was the first major narrative attempt to explore the implications of German reunification. The novel met with a witheringly hostile reception by German critics. Even before its appearance, Grass had long since made himself highly unpopular by his outspokenly negative views on German reunification. Auschwitz, Grass had repeatedly declared, made the notion of a single powerful German state unthinkable.

In *Too Far Afield*, five years after reunification, Grass undertakes a narrative exploration of the impact on the former East Germany of what is presented as essentially a ruthless West German corporate takeover. Such a theme could obviously have led to a tiresome political tract – and that is exactly how the novel was judged in almost every major German reviewing organ, Grass's already well-known renegade views on the matter of reunification being roundly and almost universally denounced, while the novel's status as a literary rather than a political text was almost equally universally ignored.

Despite the novel's hostile reception, Grass's technical inventiveness and structural brilliance are once again very much in evidence. The narrator, Theo Wuttke, once a war correspondent for the Nazis, then an East German cultural functionary, is now an elderly employee of the new German federal government. Wuttke's consuming passion, however, is not politics but literature, specifically the work of the nineteenth-century German novelist Theodor Fontane, which has fascinated him for a good half-century. (The German title *Ein weites Feld* derives from a favourite phrase of Effi's father in Fontane's best-known novel, *Effi Briest*, and is an idiom meaning, roughly, 'that's a long story'.) A latter-day Don Quixote, indeed, Wuttke has considerable difficulty in distinguishing late-twentieth-century reality from the fictional universe created by Fontane; sometimes he even appears to have difficulty in remembering that he is not himself Fontane. Not content with the opportunities offered by this degree of narrative complexity, however, Grass also provides Wuttke with a 'day and night shadow', one Hoftaller, who on one level is also just one more harmless senior citizen but on another is a timeless embodiment of the professional spy and traitor throughout history, especially German history, equally comfortably at home in the ranks of the Prussian secret police or the Nazi Gestapo or the East German Stasi. Hoftaller is also a flauntedly fictive creation, for he is openly borrowed (with permission) from the East German writer Joachim Schädlich's title character in his novel *Tallhover* (1986) – a piece of postmodern metafictional whimsy on Grass's part that left outraged traditionalist critics spluttering with indignation. This intricately ramified structure provides Grass with a complex presentational prism that enables him not only to interweave events from German history of the nineteenth and twentieth centuries but also to allow various characters to express opinions and embody positions entirely different from his own very publicly stated positions in his non-fictional writings and speeches. More fundamentally, it allows him to question the very role of the public intellectual – which is to say also his own role – in the course of modern German history.

The interpenetration of the German past and the German present is likewise central to *Crabwalk* (2002). German media coverage of this text was much more favourable than in the case of *Too Far Afield*, largely because the later work was seen to perform an important cultural task in breaking a long-standing taboo, namely mention of the fact that innocent citizens had also suffered on the German side during the war. *Crabwalk* takes for its subject the real-life sinking of the German cruise-liner *Wilhelm Gustloff* by a Soviet submarine in January 1945, involving the loss of some 9,000 lives, six times more than had perished on the *Titanic* and the worst maritime disaster of all time. *Crabwalk* involves three generations of a single German family in Grass's prismatic presentation of the story. The narrator, Paul Pokriefke, is researching the story of the *Wilhelm Gustloff* at the behest of an unnamed employer, the 'old man', who emerges as the otherwise unnamed author of the Danzig Trilogy. Born on the very night of the sinking, Paul, strongly reminiscent of the hangdog narrators of *Local Anaesthetic* and *The Flounder*, is a middle-aged journalist who regards himself as a hopeless failure in both personal and professional terms. His account of the event is based partly on real historical sources (duly quoted) but must also attempt to take into consideration the very different views of both his mother and his son. His mother, one of the few survivors of the disaster, is none other than Tulla Pokriefke, once the malevolent schoolgirl of *Cat and Mouse* and *Dog Years* and now, as a grandmother, a defiantly unreconstructed admirer variously of Hitler, Stalin, and the Baader-Meinhof group, her shifting political positions strongly reminiscent of Matern's conveniently shifting allegiances.

Discovering an internet website dedicated to the memory of the eponymous Wilhelm Gustloff – a real-life Nazi functionary assassinated in 1936 by a Jewish medical student, David Frankfurter – Paul gradually comes to realise that its virulently neo-Nazi author can be none other than his own teenage son, Konrad. For several months Konrad, signing himself 'Wilhelm', and a fellow teenage history buff, signing himself 'David' and claiming (falsely, as it emerges) to be a Jew, exchange views on the assassination in an internet chatroom. The exchanges are collegial, even amicable. The two eventually agree to meet, and the would-be Nazi retrospectively corrects history by fatally shooting the would-be Jew. 'It never ends' are the last words of the novel, a central theme in Grass's continuing fictional engagement with what he has elsewhere called the German *Vergegenkunft*, the inextricably interwoven three-in-one of the 'paspresenture' (past-present-future).[4]

Many a writer has come to artistic grief under the dead weight of laudable intentions. Grass's style at its best brilliantly avoids that fate by means of a consistent braiding of multiform and multifaceted variations on a single central technique: his narratives have always not only invoked but flaunted a fundamental discrepancy between matter and manner, between the (ostensible) story told and its multiple possible tellings and readings. As a writer he will long be remembered for the revolutionary freshness of vision he brought to German writing after 1945 – and for the challenging complexity with which his work provocatively interweaves and interrogates history, politics and the literary imagination. The challenge, the complexity, and the provocation alike achieved an entirely new and startling intensity with the almost eighty-year-old Grass's stunning revelation in the autobiographical text *Peeling the Onion* (2006) that he had himself, sixty years earlier, briefly been a member of the Waffen SS. The implications of that extremely belated revelation for our understanding of Grass as a man and a high-profile public moralist will no doubt long remain the subject of vigorous discussion. Whatever our personal position on that particular question may be, however, one thing is clear: Grass's ambivalent narrators and polyvalent narratives have retroactively acquired a whole new and intriguing and even more ambiguous interpretive dimension.

Notes

1. Günter Grass, *The Tin Drum*, trans. by Ralph Manheim (New York: Vintage, 1964), p. 15. Subsequent references appear in the text as *TD* with the page number in brackets.
2. Günter Grass, *Cat and Mouse*, trans. by Ralph Manheim (New York: Signet, 1964), p. 7. Subsequent references appear in the text as *CM* with the page number in brackets.
3. Günter Grass, *Dog Years*, trans. by Ralph Manheim (New York: Fawcett Crest, 1966), p. 123. Subsequent references appear in the text as *DY* with the page number in brackets.
4. See, for example, Günter Grass, *Headbirths or The Germans Are Dying Out*, trans. by Ralph Manheim (New York: Harcourt, 1982), p. 103.

4

PETER ARNDS

Günter Grass and magical realism

Magical realism is a genre in which magical elements appear seamlessly within a realistic setting. The term was first coined by the German art critic Franz Roh in 1925 to describe paintings that demonstrated an altered reality. Then in the 1960s magical realism was used by the Venezuelan essayist Arturo Uslar-Pietri specifically in the context of Latin American writers, most notably Jorge Luis Borges, Isabel Allende, and Gabriel García Márquez. The term can be extended to authors outside of the Latin American tradition, however, to Mikhail Bulgakov, who wrote under Stalin, the French novelist Michel Tournier, or the contemporary British-Indian author Salman Rushdie. Their novels of magical realism perceive history as so grotesque that they resist operating within realistic paradigms of representation and resort to other genres steeped in myth, legends and fairy tales. While these genres help Bulgakov to comment on the terrors of Stalinism in *The Master and Margarita* (written in the 1920s and not published until 1967), in Tournier's *The Ogre* (1970) the Erlking myth and the fairy-tale world of man-eating ogres conjoin as a means to represent the surreality of life under National Socialism, and in Salman Rushdie's prose Hindu myth and *The Arabian Nights*: *Tales of One Thousand and One Nights* (between AD 800 and 900) are important subtexts in the context of colonialism and postcolonialism.

Myth and the fairy-tale world also deeply pervade the structures of Günter Grass's work, primarily his novels *The Tin Drum* (1959), *The Flounder* (1977) and *The Rat* (1986). Myth, legend and the fairy tale constitute the magical realist atmosphere of these books and serve as a vehicle for historical representation, especially history's extreme moments such as genocide and euthanasia in *The Tin Drum*, world hunger in *The Flounder*, and the threat of nuclear war in *The Rat*. More recently the notion of magical realism in Grass's work has become interesting also in light of the author's own tainted past. Reading Grass's biography *Peeling the Onion* (2006), in which he confesses that he was a member of the Waffen

SS, raises the question of how fiction can conceal and reveal autobiographical fact. The conflict we see in Grass's work now is determined by his vacillation between, on the one hand, a persistent moral defence over the years of the necessity of Germany's continued attempts to come to terms with its past, and, on the other hand, his silence and repression concerning his own past. Indeed, Grass's insistence on 'memory work', even as he was apparently reluctant to speak about his own past, might lead us to think of the influential German philosopher Martin Heidegger (1889–1976), who, in the immediate postwar period, hid his own tarnished past behind abstractions. In his autobiography Grass resorts to an esoteric self-perception and self-presentation, specifically with his admission that throughout his work he has employed what he calls his 'baroque realism' – a synonym for magical realism – in order to avoid facing his personal past in a more direct way. With this term he seems to be alluding first and foremost to the genre of the 'tall tale' of the Baroque Age as well as eighteenth-century stories such as the *The Surprising Adventures of Baron Münchhausen* (1785) by Rudolf Erich Raspe. But Grass also returns time and again in his essays and interviews to his fascination with the pre-Enlightenment picaresque novel, and especially with Johann Grimmelshausen's *Simplicius Simplicissimus* (1668), to which he repeatedly refers in an attempt to parallel his early biography with the fictional wanderings of Grimmelshausen's juvenile *Schelm* (rogue).

The baroque or magical realism of many of Grass's texts has had a major impact on the work of other authors who confront the past and historical development of their own countries. In its conflation of magical or mythical elements with the realism of the fascist past *The Tin Drum* in particular influenced Salman Rushdie's *Midnight's Children* (1981) and Colombian writer Gabriel García Márquez's *A Hundred Years of Solitude* (1967) in their concern with the legacy of colonialism. Grass's novel then also became the model for American author John Irving's *A Prayer for Owen Meany* (1989) and *A Son of the Circus* (1995). In close parallel to *The Tin Drum* the latter thematises dwarfism and eugenics. As further examples for the international appeal of the theme of dwarfism and eugenics one could also mention the Swiss author Friedrich Dürrenmatt and his short novel *The Suspicion* (1951), the British writer Simon Mawer's *Mendel's Dwarf* (1998), or the German-born American writer Ursula Hegi and her novel *Stones from the River* (1994). Moreover, Grass connects, not through influence but as part of a closely knit universe of texts, with Michel Tournier and Mikhail Bulgakov and their use of myth to approach the literary representation of totalitarianism. In order to highlight Grass's position in world literature and his magical realist representation of world history I want to single out two intertextual connections, that between *The Tin Drum* and Tournier's *The*

Ogre and *The Tin Drum*'s impact on Rushdie's *Midnight's Children*. First, however, I begin with a brief analysis of Grass's most famous novel as a work of magical realism.

Grass, *The Tin Drum* and the legacy of Nazism

After Grass's confession in 2006, Oskar Matzerath, the protagonist of his densely picaresque novel *The Tin Drum*, may appear in a new light as a reflection of the author's own double identity as both a victim, in the sense of having lost his home, and as a perpetrator with his tarnished past. Oskar Matzerath is a deeply duplicitous figure. He has to be read not only as a fascist, as research has largely done since the publication of the book, but also as a potential victim of the Nazis' persecution of so-called *Untermenschen* (subhumans), the physically and mentally disabled, criminals, vagabonds, aimless wanderers and other social outsiders. These persecuted social groups form the basis for a literary representation of Nazi crimes via different manifestations of folk culture, the substance of Grass's baroque or magical realism, in which reality and history as fact are distorted into a heightened and at times grotesque fiction.

Specifically, Grass's book plays intertextually with Romantic fairy tales (for example, the Grimm brothers and the early nineteenth-century writer Wilhelm Hauff), with the figure of the archetypal trickster, the courtly fool, the harlequin, Pied Piper, Erlking, and with the tradition of the picaresque novel. Oskar Matzerath embodies all of these figures: he is the Thumbling of the fairy tale; he is the trickster that anthropologists such as Paul Radin (1883–1959) and psychologists such as C. G. Jung (1875–1961) have identified as a universal human archetype; he is the Janus-faced harlequin that reaches back to the medieval *diableries* (tales of black magic) and the *commedia dell'arte* (satirical comedies) of the Renaissance, and he is the picaro of pre-Enlightenment literature, a rootless wanderer beyond the pale of society. These figures are part of the book's Dionysian dimension, with Oskar himself functioning as a mediator between Dionysus and his counterpart Apollo: 'If Apollo strove for harmony and Dionysus for drunkenness and chaos, Oskar was a little demigod whose business it was to harmonise chaos and intoxicate reason.'[1] Apollo was the Greek god of light and the sun; truth and prophecy; poetry and the arts, and, in the philosophy of influential late nineteenth-century German thinker Friedrich Nietzsche, stands for individuality, rational thought, but also superficial semblance and appearance. Dionysus, on the other hand, was the god of wine, associated with ecstasy, and, in Nietzsche's thought, stands for darkness, irrationality, but also for the revelation of a deeper truth.

In view of Germany's and Grass's attempts to work through the Nazi past the Dionysian and Apollonian dimensions become very interesting. It seems that the Dionysian dimension in Grass's work functions as a catalyst for a national working-through of the past that disrupts the Apollonian semblance of German politics at the time, its deliberate climate of rationalism which functioned as an attempt to repress the irrationalism of the Nazi years. There are aspects to Grass's magical realism that, for Germans, initiate the process of coming to terms with their own past. Especially in *The Tin Drum* Grass seems to want to liberate myth from its ideological appropriation under the Nazi years. Although the Dionysian, magical elements in his work have the function of breaking through postwar politics of rationalism and oblivion, I would argue that Grass's magical realism, his recourse to the picaresque tradition, myths, legends, and fairy tales, is at the same time not free from the charge of concealment in the sense that it too can be interpreted as a language of silence, as metaphor rather than a direct voicing of truth, as an esoteric avoidance of certain topics of the past, including both his personal past as well as of events such as the Holocaust. Consequently, the baroque or magical realism in Grass's work is an ambivalent category. It reveals and conceals at the same time. While serving Grass to obscure his own past it also re-introduces irrationalism into a climate of political rationalism.

One of the key folk-tale references contributing to the magical realist atmosphere in Grass's work is the Pied Piper of Hamelin. In *The Rat*, for example, this legend refers to a popular theory after the war, that of the *ab*duction and *se*duction of the Germans by Hitler.[2] In *Peeling the Onion*, Grass modifies this theory from one of passive victimisation to semi-active participation: 'We were being seduced. No, we allowed ourselves, I allowed myself to be seduced.'[3] It is in *The Tin Drum*, however, that the legend is most prominent. Here, Oskar drums up a procession of remorseful Germans and leads them from the Onion Cellar, where they learn how to cry again after the war, to the Devil's Gulch where they try to regain their innocence by wetting their pants like infants: 'And the first thing I did to these post-war humans incapable of a real orgy was to put a harness on them . . . Soon they had their jaws hanging down; they took each other by the hands, turned their toes in, and waited for me, their Pied Piper' (*TD*, p. 533). This inversion of Oskar's position from nearly abducted child to a Pied Piper abducting Germany's innocent 'children' is a highly ironic statement on the cries of innocence that, in the words of the narrator, spread like weeds after the war: 'for innocence is comparable to a luxuriant weed – just think of all the innocent grandmothers who were once loathsome, spiteful infants' (*TD*, p. 499).

Oskar is a potential victim of Nazi persecution but he is also capable of great evil. He is responsible for the deaths of several people within his family and an accomplice of the Nazis. His duplicity aligns him with a host of mythological relatives of the Pied Piper, above all the Thumbling of the folk tale (Oskar watches a Tom Thumb performance with his mother and identifies with him), the courtly fool (as an entertainer to the Nazis in the front theatre), the Neapolitan harlequin, and the Nordic Erlking. In the rostrum scene, for example, where Oskar's drumming disrupts the marching music during a Nazi Party rally, Oskar sits in the very spot that the harlequin used to occupy in the medieval mystery play, that is, under the stage. This is one of many allusions to Oskar's satanic nature. The harlequin of the *commedia dell'arte* was a duplicitous character, in typical trickster fashion both funny and sly. But many variations of the harlequin figure also had a light, spiritual side. The *zanni* Flautino, for example, had a miraculous voice that emitted flute-like sounds, similar to the Pied Piper. This is a characteristic he shares with the Erlking, a Northern European spirit of the air, who deceives parents in order to steal their children, just as the *commedia*'s *zanni* deceive their masters so that the children in love can get together. What is comical in the *commedia* thus assumes sinister dimensions in Germanic folklore. The harlequin originates as the Hellequin of Boulogne, a knight who lived in the ninth century and who died fighting against the Normans, giving rise to a legend of damned devils (*la chasse Arlequin*), and he is closely related to the Erlking, not only etymologically so. As a candidate for euthanasia, Oskar is a potential victim of a programmatic abduction undertaken by National Socialism, but as a drummer, like Hitler, he is also capable of leading the Wild Hunt, *la chasse Arlequin*. A shameless rogue he also functions as a catalyst in postwar society's attempts to come to terms with the past. This is possibly the most important role of the trickster, rogue or picaro – that they must be shameless in order to change cultures. They hold mirrors up to the cultures whose products they are.

This duplicity in Oskar ranging from beneficial to sinister, communicating between rationalism and irrationalism, is of marked interest in light of Grass's own biography, which contains a similar tension. Oskar as a Pied Piper in particular seems to be a reflection of Grass's own lifestory. The Pied Piper is, like Oskar Matzerath, both a victim and a perpetrator, hounded as well as hounding others. In his homelessness, which results from his expulsion from civic society, he bears all the attributes of the wolf-man of the Middle Ages, a social phenomenon that provided material for the medieval charivari rituals. (The custom of charivari is a superstitious ceremony in which making noise by beating drums, or beating on pots or other objects to make a loud racket, was done to keep evil spirits away.) Future scholarship will have to decide whether Grass's work can be read in such a way that it reveals traces of the author's own controversial position as a sort of 'Pied Piper of Germany' in the triple sense of being – like Oskar – a wanderer expelled from his home (note that Grass was about to become expelled a second time from his home town Gdańsk after his confession in August 2006 when former Polish President Lech Wałęsa insisted that Grass give up his honorary citizenship), Germany's benefactor as a politically engaged citizen-writer, and a games-playing author who abducts his German readers into a dark subterranean world of fantasy and irrationalism. Yet Grass, the author of tall tales, and his Oskar may also have their parallels in the world of the circus, with the two traditional circus clowns, Stupid August(e) and his antagonist, the white clown, a direct embodiment of the battle between Dionysian urges and Apollonian reason. And just as early eighteenth-century writer and aesthetician Johann Christoph Gottsched once chased the traditional popular comic figure Hanswurst off the German stage, ceremonially burning his effigy in an apparent triumph of reason over irrationality, Grass managed to hide the youthful folly of the Stupid August(e) behind a White Clown who seemed to be morally intact. This Stupid August(e) then did not reveal himself until that ill-fated August of 2006. (Grass exploited the coincidence of the German word 'August', meaning both clown and the month of August, in a collection of poems, *Dummer August*, published in 2007 in which he reflects on the events of August 2006 and the furore surrounding his admission that he had been in the Waffen SS.)

Grass and Michel Tournier: Pied Pipers and fairy-tale ogres

Its mythological figures, the Thumblings of the Grimm brothers, the Pied Piper and the Erlking, and the conflation of these magical realist paradigms with Nazi crimes move Grass's *The Tin Drum* into close proximity with Michel Tournier's *Le Roi des Aulnes* (1970, translated as *The Ogre* in 1972), which none other than film-maker Volker Schlöndorff adapted as a movie in 1998, starring John Malkovich in the role of the protagonist Abel Tiffauges (Schlöndorff had already adapted *The Tin Drum* in 1979). This novel shares a number of features with *The Tin Drum* that are typical also of other books of magical realism: the use of myth in a culture of memory; the close connection between history and the inversion of the established social order that critical theorist Mikhail Bakhtin famously described in a book of 1941 as characteristic of the carnival: the fictionalisation of race issues, the paradigm of wandering and homelessness, the representation of historical time as circular, and the conflation of religious and sexual motifs.

Abel Tiffauges is only one among many ogres in this text, and he is as duplicitous as Oskar. Abel, the nomad (versus Cain, the sedentary), is imprisoned by the Nazis but in the course of his confinement in the east, first in a POW camp, then at Field Marshal Göring's Rominten Forest Reserve, and finally at the Castle of Kaltenborn, he discovers his love for fascist Germany and becomes a passionate defender of the Nazi cause without understanding the broader context of its policies. The novel makes no secret of its subtexts. It explicitly mentions Charles Perrault's *Le Petit Poucet*, the French equivalent of the Grimm brothers' Thumbling tales, and Goethe's famous poem 'Der Erlkönig' ('the Erlking', to which the French title *Le Roi des Aulnes* alludes), thus blending the French fairy-tale world with Germanic myth. A giant of a man who snatches children from their parents, Abel's job is to abduct children so that they can be turned into soldiers at the Castle of Kaltenborn, a Napola (National Political Institute of Education, or boarding school founded to raise a new generation for the political, military, and administrative leadership of the Nazi state) that prepares *Jungmannen* (cadets) for the war on the Eastern front. Hitler is the supreme ogre/Erlking in the story in comparison with whom Göring, the 'Ogre of Rominten' and Master of the Wild Hunt, *la chasse Arlequin* in his expansive game reserve, dwindles to 'the rank of a little, imaginary, picturesque ogre out of an old wives' tale'.[4] The Second World War itself takes the role of a mythological ogre with the 'Jungmannen serving and feeding the monstrous idols of steel and fire that raise their monumental jaws amidst the trees' (*Og*, p. 291). The war even supersedes the fearfulness of this mythological creature by becoming a synonym for carnival, a playground for adults. Yet the carnival of war does not function because adult seriousness, which has become death-dealing, is never interrupted by childish joyfulness. Seen in this light Oskar Matzerath's desire to remain the eternal child – at the age of three he refuses to partake in adult seriousness – may be read as an attempt to create his own permanent carnival.

Like Grass's *The Tin Drum*, *The Ogre* abounds in carnivalesque images of the kind discussed by Bakhtin, that is, grotesque and extreme images which undermine social norms. While Oskar's dwarfism contrasts with Abel's hugeness, both novels elaborate in similar ways on Bakhtinian banquet images and lower bodily functions. In *The Tin Drum* Oskar is forced to eat a revolting soup consisting of urine and a dying frog and his mother commits suicide after eating eels that recall the tripes of Rabelais's *Gargantua*. The various ogres in Tournier's novel display voracious appetites and the kind of celebration of flesh that is typical of the carnival (Göring, for example, is a greedy carnivore who eats even before his pet lion). Oskar's obsession with womb-like images (his grandmother's underskirts, his desire to return to the mother's womb) has a parallel in Abel's obsession with defecation: 'It was an interlude of solitude, calm and meditation during an act of defecation performed generously and without excessive effort, by a regular descent of the turd into the lubricated sheath of the mucous membranes' (*Og*, p. 168). Abel shares this obsession with excrement with Hermann Göring, who inspects the faeces of his game, regularly tasting their consistency. By conjoining defecation with religion, 'the altar on which he consummated his secret and fruitful union with the Prussian soil' (*Og*, p. 169) Abel conflates the sacred with the profane, similarly to Oskar, who performs blasphemous acts in churches such as touching Jesus's 'watering can'. In *The Ogre*, too, religious icons are sexualised as Abel likens his great 'phoric' joy, as he calls it, his paedophiliac passion for carrying children on his shoulders, with Saint Christopher as a protector of innocence traversing evil, long before it becomes his sinister profession of kidnapping them from their parents and taking them to Kaltenborn Castle. In *The Tin Drum*, at the end of the scene in which the Gdańsk Post Office is under fire by the Home Guards we see Oskar carried away by a soldier while Jan Bronski gets shot after Oskar has denounced him as 'a villain who had dragged off an innocent child' (*TD*, p. 246). This image of the evil child on the shoulders of unsuspecting adults contrasts sharply with Tournier's image of the innocent child on the shoulders of the ogre, which is also present in Goethe's vision of the Erlking.

The children Abel picks from trees and out of their parents' homes are used as cannon fodder but also for the purpose of racial selection. In *The Tin Drum* Oskar, the fairy-tale dwarf with criminal intentions is repeatedly threatened by the Nazi Ministry of Health, which wants to get him off the streets to feed him into the euthanasia apparatus. It is precisely this conflation of folklore and a historical reality that makes for the magical realism of this novel. In *The Ogre*, too, the folklore motif of a child's abduction, as one encounters it in the Pied Piper legend or Goethe's Erlking, is an element of fantasy that serves the representation of the historical reality of Nazi eugenics. At the Kaltenborn Raciological Centre Commander Professor Doctor Otto Blättchen continuously searches among 'the children they bring me for the grain of gold dust that justifies selective reproduction' (*Og*, p. 250). Here is another ogre, whose olfactory sense is so refined (Perrault's ogre can smell human flesh) that he can distinguish between races by their individual smell, 'black, yellow, Semitic and Nordic with his eyes shut, just by the fatty volatile acids and alkalis secreted by their sudoriferous and sebaceous glands' (*Og*, p. 252). Still unaware of the horrible consequences of the Nazis' concern with eugenics Abel expresses his fascination with these ideas, shares with the likes of Mengele – the Nazi doctor infamous for his experiments on concentration camp inmates – a special attraction for twins, and eagerly participates in a painstaking examination of their bodies, their 'brachycephalic skulls, wide faces with prominent cheekbones, pointed ears, flat noses, widely spaced teeth, green rather slit eyes' (*Og*, p. 287), and so forth. How different is this fascination with the body seen in its individual components from Abel's initial feeling of repulsion 'for members of the dreadful profession that consists in laying bare and touching without love the bodies that have most need of it' (*Og*, p. 120).

Everything Abel does during his career as an ogre he does out of love for children. The word *ogre* is therefore ambivalent in that, like the old blind moose that he encounters in the Polish forest, he sees himself as a gentle giant until he learns the true dimensions of his crimes, the horror of his contribution to Nazism. The climax of his paedophile fantasies occurs when Abel sleeps on a mattress made of the hair of the shorn *Jungmannen* before emptying the content into a fish pool and swimming in it. When he meets the little boy Ephraim, a survivor of Auschwitz, his dream world collapses as he realises the horrible ambiguity of the word 'Canada'. While Abel's life in the eastern European forests surrounded by the boys of Kaltenborn had been the realisation of a childhood dream about the cold expanses of the Canadian north, 'Canada', as Ephraim tells him, was also the name for the treasure house in Auschwitz in which were stored the possessions of the murdered. This is the ambivalence of the carnival itself with its figures, the clown, fool and harlequin, who stand for joy but also have a foot in hell. All of a sudden he realises that he shared his fascination for twins with Mengele and understands that while he was euphorically stuffing his mattress with boys' hair, this was indeed a reflection of the grim reality in the death camps where the hair of the victims was recycled for various purposes.

In the carnival the progress of history is temporarily suspended. Auschwitz in its permanence of unfathomable suffering is a kind of perverted carnival that suspends reality to the point that the progress of time, of history, becomes a doubtful dimension. This is something we see at work also in other novels of magical realism. In the absence of hope there is no time. It becomes evident how the association of carnival with fascism can vary: on the one hand carnivalesque perceptions of National Socialism include such visions as that by the American Expressionist painter Albert Bloch whose circus world in *March of the Clowns* (1941) contains a glimpse of hope, with Hitler projected onto the gallows, interrupting the death-dealing seriousness of Nazism. On the other hand, fascism itself is viewed as a devilish carnival oblivious to the passing of time. This corresponds to the conception of time at the Castle of Kaltenborn as 'not linear but circular. You live not in history but in the calendar. So it's the undisputed reign of the eternal return – the merry-go-round image is exact. Hitlerism is resistant to any idea of progress, creation, discovery, or imagination of an unknown future. Its virtue is not rupture but restoration: hence the cult of race, ancestors, the dead, the soil' (*Og*, p. 266). Grass uses the very same image of the merry-go-round for circular time determining the uninterrupted madness of Auschwitz. In a dreamlike vision Oskar finds himself on this merry-go-round among four thousand children that are to be gassed, propelled by his two cultural heroes Rasputin (the Siberian mystic healer who became the confidant of the last Russian Tsar and was murdered in 1916) and Goethe who keep throwing in coins, the forces of chaos alternating with the forces of order, 'a bit of madness with Rasputin and a bit of rationality with Goethe' (*TD*, p. 412), the two extremes at the core of National Socialism.

Grass and Salman Rushdie: The nation, myth and sacrilege

Breaking through the linearity of time is a key narrative technique in novels of magical realism and their particular perception of history. It is a key paradigm for these authors' treatment of the role of memory. In both Grass's *The Tin Drum* and Salman Rushdie's *Midnight's Children* circular time has the specific function of debunking the myth of the *Stunde Null*, the zero hour of the nation-state, which presupposes the linearity of historical time with its potential to wipe the slate clean and suppress unwanted memories. Grass's influence on Rushdie aside, the works of both writers display a high degree of intertextuality and heterogeneity and both have provoked strong reactions from the people who do not agree with their subversive ideology, although arguably conservative reactions to Grass's *The Tin Drum* fade, of course, in comparison with the *fatwa* placed on the British-Indian author after the publication of *The Satanic Verses* in 1989 by the Ayatollah Khomeini, the political leader of the 1979 Iranian Revolution that caused the overthrow of the last Shah of Iran.

One of the most interesting connections between *The Tin Drum* and *Midnight's Children* is their revival of the picaresque tradition. Rushdie's characters, too, display the kind of homelessness and dubious origin that are key attributes of the picaro, and one realises to what extent the picaro himself stems from an intercultural archetype that goes beyond the boundaries of Europe, that is, the mythological trickster. As tricksters Oskar Matzerath and Saleem Sinai are equipped with a magic weapon: Oskar's scream corresponds to Saleem's extremely sensitive nose. But as tricksters they are also figures on the threshold between two historical ages, Nazism and postwar Germany on the one hand, India as British colony and independent state on the other. The year 1945 marks the date when Oskar is transformed into a grotesquely misshapen dwarf, while precisely at the stroke of midnight preceding Indian independence in 1947 Saleem Sinai is born together with the other thousand midnight children. Rushdie's novel forms a trio with those of Grass and Tournier in its use of the grotesque body of the protagonist – Saleem resembles the Hindu Elephant God Ganesh – but also in its grotesque representation of history. Similar to Grass, Rushdie admits to having been influenced by Laurence Sterne's *Tristram Shandy* (1759–1769) and François Rabelais, the fifteenth-century French writer whom Bakhtin investigated in the course of his exploration of the carnivalesque, and both admit that their use of the fantastic and of the fairy-tale world stems from their cultures' particular literary heritages. While Rushdie emphasises the importance of *Arabian Nights* for his novel, of the stories of 'A Thousand and One Nights', Grass says: 'I was also, from my childhood, very much touched by the German romantic tradition: the fairy tales . . . I used in many books those archetypal figures of German fairy tales . . . I think using these fairy tales is bringing us to another kind of truth than you can get by collecting facts of this flat realism.'[5]

Like Grass, who destabilises the mendacity of post-fascist rationalism, Rushdie attempts to subvert an official discourse, that is, the official view of post-independence Indian history as a success story. The subversion of an official discourse is, in both cases, achieved specifically through the grotesque conflation of important historical events with the banality of the protagonist's private life and through a revival of the myths and irrationalist traditions suppressed by both new states: ' "We are a secular State", Nehru, the first Prime Minister of India following its independence, announced'.[6] In order to show how ludicrous the concept of the *Stunde Null* really is Rushdie recycles a central scene from Grass, the Onion Cellar episode, which resurfaces as Mumbai's (formerly Bombay) 'Midnite Confidential Club'. Both authors want to bring back the past and understand that nothing will disappear, that everything will return. Grass's catharsis through onions correponds to Rushdie's chutney, the sweetsour chutney of memory. Preserving the past thus becomes a central concern in both books. Rushdie's image of the pickling factory that Saleem works in is a fitting motif for this chutneyfication of history and the narrator compares his thirty chapters with pickle jars in which the past is preserved. Both writers engage in myth in order to preserve the past and a cultural heritage that the great rulers of their countries threaten to either manipulate or suppress. While Grass offers his vision of myth and folk culture in opposition to the spirit of rationalism under the first Chancellor of postwar West Germany, Konrad Adenauer, Rushdie writes against Jawaharlal Nehru's and his daughter Indira Gandhi's suppression of Hindu traditionalism for the sake of their monumental vision of history focused on great leaders but not the people. *Midnight's Children* revives Hindu myth, for example, in the character of the Widow who drains all hope from the 1001 children born at the stroke of midnight of 15 August 1947. This figure is representative for this novel as a work of magical realism, for on a realistic level the Widow symbolises Indira Gandhi and her rule of terror during the Emergency period (1975–77), while on the level of myth she is made to resemble the evil goddess Kali, a goddess often represented with protruding tongue, a necklace of skulls and hands full of weapons and severed heads, stark naked upon the prostrate body of her Shiva. Kali, of course, is often to be found in Grass's work (for example, *The Flounder* from 1977, or *Show Your Tongue* from 1988).

This revival of Hinduism becomes even more problematic in *The Satanic Verses* which takes the blasphemous mixing of religious icons to an extreme. When the Muslim Gibreel, one of the two central characters, enters the film world, one of his first roles is to play the Hindu god Ganeesha, with elephant trunk and large ears. Later he metamorphoses into Hanuman, the monkey king from the epic Ramayana. Rushdie's deconstruction of the dictatorial politics of the Indian film industry reminds us of Grass's parody of didactic prose such as the *Bildungsroman* (a novel of personal development) of German Classicism, but among the greatest offences is Rushdie's mixing of Islam with Hinduism, which is far more sacrilegious than Grass's rather mild bouts of atheism. Sacrilege though is a typical mode of the literature of magical realism, which attacks primarily the official discourses of the church and the state. Throughout his work Grass has targeted secular and church rule, but it is predominantly in satirical magical realism, a genre steeped in the picaresque traditions, that blasphemy and sacrilege, the rupturing of the sacred realm (church and state) by means of the profane, are directed towards the church's and the state's power mechanisms.

Conclusion

If we follow the argument outlined by the German-Jewish philosophers Horkheimer and Adorno in their book *The Dialectic of Enlightenment* (published in 1947 in the aftermath of the horrors of Nazism), we glimpse the way in which reason can become oppressive such that rationalism can reach a point at which it perverts into irrationalism, just as it did under totalitarian rule. In the fiction of magical realism official doctrines that are sold to the people as 'rational' become the target of satirical representations relying on irrationalism, a conflict that can be explored with the help of various cultural theories, be it Nietzsche's distinction between the

Dionysian and the Apollonian, French thinker Michel Foucault's thoughts on madness and its history of confinement, be it Bakhtin, or Heidegger.

Alternatively, we may look to the social theories of Gilles Deleuze and Felix Guattari to help us understand the clash between rationalism and irrationalism. Thus Deleuze and Guattari argue that what they call the 'arborescence' (from the Latin word 'arbor', meaning tree) of Western societies, the deep roots of their ideologies and their territorialism, clashes with what they call the 'rhizome', the shallow roots associated with deterritorialisation, nomadism and homelessness. ('Rhizome' is a botanical word for a horizontal stem in plants, that is, a stem which does not create a system of deep roots but rather grows out horizontally near or even above the soil surface.)[7] Tricksters, picaros, and other literary nomads are fictional representations that embody a rhizomatic way of living. In the novel of magical realism the official world tends to be subverted by different forms of the rhizome. We encounter these two realms, arborescence and the rhizome, in authors such as Grass, Irving, Rushdie, Tournier and García Márquez, but also in much travel writing, for example in Bruce Chatwin's *The Songlines* (1987), where the rhizomatic world of Australia's indigenous peoples collides with Western racism and its arborescence, its thinking in terms of deep roots. As jazz and blues are part of the rhizomatic world giving tragic-comic hope to African-Americans so are the songlines, that intricate web of dreaming paths as the manifestation of an ancient nomadic culture. The trickster of myth and the picaro of literature are the great wanderers and blasphemers of the mythological and fictional world challenging the gods, secular rulers and the apathetic citizens who remain passive in the face of misrule.

These tricksters are central to the three books presented in this chapter. Whether it is Oskar as Thumbling, harlequin, or Pied Piper, Abel Tiffauges as an Erlking tricking the parents of young boys so that these can be fed into the war machine, or Saleem Sinai satirically attacking post-independence Indian culture, these figures make up the magical realist atmosphere of these texts – their Dionysian dimension that has a number of different functions for the representation of historical reality. While folk tales such as the Thumbling tales or legends such as the Pied Piper may provide Grass and Tournier with a literary vehicle to represent the violence of the Nazi past, these tales rooted deeply in myth also serve the purpose of breaking through the mendacity of the postwar era, both in Germany and France. In Grass's novel, Oskar as Pied Piper has a cathartic function for the Germans in their attempt to come to terms with their own past. In Tournier's novel, Abel Tiffauges's fascination with fascism, which turns him into an ogre, becomes a reflection for the international appeal of fascism. Although Grass did not directly influence Tournier the two books are astonishingly similar in theme and their use of mythological material. Their reliance on the grotesque seems to attack bourgeois complacency, and specifically in Grass's novel the Bakhtinian carnivalesque (Oskar's grotesque body, for example, as he transforms in a railway car going west) comments on the Nazi ideology concerning degenerate bodies. Both authors' insistence on circular historical time, exemplified in the image of the merry-go-round, points to the eternal return of large-scale historical violence and the eternal return of the repressed. That the repression of the past, its glossing over through official versions of history, is being attacked by the literature of magical realism becomes nowhere clearer than in the parallels between Grass's novel and that by Salman Rushdie. In both texts we are faced with the debunking of the *Stunde Null*, the zero-hour of the nation-state; in both, myth as the opposite of reason and Western Enlightenment is re-introduced into a climate of rationalism and secularity; an official view of history is subverted in both, something that we see at work also in García Márquez's *Hundred Years of Solitude*, where official history and Miguel Abadía Mendez's (President of Colombia from 1926–30) denial of the 1928 massacre of thousands of strikers at the United Fruit Company are, in Walter Benjamin's words, 'brushed against the grain'.

While novels of magical realism manage to rewrite official versions of history, they do not, as we have seen, necessarily contribute to revealing the personal histories of their authors. And yet, despite the criticisms one may level at Grass for repressing his own past and for hiding them within an esoteric genre, his baroque or magical realism has provided him with highly artistic venues for exploring such issues as memory and its suppression or the eternal conflict caused by gender trouble (as in *The Flounder*). Other than concealing some of history's truths through metaphorical language, Grass's oeuvre has at the same time shown the power to re-enchant history. Above all, however, some of his books, and first and foremost *The Tin Drum*, have managed to escape the aura of provinciality that surrounds postwar and contemporary German literature and have advanced into the ranks of world literature.

Notes

1. Günter Grass, *The Tin Drum*, trans. by Ralph Manheim (New York: Vintage, 1964), p. 323. Subsequent references appear in the text as *TD* with the page number in brackets.

2. Günter Grass, *The Rat*, trans. by Ralph Manheim (New York: Harcourt, 1987), p. 41. Subsequent references appear in the text as *R* with the page number in brackets.

3. Günter Grass, *Peeling the Onion* (London: Harvill Secker, 2007), p. 44.

4. Michel Tournier, *The Ogre*, trans. by Barbara Bray (Baltimore: Johns Hopkins University Press, 1997), p. 236. Subsequent references appear in the text as *Og* with the page number in brackets.

5. Cited in Henrik D. K. Engel, *Die Prosa von Günter Grass in Beziehung zur englischsprachigen Literatur: Rezeption, Wirkungen und Rückwirkungen bei Salman Rushdie, John Irving, Bernard Malamud u. a.* (New York: Peter Lang, 1997), p. 145. My translation.

6. Salman Rushdie, *Midnight's Children* (New York: Knopf, 1980), p. 174.

7. Gilles Deleuze and Felix Guattari, *A Thousand Plateaus*, trans. by Brian Massumi (Minneapolis: University of Minnesota Press, 1987), pp. 3–25.

5

KATHARINA HALL

Günter Grass's 'Danzig Quintet'

This chapter explores the interconnections between five of Grass's literary works, extending John Reddick's long-standing and influential notion of the 'Danzig Trilogy',[1] *The Tin Drum* (1959), *Cat and Mouse* (1961) and *Dog Years* (1963), to that of the 'Danzig Quintet', through the inclusion of two later works, *Local Anaesthetic* (1969) and *Crabwalk* (2002). The first section of the chapter examines how the quintet is bound together through an extended family network of characters, resulting in a richly interwoven set of texts that moves back and forth between the past and the present, as well as the private and the public spheres of individual memory and history. The second and third sections explore the dual conceptualisation of memory within the texts (as a form of testimony on the one hand, and as a representation open to distortion on the other) in the context of the larger issue of engaging with the National Socialist past, while the final section uses Umberto Eco's notion of an 'inferential walk' to examine how the interactions between the quintet's narratives shapes the reader's relation to the texts.

'The Danzig Quintet'

Günter Grass's *The Tin Drum, Cat and Mouse, Dog Years, Local Anaesthetic* and *Crabwalk* were written over a period of forty years, with the first of the works appearing in 1959 and the last in 2002. In spite of the eight major prose works produced by Grass between the publication of *Local Anaesthetic* in 1969 and *Crabwalk* in 2002, on subjects as diverse as gender relations (*The Flounder*, 1977), post-apocalyptic dystopias (*The Rat*, 1986) and German reunification (*Too Far Afield*, 1995), these five texts can convincingly be viewed as a quintet, whose constituent parts are bound together both by genre and a number of structural and thematic continuities.

Grass draws heavily on the tradition and form of the *Familienroman*, or family chronicle, to bind the quintet together, focusing on the interrelated stories of a number of family groups – such as the Matzeraths, Bronskis, Liebenaus and Pokriefkes – whose histories are often traced over a series of generations. Other central characters, such as Walter Matern and Eddi Amsel from *Dog Years*, are incorporated into this extended family network through links such as shared schooling, war experiences, and sexual encounters. Together, their interlocking narratives form an off-beat, five-volume family chronicle, whose intertextuality foregrounds the characters' shared, collective history. Key figures from one book make guest appearances in others (such as *The Tin Drum*'s Oskar Matzerath in *Cat and Mouse*, *Dog Years* and *Local Anaesthetic*), or conversely, minor characters are developed to take on a more major role: Eberhard Starusch, the Störtebeker of *The Tin Drum* and *Dog Years*, becomes the narrator of *Local Anaesthetic*, while Tulla Pokriefke from *Cat and Mouse* reappears in *Dog Years* and *Crabwalk*. The author's conscious development of these family ties is particularly apparent in *Crabwalk*, where Tulla (initially envisaged by Grass as a sister for Oskar),[2] identifies the four possible fathers of her son: Joachim Mahlke (*Cat and Mouse*), Harry Liebenau and Walter Matern (*Dog Years*), and Störtebeker (*The Tin Drum*, *Dog Years* and *Local Anaesthetic*). Her son Paul Pokriefke, who is also the narrator of *Crabwalk*, is thus figured as the literal and literary offspring of each of these earlier characters and texts.

Characters from the quintet hail from the same extended community of Langfuhr, a suburb of Danzig, one of the great Hanseatic seaports, which was designated a Free State under the League of Nations in 1920, and whose key geographical and military importance led to its occupation by the Nazis at the beginning of the war in September 1939. Situating his families here, in his own former hometown, enables Grass to provide an overview of the history of the region from the late nineteenth century onwards. However, the quintet's main historical focus is the arc of National Socialism – the rise, rule and fall of the regime – and the repercussions of that period in the postwar era. Characters in each work return obsessively to the memory of Danzig ('lost' to Poland after the fall of Nazism in 1945) and the memory of their actions and experiences under National Socialism.

Each of the quintet's works is dominated by the presence of one or more first-person narrators: Oskar Matzerath in *The Tin Drum*; Heini Pilenz in *Cat and Mouse*; Brauxel (the alter-ego of Eddi Amsel), Harry Liebenau and Walter Matern in *Dog Years*; Eberhard Starusch in *Local Anaesthetic* and Paul Pokriefke in *Crabwalk*. All are shown looking back over the past from a point in the postwar present, ranging from the 1950s in *The Tin Drum* to the 1990s in *Crabwalk*. This shared temporal structure and retrospective narrative viewpoint elevate memory and its mediation through language to a primary position within each of the works. As the narrators remember the past, Grass illustrates how individual lives are shaped by historical and political events, while also showing the ways in which history, and in particular National Socialist history, is refracted through memory's subjective lens. By choosing to view this era 'from below', from the perspective of the 'ordinary' Germans who experienced the regime, family memory and German history are shown to be inevitably intertwined.

By extension, the different ways in which Grass shows the narrators remembering and articulating their pasts (the different ways, in other words, in which he conceptualises memory) open up a number of questions about the functions and implications of remembering, refusing to remember, or misremembering German involvement in Nazi persecution, as well as, in the case of *Crabwalk*, German wartime suffering. In particular, themes such as guilt, *Vergangenheitsbewältigung* (coming to terms with the past) and the need for an authentic engagement with the past are consistently foregrounded within the texts. These temporal, structural and thematic continuities suggest the timeliness of extending John Reddick's original conception of a 'Danzig Trilogy' to that of a 'Danzig Quintet' – a literary project spanning over forty years, which explores a number of key moments in the evolution of Germany's relation to its difficult past.

Memory as testimony in the 'Danzig Quintet'

A dual approach to memory is visible throughout Grass's 'Danzig Quintet'. While there is an emphasis on memory's value as a form of testimony on the one hand, suggesting that memory is a direct and reliable means of accessing the past, memory is figured as an act of recollection on the other, which mediates individual experience via language, so providing a representation of past events. These two conceptualisations of memory are not presented as mutually exclusive within the works: rather they are deployed where appropriate to illustrate key issues or patterns of behaviour relating to the postwar engagement with the National Socialist past.

The notion of memory as testimony is particularly evident within the first three works of the quintet, and functions both as a means of asserting the reality of the Holocaust and the role of 'ordinary' Germans in supporting the Nazi regime. In these contexts, memory is presented as a faculty that allows the past to be retrieved intact (echoing Freud's description of psychoanalysis as a form of archaeology, in which the past can be recovered, like an artefact, 'through the work of spades'),[3] an idea that is also broadly referenced in Grass's 2006 memoir *Peeling the Onion* through the use of the term *Gedächtnis*, or 'memory', which the author views as 'pedantic' in character.[4]

In this respect, the eponymous tin drum of Grass's first novel is given an important symbolic role through its ability to recall the past in every detail. As Oskar relates his life-story on his drum while a patient in a psychiatric institution after the war, key episodes are figured as testimony with a clear historical dimension. The most prominent of these is Oskar's eye-witness account of the national pogrom that took place on the 9–10 November 1938 and came to be known as 'The Night of Broken Glass'. Related in the chapter 'Faith, Hope, Love', with a repeated, ironic use of the fairy-tale opening 'once upon a time', this first-hand description of the Nazi assault on Jews and Jewish property in Danzig forms a moving climax to the first part of the novel. In it, the complicity of 'ordinary' Germans in the pogrom is highlighted (Oskar's Nazi father Matzerath closes his shop for the after-noon to enjoy the spectacle of the burning synagogue), alongside the high price of the persecution for individuals: the Jewish toyshop owner Sigismund Markus is driven to commit suicide as his property is attacked. Fittingly, Oskar testifies to the violent death of his childhood friend and drum-supplier by means of a drumming session in the postwar era. The value of his testimony in establishing the facts about the Nazi persecution of Jews in Danzig for the historical record (both as an act of remembrance for Markus and to assert the moral accountability of those responsible for his death) is one that is emphasised by Oskar's careful labelling of that particular drum, and the cataloguing and storage of all the drums he has played since 1945 in a home-made archive in his cellar at home.

Through this simultaneous act of remembering and remembrance, Oskar's narrative brings the memory of the pogrom firmly into the postwar present, a clear prerequisite for any authentic engagement with the past. Together with Mariusz Fajngold's memories of Treblinka, recounted by Oskar in the chapter 'Disinfectant', the account of the pogrom forms the moral heart of the novel. While Oskar documents the dramatic escalation of Nazi persecution in 1938, Fajngold provides sober testimony of the death camps, exposing the full horror of the Holocaust. His imaginary conversa-tions with his dead wife and children bear witness to the Holocaust from the alternative perspective of the Jewish survivor and graphically illustrate his profoundly traumatised state. In both cases, individual and family memories are used to illustrate the impact of larger historical events.

The notion of memory as testimony is further developed in the next two works of the quintet. In both *Cat and Mouse* and, more extensively, *Dog Years*, repeated references are made to Stutthof, the concentration camp established by the Nazis just outside Danzig in September 1939, where an estimated 65,000 to 85,000 people were murdered in the six years until the end of the war. In *Dog Years*, the narrator of the second section of the text, Harry Liebenau, relates the story of Oswald Brunies, a teacher whose unwillingness to take part in the collective activities of National Socialism, such as singing Nazi anthems or hanging out a swastika on public holidays, leads to his arrest following a stage-managed denunciation by some of the schoolchildren he teaches (including Tulla and possibly Harry). In recording this story, and Brunies' subsequent death at Stutthof, Harry, like Oskar before him, bears witness to Nazi persecution and ensures that the teacher is not forgotten in the present. In addition, Harry's memories of the time dismantle the dominant postwar myth that 'ordinary' people knew nothing of the concentration camps or what happened to those who were sent there:

> Everybody knew, and those who have forgotten may as well remember: Stutthof: Danzig-Lowlands County, Reich Province of Danzig-West Prussia, judicial district of Danzig, known for its timber-frame church, popular as a quiet seaside resort, an early German settlement . . . [B]etween 1939 and 1945 in Stutthof Concentration Camp, Danzig Lowlands County, people died, I don't know how many.[5]

Harry's narrative climaxes with the powerful sequence in which Tulla Pokriefke confronts a group of young aircraft auxiliaries, including Harry and Störtebeker, with the truth of Stutthof by crossing from the military barracks into the outer territory of the camp, and bringing back a skull as ultimate evidence of the murderous activities taking place there.

Grass's engagement with the memory of National Socialism in his early works – both on an individual and historical level – and his insistence on the need to bear witness to Nazi persecution, is best understood in the context of their moment of production. The year of *The Tin Drum*'s publication, 1959, was an apt moment for the exploration of these themes, as the final two years at the end of the decade marked a turning point in West Germany's relation to the National Socialist past. In the immediate postwar era, the desire to achieve a distance from past events resulted in a cultural amnesia about the Holocaust. This was especially the case in the political sphere, with Chancellor Konrad Adenauer pointing to the Nuremberg trials of 1946 as a symbolic settling of accounts. As Jeffrey Herf has demonstrated, Adenauer put forward the implicit argument that 'democracy required less memory and justice for the crimes of the Nazi era and more "integration" of those who had gone astray'. By the end of the 1950s, however, 'a more intensified period of West German judicial confrontation with Nazi crimes was beginning'.[6] In 1958 there were two important developments: the conviction of a high-ranking police officer in Ulm for the wartime murder of four thousand Jews, and the establishment of the Central Office of the State Justice Administration for the Investigation of National Socialist Crimes, which led to a number of important trials of former SS and mobile killing-unit members in the 1960s.

In the literary arena, Primo Levi's *If this is a Man* was also published in 1958 after many years of rejection and delay. This seminal survivor account was complemented in one important respect by the appearance of *The Tin Drum* in 1959: Grass, like Levi, critiqued the postwar mentality of silence about the Holocaust through his work, and asserted the need for Germans to engage rigorously with the past. In spite of his own recent failure to engage with the implications of his personal role as a member of the Waffen SS, Grass remains one of the earliest German writers to have articulated such a viewpoint. In particular, the foregrounding of memory within his work as a means of highlighting the involvement of 'ordinary' Germans in implementing or supporting the Nazi regime was groundbreaking, arguably pre-empting the work of historians on the *Alltagsgeschichte* of the period (the 'history of everyday life') by over a decade.

While the final work of the 'Danzig Quintet' also conceptualises memory as a form of testimony, it does so in the very different context of German wartime suffering. *Crabwalk* extends the story of Tulla Pokriefke and, via her son's narrative, records her traumatic memories of the sinking of the *Wilhelm Gustloff* by the Russians in 1945, in which an estimated nine thousand Germans, many of them children, lost their lives as they fled west at the end of the war. Positioning Tulla as a survivor of the *Gustloff* and allowing her to articulate the trauma of the sinking is an important statement on the part of the author. Both in interview and within the text, Grass asserts that a full examination of the issue of German wartime suffering, and in particular, of the sinking of the *Gustloff* – 'this shipping catastrophe, which was forgotten and repressed'[7] – was long overdue, and that this 'taboo'[8] was one that he should have challenged earlier in his *oeuvre*. As the figure of 'the old man' in *Crabwalk* puts it, who functions as Grass's authorial alter-ego in the novella:

> Properly speaking, any strand of the plot having to do directly or loosely with the city of Danzig and its environs should be his concern. [. . .] Soon after the publication of that mighty tome, *Dog Years*, this material had been dumped at his feet. He – who else – should have been the one to dig through it, layer by layer. [. . .] A regrettable omission, or to be quite frank, a failure on his part.[9]

Thus, in many respects the 2002 novella *Crabwalk* is a case of unfinished business for the author, with the references to Danzig and the 1963 novel

Dog Years suggesting that he views the work as a delayed extension of his earlier 'Danzig' project. However, Grass has drawn considerable fire from critics for his assertion that the memory of German wartime suffering was taboo: the historian Robert Moeller, for example, contends that the issue of German wartime suffering was fully represented in political, historical and cultural discourses throughout the postwar era.[10] While his critique of the novella is partly justified, it can equally be argued, as the following sections of this chapter will show, that *Crabwalk* also problematises Tulla's position as a victim, thereby promoting a full, rather than a selective engagement with the National Socialist past.

Memory as recollection and representation in the 'Danzig Quintet'

In each of the quintet's works, the notion of memory as testimony is overlaid with the notion of memory as an act of recollection, which when communicated, mediates individual experience via language, providing a representation of the past. By figuring memory in this way, there is a recognition that the reification of memory – the assertion that memory corresponds directly to the past – is problematic, in that it obscures the processes by which the past can be retrospectively shaped by language. As Nicola King argues, this viewpoint calls for a differentiation between 'first, the event; second, the memory of the event; and third, the writing of (the memory of) the event'.[11] Intriguingly, the coexistence of these distinct models of memory within the novel parallels the dual conceptualisation of memory within Freud's work, where the notion of the perfectly preserved past waiting to be accessed within the unconscious is countered by the use of the term *Nachträglichkeit* (variously translated as 'deferred activity', 'retro-activity' or 'afterwardsness'). This notion figures memory as a series of successive 'rearrangements' and 'retranscriptions', whereby 'memory is present not once but several times over' in a layered form,[12] and is further developed in the Lacanian concept of *remémoration* (recollection) with its sense of a continual 'restructuring of the event' over time in memory and language.[13]

Viewing memory as a representation of the past inevitably reworks the relation between memory and testimony in a way that has important implications. On the one hand, defence lawyers in a number of Holocaust trials have deliberately drawn attention to the elisions, mistakes or misrepresentations that can occur in the act of recollection as a means of undermining the authority of first-hand survivor accounts. On the other, it has been just as forcefully (and correctly) asserted that the representative nature of memory need not invalidate the fundamental truth of survivor testimony.

The latter position is taken up in *The Tin Drum*, where the recognition of memory as a representation of the past is never allowed to diminish Oskar's or Fajngold's testimony about the 'Night of Broken Glass' or Treblinka. What the novel's emphasis on memory as representation allows, however, is the complex nature of Oskar's (and the other narrators') engagement with the past to emerge. Thus, while Oskar is shown bearing witness to National Socialist crimes, he is also shown concealing his own complicity in certain key events through the misrepresentation of his memories within the narrative. In his memoirs, Grass links these kinds of 'tall tales' (O, p. 4) with the notion of 'Erinnerung' or 'recollection', which tends towards 'flattery and embellishment' (O, p. 3, my amended translation).

In the first four works of the quintet, the notion of memory as representation is used to illustrate the unreliability of narrators, who, in the postwar present, frequently distort or refigure the role they played in events under National Socialism. Grass foregrounds these misrepresentations by having his narrators relate two or more versions of key events, a textual device that highlights the contradictions in the narrators' accounts and encourages an awareness on the part of the reader of the central issue of guilt. For example, *The Tin Drum* shows Oskar giving conflicting accounts about his role in the deaths of his two possible fathers, Jan Bronski and Alfred Matzerath, which are in turn bound up with larger historical events. Bronski, who is Polish, is executed by the Nazis following the Polish Post Office siege (in 'The Card House' and 'He Lies in Saspe'), while Matzerath is shot by Russian soldiers during the occupation of Danzig at the end of the war (in 'The Ant Trail'). In both cases, Oskar initially provides a neutral account of his own involvement in these events, which positions him as a bystander or onlooker, before altering his accounts to reveal a more active and malevolent role. In the case of Bronski, Oskar's second version reveals that he repositioned himself on the side of the Nazis at the end of the siege, and led them to understand that Bronski was using him as a German hostage; in the case of Matzerath, Oskar confesses to having deliberately handed his father an incriminating Nazi badge, which he swallows in desperation, and on whose opened pin he then chokes, leading the soldiers to shoot him.

Similar narrative techniques are employed in *Cat and Mouse*, *Dog Years* and *Local Anaesthetic*. In *Cat and Mouse*, Pilenz's contradictory accounts of his relationship with Mahlke and his role in Mahlke's possible death are tied to an examination of Mahlke's indoctrination and subsequent rejection by the Nazi state, as represented by headmaster Klohse. In *Dog Years*, Walter Matern is shown persistently lying about his role in an SA (*Sturmabteilung* = Nazi paramilitary unit) attack on his childhood friend Amsel. The end of *Local Anaesthetic*, in which Starusch tries to prevent his student

Scherbaum from staging a dog-burning at the height of the '68 protests against the Vietnam War, makes it clear that many of the teacher's wartime and postwar memories were selective or even fabricated.

The novella *Crabwalk* differs somewhat from the earlier works of the quintet in its thematisation of memory as representation. Here, historical memory is interrogated much more directly, resulting in a deconstruction of distorted right-wing narratives about the *Gustloff*'s sinking, which are upheld in the third generation by Tulla's grandson Konny. Thus, for example, the characterisation of the *Gustloff* as a 'refugee ship' is challenged: it is pointed out that there were 1,500 military personnel on board, whose presence turned the ship into a legitimate military target. In this instance it is Paul, Tulla's son and Konny's father, who highlights the flaws in Konny's representations of the past, so performing a different function to the other narrators in the 'Danzig Quintet', whose own unreliability is the focus of the text. Notably, too, Konny is shown posting his outpourings on the internet – that is to say, in a public, globally accessible space – rather than being satisfied with the limited context of family discussions about the past. He is encouraged in this project by his grandmother Tulla, who will go to any lengths to have the story of the *Gustloff* told, and who gravitates towards right-wing discourses, because it is in these contexts that German wartime suffering has been most sympathetically discussed. Thus, by the end of the quintet, there is a discernible movement outwards from individual and familial representations of the past (consisting predominantly of the narrator's own personal memories), to a wider examination of historical discourses and the politics of memory in the postwar era.

Inferential walks: The reader's relation to the text

Grass's technique of highlighting the unreliability of the narrator through multiple versions of events, illustrates, as Terry Eagleton has pointed out more generally, that 'reading is not a straight-forward linear movement, a merely cumulative affair':

> [O]ur initial speculations generate a frame of reference within which to interpret what comes next, but what comes next may retrospectively transform our original understanding, highlighting some features of it and backgrounding others. As we read on we shed assumptions, revise beliefs, make more and more complex inferences and anticipations; each sentence opens up a horizon which is confirmed, challenged or undermined by the next. We read backwards and forwards simultaneously, predicting and recollecting, perhaps aware of other possible realizations of the text which our reading has negated. Moreover, all this complicated activity is carried out on many levels at

once, for the text has 'backgrounds' and 'foregrounds', different narrative viewpoints, alternative layers of meaning between which we are constantly moving.[14]

This is true of the 'Danzig Quintet' not just in the context of individual texts, but also on a larger intertextual level, as events that are first recounted in one book are often revisited in another. There is an observable progression in this respect: while the first two works in the quintet highlight the internal contradictions of a single narrator's account (Oskar in *The Tin Drum* and Pilenz in *Cat and Mouse*), the next work in the sequence, *Dog Years*, employs three primary narrators (Brauxel, Harry and Matern), whose memoirs, in addition to containing internal contradictions, constantly intersect with one another. In a further extension of this technique, the fourth and fifth works, *Local Anaesthetic* and *Crabwalk*, encourage the reader to see the 'Danzig' works collectively, as a set of interlocking family recollections that form one overarching text. References in these works to incidents and events that occurred in earlier works invite the reader to take what Umberto Eco terms an 'inferential walk' – defined as the process by which the reader takes a '"walk" so to speak, outside the text, in order to gather intertextual support'. Eco stresses that such 'walks' are 'not mere whimsical initiatives on the part of the reader, but are elicited by discursive structures and foreseen by the whole textual strategy as indispensable components of the construction of the fabula'.[15] These walks allow events in the last two works of the quintet to be properly contextualised in the light of earlier narratives and historical events, while also, in a reciprocal movement, deepening and furthering the stories that earlier narrators have told.

In *Local Anaesthetic*, Starusch's memories of his youthful period as 'Störtebeker', the self-styled leader of the 'Dusters', invite the reader to take an 'inferential walk' to the first work within the quintet, *The Tin Drum*. This walk is triggered by Starusch's reference to the gang's mascot, whom readers of *The Tin Drum* will know was Oskar Matzerath. This textual overlap signals the larger links between the two texts and invites the reader to compare Starusch's account of the gang's activities in *Local Anaesthetic* with Oskar's earlier account in *The Tin Drum* (in 'The Dusters' and 'The Christmas Play'). These chapters offer a valuable alternative view to Starusch's memories, which present a somewhat romanticised view of the gang's political resistance to the Nazi regime. Oskar's account of his time with the gang contains significantly more detail, and suggests that although its members did manage to cause some disruption to the regime, by stealing arms and ammunition, their motives were simply anti-authoritarian. In other words, their activities were not targeted political opposition, and

Starusch's presentation of himself as a resistance fighter is therefore flawed. Through this 'inferential walk', then, Starusch's determination to portray himself as involved in resistance work is shown to be a reflection of his desire to impress his 68er student Scherbaum, who views him rather disdainfully as a washed-up, politically impotent teacher, rather than an accurate depiction of past events.

Crabwalk is also characterised by numerous intertextual references to the other parts of the 'Danzig Quintet'. Just as Paul and the novella adopt a crab-like style, moving to and fro between different strands of the past and present, so this movement is enacted in the larger literary context of all five works. Here, the 'inferential walks' of *Local Anaesthetic* are transmuted into 'crabwalks', which once again invite the reader to read 'backwards and forwards simultaneously' (Eagleton 1983, p. 77) within the quintet's vast, interlocking web of memories and perspectives.

Given the controversy surrounding Grass's treatment of German suffering as a taboo, seeing *Crabwalk* as an integral part of the 'Danzig Quintet' is particularly valuable, because it allows the breadth of Grass's treatment of the enormously complex perpetrator/victim debates to become visible: when viewed collectively, it is clear that the quintet's works provide a full and extensive exploration of all aspects of German wartime experience. The myriad connections that are made between the different works on the levels of content, theme and narrative structure also signal Grass's own awareness of the importance of viewing the works together, rather than as separate, self-contained parts.

Thus, in *Crabwalk*, explicit causal links are made between Tulla's presence on the *Gustloff* and one of the central storylines in *Dog Years*, the selection of Harras's puppy, Prinz, as a gift for Hitler. As a reward, the dog's owner, the carpenter Liebenau, is given a cruise on the *Gustloff*, which he donates to his assistant and brother-in-law August Pokriefke. But the result of the wonderful experiences that Tulla's parents have on the *Strength through Joy* ship is Erna Pokriefke's later, fatal, insistence that the family sail on the *Gustloff* as they flee to the west. These overlapping stories make it impossible to separate the family's presence on the *Gustloff* from the preceding narrative of the Nazi years: the one is shown to be inextricably bound to the other.

The constant references within *Crabwalk* to Tulla's complex history are also significant, because they allow the quintet's dual conceptualisation of memory – as a form of testimony on the one hand, and as a representation open to distortion on the other – to be reiterated once more. Thus, in chapter five, 'the old man' recalls the episode from *Dog Years*, in which Tulla has the courage at the Kaiserhafen barracks to speak the truth of

Stutthof and the Holocaust with her declaration 'That's a pile o' bones [. . .] And I'm telling you they come straight from Stutthof' (*DY*, p. 334). While reminding the reader of Tulla's boldness at a time when all others were turning a blind eye to the concentration camp, this passage incorporates a continued awareness that postwar German memory must continue to bear witness to the Holocaust. However, a little later in *Crabwalk*, Tulla's distorted memories of her own role in an act of persecution during the Nazi era are also highlighted.

When talking with her son Paul, Tulla recalls an incident in which the half-Jewish Amsel was driven from the carpenter's yard following repeated abuse with the derogatory term 'Yid', and identifies the persecutor as her own father: 'And he said it out loud, too, before he kicked that Yid – Amsel was his name – out of our courtyard . . .' (*CW*, p. 111). Her account is used to reiterate the tendency of postwar Germans to misrepresent their actions in the Nazi past, by encouraging the reader to take a second 'inferential walk' within *Dog Years*, where this episode is first mentioned. When the reader returns to Harry's memories of the event in the *Love Letters* section of the novel, a glaring discrepancy in Tulla's later version immediately becomes clear: for while her father may have put her up to it, she is nonetheless identified as Amsel's chief persecutor, shouting the word 'Yid' at him sixteen times (culminating with a frenzied 'Yidyidyid!', *DY*, p. 183). The contrast between these different sets of memories suggests that the older Tulla in *Crabwalk* has deliberately chosen to obscure her role in this event. However, her casual use of the term 'Yid' (rather than the more neutral term of 'Jew') as she recounts the story to Paul betrays her lingering anti-Semitism and her guilt.

Subsequently, Jenny, Tulla's old childhood friend, alludes to the role that Tulla played in denouncing Jenny's adopted father, the teacher Oswald Brunies, thereby providing another crucial link back to *Dog Years'* examination of how ordinary people colluded in the operations of the Holocaust: 'It was pure mischief on her part. But it turned out badly. After the denunciation, they came for Papa Brunies . . . He was sent to Stutthof . . . But in the end things turned out almost all right' (*CW*, p. 229). Jenny, fully aware of Tulla's contribution to Brunies's death at Stutthof, shows a remarkable capacity for forgiveness, both here and at other points in the narrative: she and Tulla have somehow reached a mutual understanding about the events of that time, which appears to bind them together even more firmly than before. And yet, Jenny's inclusion of the word 'almost' in that final sentence also stresses that Tulla's past actions, and their dreadful consequences, can never be entirely forgotten: everything has 'almost' – but not completely – turned out alright.

These key, intertextual references thus take care to point the reader back to the earlier parts of the 'Danzig Quintet', to the messy, complex past that informs the postwar present of *Crabwalk*, inviting us to view all five works as parts of a remarkable narrative world, in which the reverberations of memory down the generations are traced with consummate literary skill. Together, *The Tin Drum*, *Cat and Mouse*, *Dog Years*, *Local Anaesthetic* and *Crabwalk* offer a wide-ranging portrait of postwar Germany's relation to the memory of its past, in individual, familial and historical contexts that are shown to be constantly overlapping. In the process, the quintet raises uncomfortable, but always thought-provoking questions, and it is these which ultimately forge the most fundamental link between the books that constitute it. The effect, in all cases, is the same: to steer the reader away from reductive interpretative positions, towards a nuanced, historically aware appreciation of the complexities of remembering the National Socialist past.

Notes

1. John Reddick, *The 'Danzig Trilogy' of Günter Grass: A Study of The Tin Drum, Cat and Mouse and Dog Years* (London: Secker and Warburg, 1975).
2. See Grass's 1973 essay 'Rückblick auf die Blechtrommel', *Essays und Reden II*, p. 328.
3. Sigmund Freud, 'Delusions and Dreams in Jensen's *Gradiva*', in *The Penguin Freud Library, XIV: Art and Literature: Jensen's Gradiva, Leonardo da Vinci and Other Works*, ed. by Albert Dickson (London: Penguin, 1990), pp. 27–118, at p. 65.
4. Günter Grass, *Peeling the Onion*, trans. by Michael Henry Heim (London: Harvill Secker, 2007), p. 3. Subsequent references appear in the text as O with the page number in brackets.
5. Günter Grass, *Dog Years*, trans. by Ralph Manheim (London: Picador, 1989), p. 294. Subsequent references appear in the text as *DY* with the page number in brackets.
6. Jeffrey Herf, *Divided Memory: The Nazi Past in the Two Germanies* (Harvard: Harvard University Press, 1997), p. 267 and p. 296.
7. 'Interview mit Günter Grass', www.steidl.de/grass, accessed 13 January 2006. My translation.
8. 'Exklusiv-Interview mit Günter Grass', *Kulturjournal, NDR*, http://ndr.de/tv/kulturjournal/archiv/20030728_1.html, accessed 18 October 2003.
9. Günter Grass, *Crabwalk*, trans. by Krishna Winston (London: Faber and Faber, 2002), p. 79. Subsequent references appear in the text as CW with the page number in brackets.
10. Robert Moeller, 'Sinking Ships, the Lost *Heimat* and Broken Taboos: Günter Grass and the Politics of Memory in Contemporary Germany', *Contemporary European History*, 12:2 (2003), 147–81.
11. Nicola King, *Memory, Narrrative, Identity: Remembering the Self* (Edinburgh: Edinburgh University Press, 2000), p. 21.

12. *The Complete Letters of Sigmund Freud to Wilhelm Fleiss 1887–1904*, ed. and trans. by Jeffrey Moussaieff Masson (Cambridge, Mass.: Harvard University Press, 1985), p. 207.

13. Jacques Lacan, *Écrits: A Selection* trans. by Alan Sheridan (London: Penguin, 1991 [1977]), p. 48.

14. Terry Eagleton, *Literary Theory: An Introduction* (Oxford, Blackwell, 1983), pp. 78–9.

15. Umberto Eco, *The Role of the Reader: Explorations in the Semiotics of Texts* (Bloomington: University of Indiana Press, 1979), p. 32.

6

HELEN FINCH

Günter Grass and gender

'The truth', said Siggie, 'is that we're through. Completely washed up and useless. We men just don't want to admit it. From the standpoint of history, the one thing men were good for, we've failed.'[1]

In Grass's *The Flounder*, the male narrator or narrators weigh up the contribution of the male gender, including the narrators themselves, to human history to date. In the end analysis, as we see from the opening quote, the men are found wanting. The novel ends with the lines 'Ilsebill came. She overlooked me, overstepped me. Already she had passed me by. I ran after her' (*F*, p. 547). Ilsebill is at once the narrator's wife and the fisherman's wife from the Grimm fairy tale, 'The Fisherman and his Wife', on which this novel is based. In this passage, she symbolises the progress of womankind in general. Thus, *The Flounder* concludes that, towards the end of the twentieth century, women have overtaken men, and men have comprehensively proven themselves to be useless, power-hungry, warmongering and violent.

Yet, despite this apparent defence of women, and this copious self-criticism on the part of the narrator, *The Flounder* unleashed a torrent of condemnation from feminist critics. Far from empowering women through a sympathetic rewriting of history, critics accused Grass of writing a novel that rejoiced in male chauvinism, sexual objectification, gratuitous violence, self-indulgence, narcissism and more besides. This chapter seeks to understand the virulence of such criticism in the context of the feminist movement of its time. It argues that, while much of the criticism of *The Flounder*'s presentation of women is valid, *The Flounder* is still a text that archives many historically influential constructions of gender, while at the same time playing with the possibilities of a postmodern or 'performative' model of gender that, in the end, it abandons. To read *The Flounder* is to read a contemporary document of the women's movement in Germany written from the outside, and to gain an insight into how narrative itself constructs gender.

The Flounder and feminism: The women's movement in 1970s West Germany

The Flounder has an intricately plotted narrative based around two framing narrative strands. One is the relationship of the narrator with his pregnant wife, Ilsebill, a humourless feminist who, like the fisherman's wife in the Grimm fairy tale, is never satisfied in her demands. The second is the trial of the fairy-tale flounder himself. In the opening pages, the flounder allows himself to be caught by a group of feminists who then put him on trial for having incited the male gender to instrumental rationality. This, they argue, has led to the pursuit of progress, war, and the impending apocalypse awaiting humanity. The trial takes as evidence the story of the narrator's relationships with nine (or eleven) cooks in and around Grass's home-town of Danzig/Gdánsk, from the Stone Age to the present day. (Nine of these cooks are historical, two more 'are fuzzy of outline, because I came to know them both too well' (*F*, p. 18).) These cooks are each a representative of their age, and the narrator's relationships with them function as exemplars of man's dealings with woman for the past four thousand years. Already, several of the problems that avowedly feminist (and indeed many other) critics have had with the text become clear: *The Flounder* is founded on an essentialist concept of gender that reduces women to a series of nine (or eleven) stereotypes or archetypes, from the outset defined by the traditionally domestic role of cook, and it is narrated from the point of view of a (magically immortal) man.

To understand Grass's depiction of the 'Feminal' (the name the Flounder gives to the tribunal of feminists), it is useful to look at the socio-historical context in which *The Flounder* was written, and in particular, at the history of the German women's movement. *The Flounder* was written over a period of at least five years, from 1972 (when *From the Diary of a Snail* appeared), to 1977, years that were crucial in the development of the German women's movement. The women's movement of the 1970s (often known as the feminist movement, 'new feminism' or second-wave feminism) largely emerged out of the German student movement of 1968. The women who took part in this movement began to question the way they were relegated to the status of wives, girlfriends and helpmeets of their male activist colleagues. Although Germany had a long history of women's organisation and agitation – which Grass refers to, obliquely, in *The Flounder* – the movement of the 1970s was unique in the emphasis that it put on the politics of the private sphere. In particular, the *Weiberräte*, or women's councils, formed mostly by young, well-educated women living in university cities in West Germany, campaigned on the issues of access to abortion, woman's unpaid labour in the home, and domestic violence.

From the very beginning, the women's movement was elitist and often divided on issues such as the status of Marxist analysis within feminist theory and practice. Nonetheless, from 1971 to 1976 the West German women's movement was catalysed and unified by the campaign to abolish article 218 of the criminal code, which made abortion illegal, in the face of opposition from the Catholic Church and the CDU. At the same time, German women writers (both West German and East German) sought a new means of self-expression that rejected the supposedly bourgeois norms of male literature, and which both recorded the truths of women's lived experience and attempted to find a new, female language that was unpolluted by the rationalist structures of masculine history and thought. One such means of reclaiming the German language and cultural heritage for women was the so-called *Märchenwelle*, or fairy tale wave, which sought to re-appropriate myths, fairy tales and prehistoric matriarchies for a new female self-understanding. *The Flounder* can certainly be seen in the context of this feminist wave of fairy tale retellings, although it is written by a man and from a distinctly masculine standpoint. By the time *The Flounder* appeared, though, the women's movement, such as it was, had lost much of its impetus. On the one hand, many of the goals of the movement, such as a freeing up of the restrictions on abortion and a greater social consciousness of the socio-economic structures that oppressed women had been achieved. On the other hand, many women felt that a conservative backlash against all forms of radicalism, fuelled by the West German government's response to the RAF terrorists (left-wing terrorists often also known as the Baader-Meinhof gang), was gathering momentum. The women's movement, instead of becoming a broad-based revolutionary structure throughout society, as it had hoped, became relegated to a sub-cultural phenomenon by the mid-1980s.

As we have seen, by appropriating a Grimm fairy tale – 'Von dem Fischer un syner Fru' (The fisherman and his wife) – and attempting to rewrite its misogynist message of the woman who can never be satisfied, *The Flounder* is very much of its time. Similarly, it rewrites the classical founding myth of Prometheus to make a female demi-goddess, Awa, the figure who steals fire from heaven to separate man from the beasts (*F*, 52). Moreover, the novel seeks to uncover a hitherto silenced German history 'from below', one experienced through the daily lives and domestic spheres of nameless women – only one of whom, the High Gothic mystic Dorothea Montau, left a trace on conventional 'masculine' history. The Feminal and the Flounder together seek to re-evaluate the contribution of these women to the development of culture, as well as the ways in which they were exploited by (and in a very few cases, also exploited) the men in their lives. As shown by the opening quote, ultimately both the Flounder and the Feminal come to the conclusion that men have thoroughly botched their role as lords of creation. The seemingly rational male achievements of 'patriarchy, the state, culture, civilization, dated history, and technological progress' have led to hunger and pollution, declares the Flounder: 'In capitalism and Communism alike, everywhere I find madness impersonating reason' (F, p. 453). Further, although the Flounder initially attempts to make the case that women contributed more to history than has been heretofore recorded – Amanda Woyke, for instance, the Enlightenment cook, turns out to have been instrumental in introducing the potato to Prussia – the lives of most of the cooks have been marked by male brutality and violence, culminating in the horrific gang rape and murder of the narrator's ex-girlfriend Billy on Ascension Day 1963.

Yet, although it deploys contemporary feminist poetic techniques, and uses a feminist tribunal as its framing device, the novel is anything but a sympathetic depiction of the women's movement. Although the novel ostensibly constructs a feminist re-reading of the lives of these oppressed cooks, the contemporary feminists themselves who practise this reading are, like Ilsebill, shrill, irrational and hypocritical. Although claiming to represent disinterested female justice, they are addicted to faction fighting and cannot agree on a concept of feminist utopia. 'Pathetic! The League of Socialist Women refused to take seriously what they called the "sexual pecking order" of Lesbian Action, while the liberal-extremist Bread and Roses group condemned the contribution of the "debating societies" as "social romanticism"' (F, p. 47). The factionalism appears all the more hypocritical as, once the members of the tribunal are away from the courtroom, almost all of them fall into bed with the narrator, at one time or other. 'No single one of them could ever hold me', he brags (F, p. 380). Moreover, their feminist goals appear either ludicrously utopian or preposterously narcissistic – sometimes both at once, as when the feminists meet to discuss Amanda Woyke in 'Ilsebill's Barn':

> And yet, despite all the playfulness – a few young women wore necklaces of (sprouting) winter potatoes – the earnestness of the original intention was maintained: working groups discussed the nutritive value of the basic foodstuffs . . . the necessity of combating hunger on a global scale, the ultimate goal, the Chinese world food solution, and over and over again the Great Leap, which was said to have already begun. (F, p. 335)

Far from pursuing the concrete goals of abortion rights and state funding of women's shelters, which were the real-life feminist campaigns in train at the time of writing, the feminists in *The Flounder* follow only wildly abstract goals that are destined to fail. Although the Feminal, and the narrator, reassess the lives of the nine historical cooks in their particular socio-political context, the same historical contextualisation is not extended to the representation of the West German women's movement.

The narrator's wife, Ilsebill, exemplifies the humourless, self-important feminists of the Feminal. In the poem which appears in the text, 'Libber, Libber', the narrator accuses, 'She has smashed what is dear and precious. / With a dull ax she had destroyed our bit of one-and-only' (F, p. 140). Thus, the narrator details how her tantrums and scorn destroy the love between her and her husband, while she all the while demands that he buy her a dishwasher. She reads 'books of all sizes in which the overcoming of inhibitions is said to be the first requirement for a free society', but 'has never, no matter how devoutly I get down on my knees to her, licked my ass, because she's afraid her tongue would drop off with her last shred of modesty' (F, p. 204). When Ilsebill is shown in a positive light, it is only when she is performing the function of Awa, of a gentle universal mother – when, under the influence of hallucinogens, she allows him to suckle at her breast (F, p. 395), or when, at a late stage of pregnancy she becomes transformed into a mystical landscape, 'closed to all interpretation. Let me in! I want to crawl into you. To disappear completely and recover my reason' (F, p. 515). The narrator's attitude to Ilsebill is by turns resentful, whining and aggressive, but he hardly ever acknowledges that, like the ideologies of the Feminal, her complaints and demands have formed in a specific historical context and are a (frequently justified) response to those circumstances.

Gender essentialism

The virulence of this portrayal of the women's movement demonstrates clearly why feminists and feminist critics such as Ruth Angress took such exception to the novel. Although the narrator starts out by claiming that he is looking for 'A third something. In other respects as well, politically for instance, as possibility' (F, p. 7), the possibility of a 'third something' soon gets lost in the gender wars of the text, which are restricted to the masculine/feminine binary. Despite his passive-aggressive remark to Ilsebill, 'Get that sulky look off your face. I'm all in favour of the libbers' (F, p. 6) at the outset of the text, the narrator hardly displays a very enlightened attitude towards the women who have been his partners throughout history. Thus, he resents Awa, the three-breasted Stone Age matriarch, because she keeps him in a state of ignorant tutelage. Again, Gret, the Renaissance nun, whom the Flounder declares could be one of the great comic protagonists of world literature, is in fact mostly reduced by the narrator to her abundant fleshy arse. Agnes Kurbiella, the poet Opitz's muse and mistress, is lauded for her silent selflessness when she acts as 'the bucket into which we vomited our misery' (*F*, p. 266). As we have seen above, moreover, the narrator feels most tenderly disposed towards Ilsebill when she ceases to be a 1970s feminist, and instead appears as the Eternal Feminine.

The Flounder's essentialist presentation of womankind is grounded in the early twentieth-century theories of gender that inform much of the novel. Thus, Gret bites off the testicle of her lover Hengge, an act of castration straight from Freud's theories of the unconscious. The fierce and dictatorial Awa – the first cook – resembles the matriarchs in Johann Jakob Bachofen's nineteenth-century work *Mother Right*.[2] In keeping with Bachofen's theory of a necessary progression from a timeless matriarchy to a progressive patriarchy, which establishes the father and his law above the undifferentiated rule of the matriarchs, the narrator must break away from Awa to gain power, and must repress his desires for endless sanctuary and to suckle on her breasts. The Flounder represents the snake in this Eden, trying to tempt the narrator into emulation of Minoan high culture and, later, into Christianity, instead of living a life of ease under Awa's kind tyranny. 'The only hope was to push off. Into the wide world. Into history', declaims the Flounder (*F*, p. 75), drawing a categorical line between female immanence and male transcendence. In leaving behind Awa's rule, after much nagging by the Flounder, the narrator creates both history and culture in his small section of the Baltic coastline. 'All she wants,' says the Flounder, 'is constant self-affirmation. Everything outside of her is ruled out. But art, my son, refuses to be ruled out' (*F*, p. 23).

To create art – whether that be a doodle of a flounder on a river shore or to write, as the narrator at one point plans, a complex novel about gender called *The Flounder* – is, in these models, a masculine activity that requires the abandonment of circular self-gratification. Thus, throughout history, the Flounder is doubly on trial, both for the crimes of mankind as visited on the suffering female cooks, and for the incitements that he whispers to the narrator to ensure the continuation of patriarchal and patrician rule. The Flounder initially defends his actions in blustering male-chauvinist form – approving the relegation of Agnes Kurbiella to the passive status of poet's muse rather than artist in her own right: 'She had no need to be creative. Because she was a creature – and perfect as such' (*F*, p. 257). The Flounder, then, appears to be the mouthpiece for the essential spirit of male identity, or even, as the trial goes on, Hegel's *Weltgeist*, the impersonal spirit that drives history inexorably forward. Yet the Flounder increasingly claims that he is tired of his position of *Weltgeist* and disappointed in the men that he has supported throughout history:

To prop up your superstructure, I have even, in my desire to be helpful, invented gods, from Zeus to Marx [. . .] Even for the much-invoked *Weltgeist*, there's not much fun in it. On the other hand, I'm coming more and more to like these ladies who are judging me.   (*F*, p. 150)

By the end of the novel, the Flounder has disowned the men whom he tempted to violence and hubris, and instead swapped his attention to the women: 'My Flounder no longer, her Flounder, leapt as though brand-new out of the sea and into her arms' (*F*, p. 547). The patronising, divisive principles that he espoused are, thus, not inherent to men, but instead could equally be transferred to women. Male creativity and female passivity, male violence and female suffering are revealed as an accident of history, as symbolised by the Flounder himself, and the novel ends with the prospect that the roles are about to be reversed.

Masculinity and narrative

As such, the construction of gender in *The Flounder* is no straightforward binary model that rests on timeless (or, indeed, late nineteenth-century) clichés of inherent masculine or feminine traits. Equally, the immortal male narrator of *The Flounder* is not the Flounder, and his personal model of history, literature and gender is not the straightforward catalogue of pro-gress, invention and oppression that the Flounder lays out for him. While the Flounder adheres to an ontogenetic model that reads the 'primitive stages' of human history as its psychological 'infancy', the narrator himself does not adhere to the Flounder's strict binary of immanence and transcend-ence. Far from engaging in a consistent and linear trajectory of masculine self-realisation throughout the course of two thousand years, he slides in and out of characters at will and on the instruction of others. In the course of one paragraph about the seventh cook, the Romantic revolutionary Sophie Rotzoll, he declares first that he was her lover Fritz, then that he would rather be the tyrannical Governor Rapp, and then, finally, that he was Sophie's kindly pastor friend, 'I wasn't Rapp (the traitor)' (*F*, p. 385). Whereas the Flounder promises the narrator a patriarchal history that, in the end, leads inexorably to repression and disaster, the narrator slips backwards and forwards through the chronological framework of the novel, escaping the twentieth century to greet the Baroque kitchen maid Agnes (*F*, p. 112), or, in a hallucinogenic moment, gathering all of his historical cooks together at one kitchen table (*F*, p. 394). Equally, the narrator is by no means an enthusiastic disciple of the Flounder; he takes much convincing to adopt the Flounder's historical programme in the first place. Throughout the Feminal trial, late at night, he sneaks into the cinema where the tribunal sits and the Flounder lives to harangue the Flounder about his mistakes and shortcomings. To return to a Freudian model, it would seem that, while the Flounder, with his insistence on patriarchy and sexual reproduction represents Eros, the narrator, whose overwhelming desire seems to be to stop history and crawl back to the womb, is governed by Thanatos.

In a sense, then, although the narrator abandons the search for a 'third possibility' between masculine and feminine, a truce in the gender wars, the narrator positions himself as the third party in the battle between the two extremes of feminist ideology and the Flounder's urbane sexism. Indeed, it is this precise dislike of ideology that informs the narrator's self-image. At a hallucinogenic meal, attended by the narrator together with Ilsebill and Griselde, a member of the Feminal who is also the narrator's lover, the women complain that the narrator could never make up his mind; it was always on the one hand and on the other hand. His absurd dislike of ideology had become an ideology with him (*F*, p. 388). Whereas the Flounder links the production of art to the foundation of the patriarchy, for the narrator art is fundamentally opposed to ideology, whether this be patriarchal, feminist or otherwise political. His idyll is that of the *Kürbishütte* (gourd arbour) where he can hide with Ilsebill and their child, like Simon Dach, the Baroque poet. In an appellative passage, he asks Ilsebill to shelter with him there:

> A gourd-vine arbour would give us and our little boy when he gets here a place to think in without having to travel, because a gourd-vine arbour would be just perfect for you and me . . . Thus camouflaged with gourd leaves and biblically secure, I could commit my lamentations about the rising price of copper and the Yom Kippur War to writing; just as my friend Dach wept aloud in his gourd-vine arbour when Field Marshal Tilly broke all records in the field of Catholic atrocities. (*F*, p. 93)

Ilsebill counters this suggestion as just one more form of patriarchal ideology: 'It's the old male-chauvinist trick. The gilded-cage routine' (*F*, p. 95).

Yet the longing for a third place, away from the strife of the world's politics, where the narrator can write and be at peace with his beloved, informs the rest of the novel. It helps us to understand why, for instance, the portrayal of the sole historically attested woman in the novel, the Gothic mystic Dorothea von Montau, is so uniformly vicious. Not only does Dorothea refuse to provide the narrator with the unpaid domestic services that would provide the narrator with this tranquil environment, but she refuses because of a sanctimonious Christianity that, as far as the narrator is concerned, is a hypocritical ideology covering up her sexual drives. Dorothea's erotic verses about her 'Jesu swete' are, in the narrator's understanding, a perversion of true aesthetic values, just as the dainty silver flail that she uses to mortify her flesh is a perversion of her swordmaker husband's skill. This flail becomes the site of another disagreement between the narrator and Ilsebill:

> Ilsebill's rage was High Gothic in origin and had been storing up ever since I exchanged her little silver scourge – a fine piece of swordmaker's craftsmanship – for a Venetian (Murano) goblet. This beautifully blown piece, which would have cost a fortune today, was the last to be shattered by Ilsebill. 'Trying to make a witch or a saint out of me, whatever serves your purpose at the moment. This isn't the Middle Ages!' she cried as she hurled.   (F, p. 129)

Yet it is not, in fact, the narrator who attempts to instrumentalise Dorothea's piety, either to canonise her as a saint or to demonise her as a witch, or indeed to rewrite her story as the tale of a feminist before her time. The narrator attempts to sidestep all ideological judgments on her life and to instead remember her as the flawed, complex historical person who was his wife. At the session of the Feminal that deals with her case, he begs the reader 'to consider my compromise proposal, halfway between the Catholic and the feminist positions' (F, p. 167). Given that 'neither of us knows what Dorothea wanted' (F, p. 168), the narrator confines himself to admitting his guilt in having beaten Dorothea as her husband, and to praising Dorothea's cooking.

Equally, this determinedly anti-ideological positioning can be viewed as the reason why Lena Stubbe, the nineteenth-century socialist cook, is portrayed in such a positive light. Lena's socialism develops in the context of the growth of the German Social Democratic Party (SPD) – when that party espoused many Marxist ideals and aims – and represents a pragmatic response to the impoverished conditions of the Danzig working classes, rather than the fossilised ideology that state-sponsored socialism has become by the 1970s. Moreover, within the revisionist debates in the SPD of the 1890s, Lena occupies the middle ground beloved of the narrator. She mediates between Rosa Luxemburg's revolutionary radicalism and Robert Michels's authoritarianism by telling both, 'the only thing that didn't change was the real world, its poverty, for instance' (F, p. 442). Lena's lifetime conveniently spans the entire period of German socialism before it lost its innocence with the formation of the communist German Democratic Republic. Indeed, through her death in the Nazi Stutthof concentration camp, she in fact becomes a socialist martyr. Yet although she espouses an orthodox socialist world-view, this orthodoxy manifests itself in a scrupulously fair distribution of soup to the poor of Danzig. Lena's practical, pragmatic feminist socialism is favourably contrasted with the fashionable Maoism of the radical feminists. Ilsebill, in common with the radical members of the Feminal, supports this Maoism: 'You with your snail philosophy!', she tells the narrator. 'How's there going to be any progress if we have to crawl all the time. Look at Mao and China. They weren't afraid to take a Great Leap Forward. They're ahead' (*F*, p. 330). The 'snail philosophy', here, is a reference to Grass's previous work, *From the Diary of a Snail* (1972), which detailed his participation in the 1969 SPD election campaign. This phrase is one of many links between the persona of the narrator and the author himself, Günter Grass. Given that Lena's gentle socialism can also be viewed as a 'snail philosophy', slow and earth-bound, it is perhaps unsurprising that hers is the only philosophy towards which the narrator is sympathetic. And indeed, the 'earthiness' of Grass's snail philosophy can also be seen to encompass the 'earthy' home cooking of all of his nine or eleven cooks, and the narrator's 'earthy' attitude to sex, which focuses on uncomplicated enjoyment of a woman's breasts and bottom. This, then, is the 'third way' that the narrator espouses between arrogant patriarchy and ideological feminism.

Can it then be said that the narrator does, in fact, clear himself from the charges of a crude sexism? Alas, no. Although the narrator occupies a space between these two ideologies, the gender of the novel's narration is most definitely male. As we have already seen, the narrator occupies a privileged position in relation to the Feminal and in relation to his nine or eleven cooks. He is the one figure who can authoritatively provide evidence about the cooks throughout history, although neither Flounder nor Feminal are disposed to hear it:

> My contention, supported by documentary evidence, that from neolithic times to the present I had lived in a relation of intimacy with Awa, Wigga, Mestwina, the High Gothic Dorothea, the fat Gret, the gentle Agnes, and so on, was not corroborated by the Flounder – 'Men', he said, 'have at all times been interchangeable' – and was ridiculed by the associate judges: 'Anybody can make such claims. What is he, anyway? A writer looking for material. Trying to ingratiate himself, to latch on, to grind literature out of his complexes.' (*F*, p. 73)

Despite these initial objections, the narrator does manage to ingratiate himself with the Feminal, and, as we have seen, does indeed manage to grind literature out of his many complexes. As the Agnes episode shows, male narration and creativity is bought at the expense of female subservience. Yet throughout the novel, although the inequality of this relationship is acknowledged, transcendent male creativity is constantly privileged above an immanent female creativity (which is usually expressed through cooking.) The male narrator is not only involved with all nine or eleven cooks, but also seduces all of the members of the Feminal in turn: he is not only the patriarch who has dominated all of the historical cooks, but the man who undermines the supposed female solidarity of the feminists.

On the narrative level of the text, this male dominance asserts itself as an asynchronous narrating moment as well as a binding moment of memory. This can be seen at the beginning of the novel when, together with the Gdánsk artist Richard Strya, the narrator explains their common male creative power:

> We, with the help of modest sips out of water glasses, drank ourselves back to the past. Strya and I can do that. We are contemporary only for the time being. No date pins us down. We are not of today. On our paper most things take place simultaneously. (F, p. 123)

If the women of the text pass on oral narratives, it is only men who can write them down. Not only does the male narrator write *The Flounder*, but also the male painter Philipp Otto Runge writes down the two versions of the oral folktale of the fisherman and his wife from the old woman of Rügen. When the men and women of his party of Romantic writers debate which version he should publish, Runge is another privileged third moment who decides between the misogynist and the misandrist versions of the fairytale – and ultimately decides for the misogynist version.

This privileged moment is inherently bound with the gender of narration: none of the women in the text have such a sovereign freedom from the linearity of history. They are each confined within their own time and concerns, and even those literate female visionaries such as Amanda Woyke and Lena Stubbe can only write about the future in a linear, Enlightenment fashion that is doomed to failure. Thus, Woyke's written fantasies of a perfectly ordered future appear naïve and excessively hopeful to late twentieth-century readers, and her humanitarian advice is twisted by her correspondent, Count Rumsford, into punitive and authoritarian policies. Stubbe's dreams of a proletarian future end when the Nazis systematically destroy all that she has worked for. Her sole writing, the Proletarian Cook Book, goes up in flames when the Soviets (ironically, a supposedly socialist power) bomb Danzig. The voices of the women whom the narrator claims to represent are never heard in their own right. It is no wonder, given the sorry fate of these women's writings, that the narrator prefers women to use an oral style of narrative whose rhythm is determined by the rhythm of repetitive physical labour: 'But speaking of my Mestwina's evocations, of Fat Gret's undimmed flow of speech, and of Amanda Woyke's mumblings, I must insist that in every case (for all their reprehensible attachment to the past), the style was determined by work being done in the present.' He laments that 'work norms and conveyor belts do not admit of storytelling'. Ilsebill once more makes the feminist objection that 'we women will never again consent to pound acorns into flour', at which point the narrator simply exercises his dominance over the narrative and 'wandered off into the next story' (*F*, p. 299).

Moreover, the language used by the narrator to describe his female protagonists contains multiple examples of the tired vocabulary of male chauvinism and sexual objectification of women. This crude use of language does justify the feminist disgust of, for instance, Angress, who says that in *The Flounder*, 'It's all tits and cunts, business as usual in current male fiction.'[3] Thus, the narrator looks at a group of women poets in India and considers 'which of the lady poets he would like to fuck if the opportunity presented itself' (*F*, p. 185). To name but a few more examples, when the narrator ritually eats Awa after her eventual death, he comments, 'She didn't taste especially good. Like a superannuated cow' (*F*, p. 261). Or, although the supposedly subversive Gret instructs her novices to lead a life of feminist solidarity in her convent, her novices apparently 'kept squirming on their stools and persisted in seeing harder and more lasting promise in their buttered carrots' (*F*, p. 197), a preposterously phallocentric notion of adolescent female sexuality. Gret's own sexual play apparently 'solves the bitterly earnest question of the century, the question of how to serve up the bread and wine, the Lord's Supper, in her own way, to wit, bedwise, by acrobatically moving her twat into the vertical and offering it as a chalice' (*F*, p. 209). Such an act would seem more to gratify the childish anti-clericalism of the narrator than the sexual desires of any woman. But throughout the text, women's sexuality is reduced to their genitalia, which are portrayed as cavernous, cleft or otherwise empty, ready to be filled with a male phallus.

Further, the relentless chronicle of violence towards women throughout the text, even if offered up as evidence for the brutality of the patriarchy, is dispiriting. For instance, the narrator's brutality towards Dorothea is not merely expressed in a series of vicious beatings. On the narrative level, it is demonstrated by the fact that he insistently imposes his own interpretation on her religious poems. The narrator denies her own creative account of her visions of Jesus, in favour of a vulgar Freudian reading of her poems, one that contends that expressions of religion are merely sublimations of sexual drives. Dorothea's place in the complex Late High Gothic culture of ecstatic mysticism, which expressed Christian spirituality in erotic language, is denied by the narrator's phallological interpretation. This symbolic level of violence meets with the narrator's actual violence towards Dorothea to form a thoroughly misogynist episode that sours the whole text. Moreover, the Dorothea episode foreshadows the most profoundly disturbing and violent episode of the novel, 'Father's Day', which also paradoxically provides the most radical disruption of the gender binaries in the entire novel.

Father's Day: Gender transgression

The 'Father's Day' episode is set close to the present of the narration: it takes place on Ascension Day, 1963, and involves the three members of the Feminal, Siggie, Maxie and Frankie, who later catch the Flounder and bring him to trial. Also present is Billy, who had been engaged to the narrator, and is now Maxie's lover. All four women have rejected not only heterosexuality, but normative female gender presentation. They have abbreviated their female first names into masculine nicknames, wear masculine clothes, drop their voices 'to cellar pitch' (*F*, p. 456), and hence also want to celebrate the traditional men's festival of Father's Day or Ascension Day. The four women embark on an expedition, along with every other male in Berlin, to the lakes surrounding the city. Here, they swig beer, barbecue meat in the open, and indulge in male bonding rituals. A power struggle then develops between the previously dominant Billy and her lover Maxie, as a result of which Billy is first humiliated and then gang-raped by the other women. Distraught, she stumbles off alone into the forest, where she is gang-raped by a group of Hell's Angels outraged at her transgression of the strict gender divide, and then run over by their motor bikes until she is dead.

The episode is unique in the novel for its horrifying violence, and also unique in the stark drive of its narrative voice, which features no wry asides from the Flounder and hardly any pontificating on the circular nature of history from the narrator. It is also unique in the novel in decoupling biological sex from social gender, and subsequently deconstructing the idea of biological sex altogether. The rest of the novel, as we have seen, rests on tired clichés of maternal, passive women and phallic, violent and creative men. By contrast, the 'Father's Day' episode takes seriously the notion that masculine gender is not something which is inherent to those who are born men, but a set of what the gender theorist Judith Butler calls performative 'acts, gestures, enactments' that constitute gender.[4] By performing as men, wearing male clothes and the ritual hats of Father's Day, the four women in fact become men. Their successfully transgressive performance constitutes the apotheosis of the separation of nature from culture that the Flounder initiated in the Stone Age: gender becomes not natural, but constructed. Siggie, Frankie and Maxie even urinate by means of a plastic dildo. 'That's what distinguishes man (or woman) from the beasts,' comments the narrator. 'For everything that's lacking under the sun we find a substitute.

Where there's a will there's a way' (*F*, p. 487). On Father's Day, not even the body is inherently gendered; technology has made possible gender transgression at will. 'For if a wafer can be the flesh and a swig of undistinguished wine the blood of our Lord Jesus, then an artfully conceived stopper . . . can bring salvation or at least a little bit of redemption' (*F*, p. 487).

Yet *The Flounder* approaches the notion of utopian and cyborg gender transgression that only gained widespread theoretical currency more than ten years later in the works of Butler and Donna Haraway, and pulls back from the radical implications of such transgression. *The Flounder* allows Siggie, Frankie and Maxie to change gender, but once they have done so, they are subject to the same ruthless drives of patriarchy as the other men in the novel. They use the same dismissive language towards women, calling them 'chicks' and 'femmes' (in the original German, 'Trinen'). They engage in violent fights and braggart contests, and when, tired out, they fall asleep, they dream 'the great, the unmistakable dream of procreation' (*F*, p. 486). And, having dreamed this dream, they gang-rape the sleeping Billy, thus replicating the cycle of misogynist violence that structures the novel. When the Hell's Angels murder her for her gender transgression, they are only continuing the punishment that Siggie, Frankie and Maxie, the new men, initiated. Masculinity and patriarchy become renaturalised as forces of history that cannot be deconstructed and made safe by performative parody. The quote that opens this chapter – ' "The truth," said Siggie, "is that we're through. Completely washed up and useless. We men just don't want to admit it. From the standpoint of history, the one thing men were good for, we've failed" ' – takes on a horrible new force when we realise it is uttered by a woman who, ten years previously, had as a man been responsible for the rape and murder of another woman.

Conclusion

It is this note of eternal violence against women that remains. Although *The Flounder* does provide a historical snapshot of the debates surrounding feminism at the time of its writing, it derides them unremittingly. While the narrator provides an ongoing record of the feminist arguments of the Feminal against the patriarchy, these arguments are revealed as hypocritical and meaningless once the reader realises that the chief advocate of the Feminal, Sieglinde Huntscha, is the Siggie who raped Billy years ago. Yet the 'third way' of the narrator is, as we have seen, no utopian solution to the gender wars, but in itself a form of creativity that perpetuates misogyny.

It would of course be illegitimate to identify Grass with the whinging narrative voice, despite the fact that *The Flounder* appeared at a time when he was playing with the introduction of more autobiographical material in his work. Rather, Grass is the author who has constructed an extremely sophisticated narrative that binds history, gender, cooking and poetics into a complex and rich novel, not the misogynist narrator himself. Nonetheless, although *The Flounder* contains within it the promise of a truly radical rewriting of gender, it ultimately relapses into tired gender stereotypes that have persisted in Grass's writings right up until his most recent work, his autobiographical work *Peeling the Onion* (2006). At the end of the novel, the Flounder leaps into a woman's arms; it appears that women are now going to be given history's upper hand. However, *The Flounder*, in its plot, in its language and in its narrative strategy suggests that this will only mean the continuation of patriarchy and of gender stereotypes under another name. *The Flounder*, ultimately, perpetuates the same gender stereotypes at the same time as it claims to deconstruct them.

Notes

1. Günter Grass, *The Flounder*, trans. by Ralph Manheim (London: Minerva, 1978), p. 480. Subsequent references appear in the text as *F* with the page number in brackets.
2. Johann Jakob Bachofen, *Das Mutterrecht (Mother Right: An Investigation of the Religious and Juridical Character of Matriarchy in the Ancient World)*, first published in 1861, now available as *Das Mutterrecht: eine Untersuchung über die Gynaikokratie der alten Welt nach ihrer religiösen und rechtlichen Natur. Eine Auswahl*, ed. by Hans-Jürgen Heinrichs, 8th edition (Frankfurt am Main: Suhrkamp, 1993).
3. Ruth Angress, 'Der Butt – A Feminist Perspective', in *Adventures of a Flounder: Critical Essays on Günter Grass' Der Butt*, ed. by Gertrud Bauer Pickar (Munich: Wilhelm Fink, 1982).
4. Judith Butler, *Gender Trouble* (New York and London: Routledge, 2006), p. 185.

7

REBECCA BRAUN

Authorial construction in *From the Diary of a Snail* and *The Meeting at Telgte*

When, in late 2006, it was revealed that Günter Grass had served for a short time towards the end of World War II in the Waffen SS, shock waves spread not just through Germany but the world. The German weekly news magazine *Der Spiegel* summed up much of the hostile media coverage with a belligerent cover page and title story, 'The Tin-Drummer: A Moral Apostle's Late Confession' (21 August), while fellow author John Irving fought back, writing in the British newspaper *The Guardian*, 'Günter Grass is my hero, as a writer and a moral compass' (19 August). At stake throughout the debate was Grass's public renown as Germany's leading commentator on moral issues, since the 1960s often summed up in the trite phrase 'Gewissen der Nation', or 'conscience of the nation'. The fact that Grass had not given an entirely accurate account of his actions during the war whilst at the same time shaming other public figures with skeletons to hide was not only felt seriously to undermine his moral standing. In the eyes of some of the author's harshest critics, it also called for a complete re-evaluation of his literary work to date, including a return of the Nobel Prize for Literature awarded in 1999.

Such outrage can only properly be understood in the wider context of Grass's public image. Like him or loathe him, media commentators and readers alike have been unanimous in seeing in Grass a straightforward example of a politically engaged author whose fiction can be readily interpreted in the context of current socio-political issues. In 1969, following Grass's high profile support of the left-wing Social Democratic Party (SPD) from 1965 onwards, the fellow-author and literary journalist Horst Krüger said of him:

> Grass – the perfect synthesis of individuality and image. An advertising picture that's always accurate. He really does look like his mass media reproductions [. . .] He almost seems as established as a leading brand-name product. National representativeness plays a part here, like with the Mercedes star. That's well known all around the world too and you know what you've got with it.[1]

Engaging with Krüger's metaphor of the 'brand-name product', this chapter questions Grass's role as a 'national representative' who is easily reducible to his mass-media image.

Indeed, I will argue that Grass presents a kind of authorship that is precisely *not* all it seems and that this is something that can be discerned in the manner in which he presents versions of his own person in his literary fiction long before the 2006 autobiographical revelations. In fact, as far back as 1972, when Grass was at the height of his success as a political commentator and public intellectual, he began to develop a contrasting image of the author as a whimsical textual construct in the semi-autobiographical *From the Diary of a Snail*. A later text from the end of the decade, *The Meeting at Telgte* (1979), builds on this, setting against the dominant image of Grass as a public advocate of responsible socio-political intervention an image of authorship as intrinsically unaccountable. Taken together, these two texts reveal a great deal about Grass's understanding of the authorial role both within literature and the world. This is an understanding that has gone on to inform almost all Grass's subsequent literary and political activities and, in its very complexity, has helped generate an oeuvre that is as rich in aesthetic innovation as it is in socio-political comment.

From the Diary of a Snail

Given the political path that his public appearances took in the 1960s, it is hardly surprising that *From the Diary of a Snail*, a first-person narrative that draws heavily on Grass's experiences in the 1969 West German election campaign, during which he travelled the length and breadth of the country delivering speeches on behalf of the SPD candidate Willy Brandt, has been read as a literary account of the author's political activities. Addressed to his children, the *Diary* follows two main strands, one fictional, one factual. On the factual level, Grass records his experiences on the campaign trail, with the book culminating in the victory of his party, the SPD. This is the 'diary' part of his text. Interwoven with this is the fictional strand of Hermann Ott, alias Dr Zweifel – the German word 'Zweifel' means 'doubt', an aptonym, or 'speaking name', that is central to this strand of the text. Zweifel witnesses the expulsion of the Jews from Danzig and spends the Second World War hiding in a cellar in the Polish countryside. Grass overtly introduces this story into the narrative in order to try to explain to his children back at home why he is so concerned about contemporary political developments in West Germany.

The fictional strand appears therefore in the first instance to be merely a device to help fill in the author's own political background, and this is how it has been largely understood to date. However, it also has important wider ramifications. Most notably, it allows the author to draw attention to the way he presents himself within his text. This is particularly evident in the way he develops the metaphor of the snail, the second part of the book's title. Within the fiction, Dr Zweifel is an avid collector of snails and derives his own personal philosophy from them, that is, from their slow, deliberate progress and their sticky adhesion to the earth beneath them. This is something he shares with the author. With his emphasis on the daily toil of electioneering, Grass presents himself to his children as measured, resisting the temptation to be either carried away by euphoria or plunged into the depths of despair. Indeed, this is presented as the credo of the whole book:

> Since in my thoughts, words, and deeds I am categorically earth-bound and even aboard a Super 111 am at best an unauthentic flier, nothing, not even an election campaign, can speed me or any part of me up. Accordingly, I request you to dispense with cries such as 'Faster!' or 'Get a move on!'. I mean to speak to you by (roundabout) bypaths: sometimes offended and enraged, often withdrawn and hard to pin down, occasionally brimful of lies, until everything becomes plausible. [. . .] And so, if my sentence twists and turns, and only gradually tapers to a point, don't fidget and don't bite your nails.[2]

Grass describes his own measured approach to life and literature in physical terms – he is 'categorically earthbound' – that are reminiscent of the snail, and then explicitly applies this to his activity within the narrative. As an author speaking within the text he takes on some of the snail's most striking physical attributes, namely its vulnerability and corresponding tendency to 'withdraw', and then links these to the twists and turns that his tale will take.

Such self-presentation squares well enough with the conventional reading of the snail as a metaphor for slow but steady political progress. Somewhat more difficult to reconcile, however, are the lines beginning 'I mean to speak to you by (roundabout) bypaths' that draw attention to the author-cum-snail's predisposition for untruths. Following detours and red herrings, he is not only 'hard to pin down', but would appear to be deliberately sowing confusion in order to blur any straightforward sense of causality or offer any clear political guidance. His remit is simply to narrate 'until everything becomes plausible'. This may be understood as a direct reference to Grass's tendency throughout the piece – and indeed in many of his other works – to blur the boundaries between fact and fiction. A little later on, this tendency is described as a fundamental aspect of Grass's character: 'I talk and talk; I listen to myself talking about things already talked to death, such as worker participation in decision making. I'm with it, but I'm also far ahead, exploring realities that pant for a different kind of justice. I spin thoughts, chase after the thread, tangle myself up, lie my way out [. . .] Then, children, I make words' (*DS*, p. 73). Accessing the fictional realm ('making words') is described as a compulsive act on the part of the author which is both liberating and treacherous and ultimately necessitates authorial elusiveness. The image of the author emerging here is quite different to that of the election campaigner slowly but surely edging closer towards his goal.

Against the laudable model of political commitment, then, is placed a second understanding of the author within his text. This is the author who is so fundamentally indebted to the fictional realm that he characterises himself as a snail not simply in order to send a clear political message, but rather in order to use the slippage between fact and fiction to question the very nature of his existence both inside and outside the text. Such a technique comes particularly to the fore when Grass depicts himself responding to his children's requests for intimate information about his person. Demanding '"Tell us something about yourself. About you. What you're like." "But tell us the truth. Don't make it up"' (*DS*, p. 70), they request an autobiographical narrative that, according to a traditional understanding of this mode of writing, should have a serious truth-telling mission at its core. Grass, however, immediately sets about questioning the assumptions underlying such self-presentation, asking 'Where does the peeling of a personality begin? Where is the tap that holds back confessions?' (*DS*, p. 71). The violence inherent in his chosen metaphors – autobiographical self-revelation is equated with 'peeling a personality' or loosening a 'tap' on 'confessions' that will subsequently pour forth – makes the reader's desire (here represented by his childeren's questions) for more intimate acquaintance with the authorial subject appear almost sadistic. Furthermore, it indicates a misplaced trust in the power of literary narrative on the part of these readers, for the very strength of the metaphors in an otherwise moderate narrative makes them stand out as objects of implicit authorial scorn.

Consequently, Grass's response both playfully shuns any sense of dramatic public self-revelation that might satisfy his readers and maintains his careful, educative tone toward his children. Continuing his snail metaphor, he withdraws from the public gaze to deconstruct his public persona from within the shelter of his cryptic literary text. Announcing rather grandly 'I confess that I'm sensitive to pain' (*DS*, p. 71), his revelations amount to nothing more than confirming that, like the 'slug' (*DS*, p. 71) with which he compares himself, he has a nervous system. 'Where am I now?' (*DS*, p. 72), he asks, and locates himself solely through external objects – shreds of tobacco and marks on white paper – before declaring himself missing entirely: 'I look out to see what the clamor is; actually it's me that's clamoring and somewhere else' (DS, p. 72). It would seem that in this pseudo-autobiography only the shell of his text offers the author any substance at all, and it is certainly in this vein that he offers his children a potted biography, which, far from providing an overarching narrative of the author's life, is characterised by an utter lack of causality. The distance that the literary author takes from his famous public persona appears as the final stage in what is effectively a systematic destruction of this persona. Personalising his literary fame and turning this character into a tenant ('Fame has been with us as a roomer', DS, p. 75), he claims of this individual:

> It's only because he's so lazy, and so useless when he besieges my writing desk, that I've taken him with me into politics and put him to work as a receptionist: he's good at that. Everybody takes him seriously, even my opponents and enemies. [. . .] He's beginning to quote himself. [. . .] He likes to have his picture taken, forges my signature to perfection, and reads what I scarcely look at: reviews.
> (DS, p. 75)

Not only does such a description of Grass's entrance on the political scene make a mockery of the serious motives that can be discerned elsewhere in the text, it is also a travesty of a conventional autobiography. The public personage is neither elucidated nor reassessed by the revelations of the writing subject, but is shown up to be an entirely fictional construct. He is nothing more than an image that has grown out of the coverage he receives across the public sphere. The hollowness of this image is underlined by its lack of substance – it feeds off untruths and self-citation – and its obsession with public perception (eagerly encouraging photographs and reviews).

Grass is not content to stop here, however. Having seriously undermined the integrity of his public persona, he turns his attention to his writing persona. In this context, he develops two metaphors, again ostensibly aimed at explaining his professional person to his children: 'A writer, children, is someone who writes against the passage of time' (DS, p. 141), and 'In case you didn't know, children, a writer these days is just a fug measurer. What they call stable smell' (DS, p. 222). Both images have clear political overtones. 'Writing against the passage of time' is developed in a particularly political chapter: Grass and his family visit friends in Czechoslovakia, inspiring reflections on Germany's recent past, the persistence of German perpetrators into the present day, and the continued existence of brutal, totalitarian regimes in the Eastern Bloc. The chapter in particular, and Grass's text in general, clearly reflect critically on these socio-political concerns, with the author drawing attention to his belief that it is his job as an author to write against the public tendency to forget the lessons of history. Likewise, his later reference to the author's role in perceiving and exposing unpleasant smells has a primary, obviously political connotation. This reference is developed within a chapter that details the extent of his travels across Germany as part of the election campaign where exposing the fug is directly linked to taking on staunchly conservative areas.

Both metaphors, in their most obvious interpretations, therefore fit well with the dominant public image of Grass as a politically motivated author who takes a strong moral stance on Germany's recent past. If we look a little more closely at the wider textual context in which each metaphor is developed, however, the case for a solely political reading of Grass's authorial self-presentation begins to weaken. While the chapter detailing his visit to Czechoslovakia appears to debate at length the author's public responsibilities in difficult political times, much of this discussion shields painful personal information about his marital break-up. Conversation with his wife, Anna, is awkward throughout the stay and discreetly managed to avoid full-scale arguments. In these strained circumstances, consideration of Germany's recent past is alluded to by the author as just one attempt at covering over the couple's difficulties: 'Anna looks about as if she'd forgotten something. Lost syllables and other arrears. Now we stop talking about the time that has passed. (Since all have their parts, I'm left with the role of morale builder)' (*DS*, pp. 142–43). Not only does his trumpeted political role of writing against political forgetfulness emerge here as something of a front (resurrected and abandoned as underlying emotions allow), the very metaphor itself becomes tinged with the author's personal circumstances and is rendered ambiguous. The 'time that has passed' can refer just as much to problems in the couple's marriage as recent German politics. By the end of the chapter this is almost certainly the case, where the time that passes now is of a solely personal significance – 'when even more time had passed' (*DS*, p. 145) alludes to the obviously uncomfortable year in which Anna's lover Vladimir began to die of cancer and it became clear to all concerned that the Grass marriage was no longer viable.

Such personal difficulties shielded in an apparently overtly political self-conception can also be found in the text's wider structure. As we have already seen, Grass draws attention to his own writing project, reflecting on his narrative style and self-presentation as he progresses. Such meditations go so far as to address directly his use of the diary form, both in his own text and in his characterisation of Dr Zweifel as an avid diary writer. Self-consciously attesting to his fragmentary attempts to record his increasingly fragmented life, he muses '[German scientist and satirist] Lichtenberg's name for the waste book used by English merchants was *Sudelbuch* ['botchbook']; This method of writing casually against time was recommended to me by Doubt . . .' (*DS*, p. 128). Just as Zweifel – Doubt – writes letters (that are never sent) and composes charts and tables to pass the time, Grass here presents himself as turning to writing as a means of gathering his thoughts and committing to paper – and therefore to memory – the various aspects of a difficult and yet fulfilling daily existence. This process of literary reflection is, furthermore, an agreeable one (done 'casually') – a kind of time-out that stops the passage of time in quite a different way to the political reading implied above. This is a far more personal, not to mention self-consciously textual, understanding of his authorial activity.

The slippage from a coherent political self-conception into a far more idiosyncratic understanding of authorship within the text and the author's own personal world is further supported by his self-description as a 'fug measurer'. 'Fug' attracts Grass's attention from early on, when he specifically records the smell of his own unwashed shirts ('fug-saturated shirts', *DS*, p. 27) at the end of a week's campaigning, and relishes in the smell of local politics 'because I collect fug' (*DS*, p. 82). This interest in the smell of his political environment, however, leads into a far more existential depiction of his authorial activities than political activism alone would justify. Expanding on his self-conception, Grass states unequivocally: 'A writer, children, is a man who loves fug and tries to give it a name, who lives on fug by giving it a name; a mode of life that puts calluses on the nose' (*DS*, p. 223). This sort of existential attachment to the metaphorical 'fug' could be a very strong statement of political commitment on the part of an author who has already established his public responsibility to 'write against the passage of time'. Given the text's wider self-conscious reflections on the author's use of the narrative form, however, it may also be read as a far broader statement concerning the author's need to experience himself as someone who continuously engages with the world around him, committing these experiences to paper almost in spite of himself. This is certainly substantiated by subsequent statements in the same chapter, where the author's need to write has become an obsession that controls him entirely: 'Everywhere all the time. I write while I talk listen answer' (*DS*, p. 227), he says, drawing attention to the existential nature of his textual affliction: 'often I write only to prove to myself that I exist, that it's me who's writing words on slips and throwing them out the window' (*DS*, p. 228). The author's textual motto could be summed up as 'I write, therefore I am', but even this 'I' is nothing more than a textual construct, the product of a writing process that churns out identities on a metaphorical conveyor belt: 'I write on rain-splattered slate roofs, in puddles of beer, on a conveyor belt: I I I' (*DS*, p. 228). Thus while the whole text is apparently geared towards elucidating Grass's public persona, the very process of self-presentation this entails undermines such an aim from the start. In presenting himself, Grass is brought to reflect on what exactly constitutes the personal 'I' of the text and the public 'he' of politics. In both cases, the answer appears to be little more than empty discourse.

These considerations are problematic for the conventional interpretation of the text as an intimate account of Grass's public political persona. While they do not deny his public commitment to the political cause, they certainly challenge the idea that the author Günter Grass and his texts can be reduced to a political line. Rather, Grass draws attention to the innately constructed nature of authorship in both the public sphere and the text. The issue of 'peeling a personality' (*Enthäutung einer Person*) is a red herring because actually the author consists of nothing but 'peel' (*Haut*); there is no central core to be revealed. This point is brought across strongly at the end of chapter 26, when the author expresses the wish, 'If I could shed my skin [*Sich häuten können*: translated elsewhere as 'peeling']. Be outside myself. Sticky-new', only to be addressed by an old school friend with the greeting 'What do you say, old-timer?' [*Na, alte Haut*!: literally, 'well, old skin!'] (*DS*, pp. 256–7). The wish remains hypothetical because there is no way 'out of himself'. Instead, the author is manifestly produced by the discourses in which he takes part. This would appear to be the unavoidable condition of the author compelled to reproduce himself in fiction as in the public sphere. Just as the media gave rise to one image of the author, his text creates another.

The Meeting at Telgte

I have suggested 'I write, therefore I am' as a possible motto for *From the Diary of a Snail* that gives the text relevance beyond the specific circumstances in which it was written. When *The Meeting at Telgte*, a work recounting the fictional meeting of baroque poets at the end of the Thirty Years War, was published in 1979, many critics believed that this text carried its own motto within it. It was written in honour of Hans Werner Richter, founder of the Group 47, the loose consortium of West German writers which emerged in the immediate postwar period, many of whom later became famous for their political engagement, and Grass made the parallels with this group clear from the outset. Early on in the narrative the seventeenth-century lyricist Simon Dach, Richter's alter ego, asserts the superior moral standing of poets compared to the princes, and this has been taken by many to sum up the at times rather self-congratulatory tone felt to pervade the text:

> After all, they were not nobodies. Everything had been laid waste, words alone kept their luster. And where princes had disgraced themselves, poets had earned respect. They, not the powerful, were assured of immortality.[3]

Far more directly than any of Grass's other literary outputs, *The Meeting at Telgte* deals with contemporary authors' collective attempt to take on a political role. The parallels between the seventeenth- and twentieth-century groupings endow the text with an immediate meaning: the care with which the three-day meeting, its literary and political aims, and the unfolding dynamics within the group are described indicates a deliberate attempt to provide insight into the workings of the Group 47, as well as retrospective acknowledgment of their achievements.

Certainly, the main group of authors invited by Dach appears to play out the major arguments about literature and politics that dominated the 1950s and 1960s and were of continued relevance throughout the 1970s. Where Group 47 authors were initially united in their attempts to instigate a self-aware, specifically postwar literary discourse, their baroque counterparts meditate at length on the various literary forms and styles that may be considered appropriate to the needs and mores of their time. Such concerns inform almost all of the debates sparked by the readings: poet and philologist Augustus Buchner, for example, initiates a heated versification discussion; writer Sigmund Birken finds his idea of 'appropriateness' in dramatic characterisation ridiculed, while protestant Johann Rist's contemporary drama leads to reflection on the current state of affairs in the war-torn German lands in the aftermath of the Thirty Years War (1618–1648). Indeed, a sense that the very nature and purpose of literature is under scrutiny informs the whole meeting, with stylistic and ideological differences conditioning many of the heated exchanges that underpin the group dynamics. Furthermore, throughout the meeting a small group of activists led by Johann Michael Moscherosch, the famous satirist and moralist, and Rist works on a political manifesto that seeks to exploit the poets' collective rhetorical mastery and comparatively high social standing to some kind of concrete political effect. The idea that, thanks to their commitment to maintaining the purity and integrity of their artistic production, they may themselves have managed to remain unsullied by political developments is strongly expressed in the words of an early draft for this manifesto: 'they were the other, the true Germany' (*MT*, p. 67) and echoes the earlier assertion made by Dach that 'after all, they were not nobodies' (*MT*, p. 17).

However, such an earnest self-conception is not left unchallenged within the text. Not only do the poets frequently let themselves down on a moral level (most notably in their readiness to believe the young Christoffel Gelnhausen's lies when it comes to reaping the benefits of his plunder) and reveal themselves to be poor leaders (in their repeated childish squabbling, unconsidered herd-like behaviour and tendency to be distracted by petty argument, food and sex); the limitations of the kind of publicly accountable model of authorship they represent are also thrown into sharp relief by the two outsider figures, Heinrich Schütz and Christoffel Gelnhausen. Heinrich Schütz, a celebrated composer of the time, turns up at the meeting unexpectedly, while Christoffel Gelnhausen, a mixture of Germany's most renowned baroque author Grimmelshausen (1621–1676, born in Gelnhausen) and his most famous – and indeed the seventeenth-century's best-known – literary creation, Simplicissimus, offers his military influence to provide the group with food and shelter for the duration of their stay. Both characters act as foils for the main group, and both are undeniably larger than life.

Schütz hails from what might be called a different artistic world. Where the poets meet in the name of serving literature and their country, the reality of their situation is that they first and foremost serve their patrons. Schütz, on the other hand, has refused to make any artistic compromises in his attempt to reveal the true, quasi-religious beauty bound up in the word. Likewise, where the poets are easily distracted from their task by any number of worldly concerns, Schütz never loses sight of the important potential in their meeting. He reaches the zenith of his authority at the very point when the poets, distraught by their human weaknesses, are about to abandon the meeting in despair. Schütz intervenes in almost godly fashion to absolve them of their guilt, remind them of their duty and encourage them in clear, straightforward terms: 'In the eyes of God, he said, their complicity in the horror was slight. Their undertaking, however, which would benefit the language and help their unfortunate fatherland, remained great and must be carried on' (*MT*, p. 92).

Significantly, such an antipathy to despair is reminiscent of Grass's own highly publicised stance throughout the 1960s and 1970s. In his well-known, provocative cycle of poems 'Fury Anger Rage' ('Zorn Ärger Wut'), published in the 1967 collection, *Cross-examined* (*Ausgefragt*), Grass polemicised against 'impotence' ('Ohnmacht'), suggesting that following a complicated recipe for brawn might offer a more constructive way of venting one's anger than falling into despair.[4] Similarly, in *Head-births or The Germans Are Dying Out* (1979) the author played with the image of the writer as Sisyphus, heroic challenger to the gods and champion of the absurd, and carried on in the early 1980s to champion positive action as the best response to challenging political circumstances, stating for example in 1983, 'Orwell's decade demands that we don't resign ourselves melancholically to sliding towards catastrophe, but that we dig our feet in on the downward slope.'[5] Implicitly endowing Schütz with such insight increases this character's position of authority for those familiar with Grass's work. He is meant to inspire awe not only on account of his artistic achievements but also on account of his impeccable moral rigour and intellectual clarity.

Christoffel Gelnhausen, on the other hand, is quite the opposite. Although he initially saves the poets' meeting by finding them alternative accommodation, many of his subsequent actions threaten to jeopardise the proceedings. Where Schütz's absolute authority seems at times divine, Gelnhausen's roguishness is taken to the extreme. A firm believer in the end justifying the means, he has no compunction in exploiting the power conferred on him by his military posting. He empties the inn for the poets with a mixture of trickery and intimidation, while he procures food for them by callously plundering the remains of a raid that had just been carried out on his own people. His utter lack of moral feeling is matched only by his lively imagination. Both have their roots in his hands-on experience of reality. Introduced to the poets with the words 'His lies [. . .] are as inspired as any romances [. . .] he is familiar with the seamy side of life, and wherever he goes [. . .] he knows his way about [. . .]. He might help them' (*MT*, p. 7), Gelnhausen represents a spirited approach to the world that underlines the narrowness of their poetic vision. He observes their literary arguments, and comments 'the world could come to an end, and in the midst of the rumbling and roaring these gentlemen would quarrel over the correct or incorrect use of metric feet' (*MT*, p. 31). Where the poets genuinely want to help guide literary and political developments for the greater human good but are ultimately rather clueless as to how to proceed, Gelnhausen acts as the court-fool who through his own twisted and highly entertaining understanding of the world keeps revealing their shortcomings. His explicit criticism from below combines with Schütz's implicit criticism from above.

In fact, as unlikely a pairing as the two may be, Heinrich Schütz and Christoffel Gelnhausen join forces in representing an alternative image of authorship within the text. When Schütz, the text's artistic and moral authority, advises Gelnhausen to take up the pen, the words with which he does so can be read as the motto of this second understanding of authorship: 'he told the regimental secretary never again to put his murderous fictions [*Lügengeschichten*, literally 'lying-stories'] into practice, but to write them down bravely' (*MT*, p. 92). Schütz's absolute dedication to his art contrasts with the poets' pragmatic attempts to compromise, and his decision to ignore circumstantial restraints leads to a rather different understanding of literature and the author's accountability within it. Endowed with outstanding moral acumen, the author can ignore conventional understandings of right and wrong in the greater name of artistic production. For Gelnhausen, this means that his trickery will become his most prized asset, as his ability to deceive and to shirk responsibility help him to construct a spirited fiction that opens his readers' eyes to the world in which they live. As numerous critics have noted, it seems significant that the major text he will go on to write was a clear source for Grass's *The Tin Drum*. Just as Schütz carries some of the famous author's moral authority, Gelnhausen could be described as his literary representative.

Equally significantly, Grass has also spoken elsewhere about 'murderous fictions' (*Lügengeschichten*) and the idea of different social and literary realities. In *The Tin Drum*, Oskar refers to the act of narrating his life story as a case of 'telling lies' (*etwas vor[lü]gen*),[6] while in an interview in 1971 Grass speaks of art's challenge to our everyday understanding of reality: 'All arts [. . .] confront the narrowly-defined, tangible reality with a new reality, a literary, pictorial, musical, theatre-style one, which must then, however, be conceived as such.'[7] Schütz's approval of Gelnhausen's craft thus carries a triple seal of authorial approval. The role played by both characters, cast as larger than life and endowed with important aspects of Grass's own public persona, allows them to transcend the group of writers and their contingent concerns. They are brought together by their understanding of authorship, the positioning of which in the text is clearly intended to provide direct competition to the laudable but ailing notion of the writer as self-appointed 'conscience of the nation' (*Gewissen der Nation*). This may be summed up as the second model of authorship evident in *The Meeting at Telgte*, and it is exclusively text-centric. Indulging in the liberties of art, the author is by no means necessarily a socially acceptable figure. Rather, at the risk of being distanced and unfathomable like Schütz, or a dissimulating rogue like Gelnhausen, he serves literature first and society second.

The two contrasting models of authorship I have outlined above – a publicly accountable, cohesive grouping on the one hand and a lone exist- ence answerable only to the laws of the text on the other – is a productive tension that not only goes through *The Meeting at Telgte*, but also Grass's writing as a whole.[8] Thematically speaking, the two models relativise one another within the text. The charge that the main group of writers, together with their politicised self-understanding, is presented in a self-congratulatory manner is easily rebutted with reference to the serious challenge that Schütz and Gelnhausen pose to their literary credentials. At the same time, the laudable intention underlying their meeting is never really called into doubt. The literary loners, on the other hand, do not offer any practical model for socio-political improvement beyond Schütz's vague encouragement to the group to continue in their efforts. Their sudden appearance and disap- pearance underline their one-sidedness, their fundamental unsuitability to uniting the different pulls of literature and politics. The result is that neither model on its own offers a satisfactory all-round paradigm of authorship.

Likewise, the text does not have any answers: whether the manifesto that, when finally drafted, is lost in the fire that destroys the inn, would have had any impact can never be known for sure (although the narrator does dismiss it), and exactly why the manifesto never made it into the wider world – who was responsible for causing the fire? – remains a mystery. Read with Grass's exploration of authorship in mind, however, these uncertainties are not necessarily problematic. Bringing the authors together allows Grass to explore various contrasting understandings of the author without running the risk of contradicting himself.

Not only does *The Meeting at Telgte* not have any answers, it also actively poses questions. In particular, the seemingly unidentifiable first-person narrator has caused considerable speculation amongst Grass scholars. Although most commentators are agreed that any specific identity is probably untraceable,[9] Alexander Weber has gone to some lengths to identify the first-person narrator as one historical personage. Reading the text extremely closely and applying a baroque approach to possible emblems within it, he makes a strong case for identifying the first-person narrator with the little-known poet Johann Matthias Schneuber.[10] Such an identification is convincing not only with reference to the inner logic of the text, as Weber argues in intriguing detail, but also with respect to the rest of Grass's writing. Schneuber is characterised in the text as a troublemaker who enjoys spreading unkind rumours and is jealous of the success of others and keen to mock. This behaviour both marginalises him from the main group of authors and reflects the first-person narrator's own marginalisation within the text (there are comparatively few direct references to him), together with his penchant for literary intrigue.

Most importantly, in the context of my argument, elevating an untrustworthy schemer to the important position of first-person narrator introduces on a structural level the second model of authorship discussed above. The narrator deliberately causes confusion about the course of events and his own relationship to them, calling his identity into doubt and playing petty power games with the reader. 'I even knew what no one else did' (*MT*, p. 84), he boldly claims with reference to unfolding political events, yet when it comes to exactly who said what at the meeting, he cannot even remember whether he or someone else spoke: 'Someone (I?) asked' (*MT*, p. 21). This sort of narrative vagueness is familiar to Grass readers from the 'Danzig Trilogy' onwards. The text of *The Meeting at Telgte* functions as a deliberately wicked example of the turn that a text-centric model of authorship can take. Answerable only to the word – and the narrator first introduces himself with the words 'I am writing down' (*MT*, p. 3) – he manages to absolve himself of all responsibility for his text by thoroughly obfuscating his identity within it. His blatant disregard for narrative accountability stands in stark contrast to the event he narrates: the authors' collective attempt to take on a position of responsibility in respect of their literature and their country.

Not only within the text (the two different conceptions of authorship), but also across the text (form and content) Grass thus plays different models of authorship against one another. The open-endedness of the text arises because Grass wants to allow space for both conceptions of authorship, not pitch one against the other. In so doing, he carefully avoids placing a clear self-image into any one of the characters, the narrator included. Instead, aspects of himself and his authorial credo are scattered across the text. It is no accident that there are similarities between Gelnhausen's trumpeted literary style and that of the author of *The Tin Drum*, that Schütz speaks Günter-Grass words of authorial defiance, or indeed that much of the author's personal experience of the Group 47 informs the generally positive description of the baroque poets while the first-person narrator is unrepentantly untrustworthy in the best Günter-Grass fashion. Grass is both everywhere and nowhere in his text, not least because it feeds off a tension that is fundamental not only to contemporary debates about literature and the world, but also to his own self-conception as an author functioning in the public sphere.

Conclusion

In both of the texts discussed in this chapter, Grass overtly develops a familiar image of authorship as publicly accountable and politically motivated. This understanding of authorship has largely conditioned not just the reception of these two texts, but also of Grass's work as a whole. This essay has argued that these works are far more ambiguous than such straightforward readings allow, and this in turn encourages us to reassess Grass's own understanding of authorship. The idea that the author is somehow complicit with his text, both enabling its 'untrue' fictional inventions and himself becoming a textual construct in the process, permeates both pieces. In *From the Diary of a Snail* such considerations lead into extensive reflection on the writing subject and the process of writing as an existential necessity, while in *The Meeting at Telgte* a new complexity is brought to the question of how authorship relates to the world by the various models of authorship explored within it. These contradicting images of authorship, common to both texts, sum up an intriguing contradiction in Grass's understanding of his own authorial position. From *The Tin Drum* (1959) through to *Peeling the Onion* (2006), which appeared shortly after his revelations concerning his SS service discussed in the opening lines of this chapter, he has repeatedly drawn attention to the social and political role of authors in the world. Much of Grass's literary technique, however, from the innovative use of extended metaphor through the blurring of fact and fiction and ironic subversion of genre to his trademark manipulation of unreliable narrators, is reliant on a textual conception of the author as a deliberately elusive and unstable construct.

Notes

1. Horst Krüger, 'Das Wappentier der Republik: Augenblicke mit Günter Grass', *Der Spiegel*, 25 April 1969, my translation; also quoted in Franz Josef Görtz, *Günter Grass: Zur Pathogenese eines Markenbilds* (Meisenheim am Glan: Hain, 1978), p. 51.
2. Günter Grass, *From the Diary of a Snail*, trans. by Ralph Manheim (New York: Harcourt, 1976), p. 9. Subsequent references appear in the text as *DS* with the page number in brackets.
3. Günter Grass, *The Meeting at Telgte*, trans. by Ralph Manheim (New York: Harcourt, 1990), p. 17. Subsequent references appear in the text as *MT* with the page number in brackets.
4. This poems that make up this cycle are 'Powerless, with a Guitar' ('In Ohmacht gefallen'), 'Do Something' ('Irgendwas machen'), 'The Jellied Pig's Head' ('Die Schweinekopfsülze') and 'The Epilogue' ('Der Epilog') and they can be found as parallel translated texts in Günter Grass, *In the Egg and Other Poems*, trans. by Michael Hamburger and Christopher Middleton (London: 1978), pp. 94–115. The title 'Fury Anger Rage' ('Zorn Ärger Wut') is not included in this parallel text version.
5. Günter Grass, 'Orwells Jahrzehnt II', in Günter Grass, *Werkausgabe*, vol. 16, ed. by Volker Neuhaus and Daniela Hermes (Göttingen: Steidl, 1997), pp. 71–9, 78–9, my translation.
6. Günter Grass, *Die Blechtrommel*, in Günter Grass, *Werkausgabe*, vol. 3, ed. by Volker Neuhaus, p. 9. My translation. I have chosen not to follow Ralph Manheim's translation here, as he strays quite far from the German.
7. Günter Grass in interview with Getrude Cepl-Kaufmann, 'Ein Gegner der Hegelschen Geschichtsphilosophie' (1971), in Günter Grass, *Werkausgabe in zehn Bänden* (1987), vol. 10, pp. 106–20, at p. 113. My translation.
8. For a full discussion, see my book, *Constructing Authorship in the Work of Günter Grass* (Oxford: Oxford University Press, 2008).
9. Wimmer argues quite convincingly that the text resists any specific author-character identification, Ruprecht Wimmer, '"Ich jederzeit": Zur Gestaltung der Perspektiven in Günter Grass' "Treffen in Telgte"', *Simpliciana*, 6–7 (1985), 139–50.
10. Alexander Weber, 'Johann Matthias Schneuber: Der Ich-Erzähler in Günter Grass' "Das Treffen in Telgte": Entschlüsselungsversuch eines poetisch-emblematischen Rätsels', *Daphnis*, 15 (1986), 95–122.

8

MONIKA SHAFI

Günter Grass's apocalyptic visions

'War always raged whether it was close to home or far away', Grass stated in his opening speech 'The War Has Run Out of Steam', held at the 2006 International Pen Congress in Berlin. A world perpetually void of peace, he continues, sets the moral and literary agenda for authors: 'We authors are late bloomers . . . because events that happened and continue to happen . . . never quit escaping us. What historians are willing to write off, remains present to us.'[1] While Grass is reacting specifically to the invasion of Iraq in 2003 in this speech, his principal argument that writers are charged with the task of accounting for individual suffering and of taking those in power to court for their lies, profiteering or megalomania characterises his entire oeuvre. Guilt and responsibility, be they of nations or of citizens, are the twin forces Grass does battle with, and in each of his four major works written in the decade between 1980 and 1990, *Headbirths or The Germans Are Dying Out* (1980), *The Rat* (1986), *Show Your Tongue* (1988), and *Dead Wood: An Epitaph* (1990), he depicts how (West) Germany and Third World countries engage with the political, economic, social and cultural conditions of late capitalism.

Not only is the spectrum of problems addressed daunting, ranging from the abject poverty of the metropolitan slums belts in India or Indonesia, worldwide ecological devastation, threat of atomic annihilation to the spiritual malaise of prosperous West Germans or their dismal politicians, but Grass also experiments with time-frames and narratives styles that dislodge traditional genre patterns. Moreover, these challenging, at times bewildering, works, combine multiple media, attach plots to his own biography and frequently reference German literary giants such as Lichtenberg, Lessing, the Brothers Grimm or Theodor Fontane. Grass is also fond of including authorial self-reflections or ruminations on the genesis of the text. Such a thematic and narrative mélange has not always resonated with critics and the initial reception of these four works has been quite mixed, and outright negative in the case of *The Rat*.

The question, 'And how will Sisyphus react to Orwell's decade?', from *Headbirths*,[2] hovers umbrella-like over the four texts, each providing a different narrative take and conceptual approach. With Sisyphus and Orwell as place makers, referencing both the myth of Sisyphus and Orwell's dystopian vision of the future (now present) in *Nineteen Eighty-Four* (1949), Grass probed whether the world still allows for hope, activity, and future, or whether it is finally void of reason and justice. Is the apocalypse, as in the past, still an event to be fearfully awaited or has it become a quotidian reality, a daily onslaught of pollution, poverty and hopelessness? These are global questions, yet in their core these texts revolve around Grass's life-long fixation on the history and fate of the German nation and, by implication, on his own contributions to its cultural pantheon and political path. German nationhood and (apocalyptic) future are also repeatedly linked to the figure of the child and to a key body of children's narratives, the Grimms' fairy tales. The tension between children's time and realm, alternately characterised as future, fairy tales or forests, and the destruction of these spaces, runs through all of these works. A recurring theme is also the feeling of shame with which Grass responds to sights that threaten to render him speechless. This fear of material annihilation and narrative void is a key feature in all four works, and in each Grass struggles to affirm the power of (his) words against the dual threat of extinction and silence.

Headbirths or The Germans Are Dying Out

In Grass's prolific oeuvre, this hybrid narrative probably features the most intriguing title. Headbirths, a literal translation of 'Kopfgeburten', an unusual German compound, indicates creative powers but also hints at male birth envy, since headbirths can only produce abstractions. Their lifelessness is heightened by the subtitle with its ironic allusion to doom-laden right-wing rhetoric. Indeed, one of the text's narrative strands features a German couple in their mid-thirties, the high school teachers Harm and Dörte, textbook examples of tall, blonde Lower-Saxons, who cannot commit to having a child. Alternately wanting or rejecting parenthood, their constant vacillations, 'The Yes-to-baby No-to-baby dilemma' (*HB*, p. 104), frame all of their pursuits and disputes, particularly during their five-week travel to India, Thailand, and Indonesia undertaken in the summer of 1980. They had booked this tour with the travel agency 'Sisyphus' (*HB*, p. 25) because in addition to sightseeing and beach fun it had promised Asia unadorned (*HB*, p. 25). The young couple's voyage, their 'slum tourism' (*HB*, p. 24), parallels Grass's own travel to Asia in 1979 and the description of his travel, undertaken in the company of his wife Ute and the German film-makers Volker Schlöndorff and Margarethe von Trotta, forms the text's second plot. Added to these two journeys, the empirical as well as the fictive one, are depictions of all the characters' everyday life in West Germany and their views on the election of 1980. Grass also reports on his friend Nikolas Born dying of cancer.

Travelling in Asia, both Grass, the author-narrator and Harm and Dörte face similar misgivings about the twosome of (Western) privilege and (Asian) poverty. Yet by splitting the burden of shame and guilt, typical of self-conscious Western travellers to so-called Third World countries, among several protagonists, Grass introduces multiple, often contesting perspectives that eschew firm ideological or narrative positions. He also lays claim to a new time concept of simultaneity, the 'paspresenture' (*HB*, p. 103), which would supersede the linear unfolding of time. This disregard for boundaries, fixed forms and conventional logic render *Headbirths* very much a postmodern narrative. Though the text's dominant mode is irony, particularly in its portrait of the fictive couple, its undercurrents are fear and shame. All figures fear the long-term consequences of overpopulation, demographic changes, ecological devastation and monumental income inequalities, and they struggle to find personal as well as political responses to problems whose complexities defy solutions. From the hindsight of the early twenty-first century, Grass's keen awareness of early signals of economic globalisation and its devastating effects on the world's poor is impressive.

Fittingly, the text begins with a nightmarish demographic scenario. Strolling among cyclists in Shanghai, Grass, the author-narrator and his wife Ute suddenly imagine, 'what if, from this day on, the world had to face up to the existence of nine hundred fifty million Germans, whereas the Chinese nation numbered barely eighty million . . . In the midst of the cycling multitudes we were seized with terror. Is such a thought possible? Is such a thought permissible?' (*HB*, p. 3). The fear of such numbers is, of course, unfounded since Germans are, in fact, a dying nation (*HB*, p. 5), in part because educated and well-to-do middle class couples such as Harm and Dörte cannot commit to procreation. But Grass's inversion, the text's initial headbirth that spawns all others, also raises the spectre of Germany's historical legacy as well as this nation's future. Perhaps Germany warrants extinction (*HB*, p. 6)? The ambiguity of this speculation, a rather problematic correlation of national history and character with growth rates, marks the text both formally and thematically. For one, Grass is unsure whether the discussion of Germany's future calls for a narrative or a film. He opts for both, thus presenting Harm's and Dörte's trip as an independent narrative as well as a film script in the making to be frequently discussed with Schlöndorff. Grass seamlessly shifts from the fictional couple's travels to his own empirical experiences as presented by the author-narrator. In this manner, he tells Schlöndorff in direct speech that if they agree on the film it should be shot in India, then switches to a descriptive mode comparing the fictive couple with Ute and himself (*HB*, p. 10). These constant narrative shifts are mirrored in the figures' inability to take a firm political stance. All of them play 'the Central European "Ontheonehand-ontheotherhand" parlour game' (*HB*, p. 11), allowing them to neatly list the pro and contra arguments for key issues West Germany is faced with in the election year, specifically the plans for building an atomic reactor in Brokdorf. The narrator, too, has 'two opinions about everything' (*HB*, p. 10), but he also knows that time is running out for such privileged game-playing.

Like Grass himself, Harm and Dörte are engaged in local party politics, giving speeches either for the Social Democratic Party (SPD) or the liberal Free Democratic Party (FDP), but their activism, full of rhetoric reminiscent of their student protest days, falls flat even in their home town of Itzehoe. The text's satirical depiction of the couple, centred on their reproductive indecision, reflects Grass's critique of the generation of '68 whose revolutionary fervour he has repeatedly depicted as misguided and self-aggrandising. Interestingly, the couple's wavering is almost entirely prompted by political considerations, culminating in Dörte's memorable final verdict, 'Under Strauss there's no way I'll bring a child into the world' (*HB*, p. 134; the reference is to Franz Josef Strauss, a conservative politician deeply unpopular amongst left-wing Germans of the time). Surprisingly, however, the professional implications of child-bearing hardly concern Dörte. Her lack of practical foresight may be proof less of her self-absorbed naïvety than of Grass's own patriarchal bias that, in this instance, conceives children only as a political and demographic issue, not as a life-changing event in individual women's biographies.

Haunted by the dual problems of German nationhood and abject poverty in Asia, linked through the topos of children, Grass develops different conceptual scenarios. To address the first problem, he advocates German national identity solely as a cultural and literary force, and this concept of Germany as a 'cultural nation' will later also buttress his opposition to reunification. Secondly, on New Year of 1979, with Orwell's decade about to begin, he thunders against the perverted logic of reason: 'In the quavering voice we know so well, reason teaches us to look upon the latest madness as relative progress . . . That's the way it is: since the sacred cow of enlightenment went dry, no sap can be milked from progress' (*HB*, pp. 67–68). Yet despite such far-reaching verdicts regarding the dwindling power of reason, the narrator opts for resilience and curiosity and his deep and lasting shame will not yield to resignation (*HB*, pp. 121–22). The text's surreal final scene, in which groups of cheerful Indian, Chinese, and African children surround Harm and Dörte in their Volkswagen car, who for once do not know 'what to say in German' (*HB*, p. 136), brings the work full circle. Confirming the vitality of children and the unstoppable force of migration, the conclusion inverts the narrator's initial demographic nightmare, thus ending the narrative in a light-hearted and ironic manner. Alternately sombre and playful, moralising and ironic, or self-critical and indignant, *Headbirths* is the least gloomy of the four texts since it juxtaposes a dire prognosis with some hope for the future. Grass starts Orwell's decade disillusioned, but ready to roll Sisyphus's stone.

The Rat

Only six years later, such defiance had given way to a deeply pessimistic outlook, the apocalyptic scenario presented in *The Rat* (1986). This book radicalises themes and forms explored in *Headbirths* but now, the ultimate disaster, atomic annihilation, has already happened. In this set-up Grass responds to fears prevalent at the beginning of the 1980s which witnessed the final show-down of the Cold War, with West Germany as one of its main stages. In the escalation of the nuclear arms race between the United States and the Soviet Union, Cruise and Pershing missiles were stationed in West Germany, leading to fierce mass protests. To Grass, the logic of nuclear deterrence was as misguided as the pursuit of continued economic growth, and he depicted both as destroying civilisation and the force of reason. He had articulated this far more negative view of the current state of affairs in his acceptance speech of the Antonio-Feltrinelli prize delivered in Rome in 1982. This often quoted lecture, 'The Destruction of Mankind has Begun', is generally regarded as a decisive turning point in Grass's works of this period. He argues that through 'poverty, hunger, polluted air, polluted bodies of water, forests destroyed by acid rain or deforestation'[3] human beings have systematically eroded the foundations for their survival. While prophesies of ecological and atomic devastation are quite typical for this period, Grass is also troubled that fiction will be wiped out. In the narrative no-future scenario he so deeply fears, those in power would have finally triumphed over literature's quest for justice and meaning.

The Rat offers by far the most extreme and most complex approach to the topic insofar as the first-person narrator juggles several distinct plot lines densely packed into twelve chapters and frequently interspersed with lengthy poems. In each of these stories he struggles with the work's basic paradox, that is, how to survive as a narrator when the complete extinction of mankind renders this very position impossible. Grass addresses this contradiction by inventing a non-human survivor, a she-rat, to whom the narrator talks in lengthy dream sequences. While the dream-mode could indicate that doomsday exists only in the imagination of the narrator but has not yet become an empirical reality, this ambiguity does not weaken the diagnosis of a world beyond repair and hope. This bleak assessment is delivered by 'the She-rat in my dream'.[4] It is she who depicts human beings as monstrous in their greed, cruelty and hate, who, from the very beginning, were bent on destroying what they dread: the fears that they project onto the rat. The author-narrator's role is to argue against her apocalyptic condemnation: 'Finished! she says. You people used to be, you're has-beens, a remembered delusion' (R, p. 3).

This scenario takes up crucial elements of the apocalypse, a complex biblical and historical textual tradition that attempts to give meaning to the chronology and finality of human existence. The Western apocalyptic tradition, though elaborate and profuse in character, can broadly be described in relation to two main features. One is the foretelling of catastrophe, the final end, often expressed in images of natural disasters, or of filth, an archive Grass clearly draws on. The other is the foretelling of hope, of a new beginning and a new order. Yet, *The Rat* neither provides for salvation nor does it dissolve the dualism; it is, as the critic Thomas Kniesche argues, 'post-apocalyptic' since it substitutes the narrative foretelling of glory with intertextual references.[5] Alluding in his opening sentence to the eighteenth-century German playwright G.E. Lessing's *Die Erziehung des Menschengeschlechts* (The Education of Humankind) which substituted education for revelation, the narrator allies himself with reason, but it remains open whether he still believes in its power.

Grass wants to simultaneously depict annihilation, warn against it and account for the loss of the world; and he attempts to narrate in the manner of the 'paspresenture', first advocated in *Headbirths*, challenging readers to follow him through multiple plots and parodies aimed at superseding chronology. The apocalyptic narrative generally follows a tripart structure of beginning, middle – the position from which the text speaks – and end thus allowing for meaning and action to continue, for even when faced with the abyss, we do *something*. For Grass, that 'something' is narration, first and foremost, and he crafts a text that both confirms and invalidates story telling. On the one hand, the narrator states that everything has been said (R, p. 89) and it is time to bid farewell, but this parting involves, on the other hand, naming the world and all that will be lost. Grass has thus set a huge task for himself. This might explain the need for multiple story lines and yet their excess threatens to overpower his message.

The text's opening scene depicts the narrator observing the Christmas present he had wished for: a rat. Though happy about the unusual gift, the Christmas festivities had caused him more ennui than joy: 'Oh, the misery of not knowing what to wish for. Every wish has come true. What's needed, we say, is need . . . Surfeited and needy, that was my state' (R, p. 2). This paradox of abundance and lack, indicative of the perverse logic mankind has followed, provides the text's moral and political blueprint. Soon the rat mutates into a dream companion, a 'she-rat', while the narrator finds himself locked in a (dream) space capsule circling the earth and trying to refute her arguments. For the she-rat humans are primarily waste-generating beings who deserve to perish. Defining humans, not rats, as abjects is only the first in a series of inversions that culminates in establishing rats as the wiser, superior and kinder race, and therefore able to survive. Compelled to rebut the she-rat's pronouncements on the history of human litter, the author both mourns the loss of (his) world – melancholically evoked in such poems as 'I dreamt I had to take leave' (R, p. 82) – and turns to narration, hoping that he can 'put off the end with words' (R, p. 8). Whether his stories or repeated pleas for hope and survival are ultimately successful cannot be determined since the ambiguity of the dream and the dreamer remain until the very end. The different plots, anchored by the exchanges between she-rat and narrator, revolve around the ambiguity of this farewell, both delaying and mourning the final destruction and, in the process, offering an interpretation of the events unfolding.

One of the text's many sub-plots describes a scientific expedition to the Baltic sea undertaken by five women who, for this purpose, have purchased an old boat, named 'The New Ilsebill' (R, p. 12). The story of their voyage, reminiscent of Grass's maritime affinities and themes, is, as both the set-up and the boat's name indicate, closely connected to his novel *The Flounder* (1977). Most of the narrator's attention is focused on the boat's beautiful captain, Damroka, who soon redirects the mission and takes course for the sunken island of Vineta, the utopian realm of women. Though they finally reach Vineta's location, rats have already taken over the city. The women recoil in horror and at this very moment are killed by the atomic blast. Paralleling Grass's novel *The Flounder*, women are again portrayed as the more reasonable and more pragmatic sex – their femininity, as depicted in clothes, habits or love-lives, is catalogued in great detail – but the topic of gender conflict is subordinate to the narrator's sadness about having to say farewell to women also. Well aware of their complete indifference toward him, he comes across as a remorseful though also self-centred observer.

Early on in the narrative, Oskar Matzerath, from *The Tin Drum* (1959), suddenly also makes an appearance and initiates yet another sub-plot. He is introduced as an old acquaintance, who, the narrator tells us, wishes to confirm 'that he still exists. He wants to make a come back. All right, let him' (R, p. 17). With 'Herr Matzerath', now a sixty-year old, successful video producer forcing himself into the story and seemingly not subject to authorial control, an outrageous intertextual zigzag unfolds that ends with Matzerath's journey to his grandmother Anna Koljaiczek's celebrations – it is her 107th birthday. The elaborate party offers a multiple finale insofar as the atomic blast occurs on the very same day, killing everybody except the grandmother. In addition, the narrator frequently confers with Matzerath about his tin drum past and his assessment of Germany in the 1950s, the era of 'Adenauer-Malskat-Ulbricht . . . "Three Master Forgers"' (R, p. 28; the references are to Konrad Adenauer, the West German Chancellor from 1949 to 1963, Lothar Malskat, postwar painter and artwork restorer, and Walter Ulbricht, leader of East Germany from 1950 to 1971). The story of the painter Malskat, who had been commissioned to restore the Gothic paintings of the Marienkirche in Lübeck in 1950 but who then passed his work off as original Gothic artwork, shapes a further story line. One of the main functions of the Matzerath and Malskat narratives is to critique the political, cultural and moral deceit of West Germany's founding years and to show how historical memory is built of facts and fiction.

Another art form that the narrator and Matzerath frequently discuss is a joint video production, to be entitled 'Grimms' Forests'. The script, the text's fifth sub-plot, offers perhaps the most forceful account of the link between material and narrative destruction. Loss of forests and loss of fairy tales go hand in hand, and the proposed film is to depict both decaying forests and the brave fight put up by Hänsel and Gretel and a huge cast of fairy tale characters. According to the narrator only a silent movie with subtitles in the manner of Walt Disney could adequately express this long farewell. Yet, in trying to transcribe the fast-paced and slapstick features of a Disney movie into narrative sequences that by their very nature are bound to chronology, Grass pushes this plot's readability to its very limits. What is meaningful and entertaining on the screen tends to lose its parodic edge when recreated on the page:

> Rübezahl threatens to punch the prince on the nose. The witch and Gretel are disgusted with the frog king. When the prince tries to run away, Rumpelstiltskin trips him up. The witch and the bad fairies shape their hands into claws, but before they can grab him, the remaining dwarfs bind him with a strand of Rapunzel's hair.　　　　　　　　　　　　　　　　　　　　(R, p. 272)

In these and related scenes, fairy tales are posited as the realm of futile resistance and utopia in which children and fairy tale figures advocate (ecological) restraint. In contrast to the adults who are caught up in the infernal logic of production and waste, desire and tedium, children and their fairy-tale companions know how to balance love, leisure, and living within one's means. Despite their constant rebellion against authority and their numerous subversive acts, which include poignant parodies of a chancellor modelled on the recently elected Helmut Kohl, this juvenile cast reflects the Romantic perception of the child as the authentic and therefore superior being. Close to nature and full of truth and wisdom, children are poised to guide the adults. Yet, the children can neither save the forests nor the fairy tales, and they proffer no hope. Not a single story allows for escape; escape is something only rats can achieve.

A didactic and moralistic work, in which narrator and she-rat alternately lecture about the causes ending all history, chief among them the misguided course of reason with its fetishisation of growth, *The Rat* in its rich inter-textuality also sums up Grass's previous works. Though the fivefold vari-ation of its themes – destruction and mourning – covers enormous historical and creative ground, its narrative profusion undermines at times the text's coherence and critical edge. Often compared to *The Tin Drum*, it lacks the earlier novel's focus, grounded in a specific locale and an ingenious protag-onist. Despite sounding a high state of alert, *The Rat* appears abstract and, not surprisingly, it has elicited the most polar responses.

Show Your Tongue

Calcutta had long fascinated Grass, and since his first visit in 1975 he had wanted to return. Both as artist and citizen he felt challenged by the city and, in 1986, deeply frustrated by German politics and the negative recep-tion of *The Rat*, Grass and his wife Ute left for an extended stay in Calcutta. *Show Your Tongue* (1988), a mixed-media work comprising a hundred-page prose section, fifteen charcoal drawings and a lengthy poem in twelve parts, is an account of the six months the couple spent in the West Bengal capital. Proceeding in chronological manner and tracing his stay largely by way of places and sites, Grass focuses all three sections on the abject poverty of Calcutta's pavement dwellers and his own helpless response.

En route to Bengal, the autobiographical narrator states: 'I know that in Bombay, or in Calcutta at the latest, the adage about wiping your ass with a hedgehog awaits me . . . So will it be the climate that is extreme and different?'[6] This initial observation shows Grass to be aware of some of the epistemological traps awaiting Western intellectuals travelling to Asia. As enlightened observers of a reality that can be alternately appalling and fascinating, they struggle with colonial legacies, cultural differences and vast socio-economic inadequacies that test their judgment. Grass continues a long line of German travellers to India and though he guards against clichéd projections of India as wondrous mysticism, he remains largely trapped in Third World misery-reporting. His focus is directed almost entirely on suffering which renders, as he states in the text's poem, not future, but current life apocalyptic.

With the exception of a few side-trips, Grass and his wife spent most of their time in Calcutta and descriptions of their daily life – overcrowded trains, sleepless nights under mosquito nets or the daily ritual of boiling water – alternate with depictions of the city. From the very beginning Grass established his interaction with Calcutta primarily as a work, not a travel mode. He responded to the daily onslaught of suffering with a deep sense of shame alluded to already in the title: the goddess Kali is often depicted with a protruding tongue, which Grass interprets as a sign of shame. The feeling of shame and its implications for the author's creativity form the undercurrent to Grass's experiences and perceptions.

Shame, an emotion seminal in establishing collective bonds, is often characterised as a largely unwanted and difficult to control sentiment that cuts to the heart of social acceptance and value. Described as the feeling of 'being in the social world as an undesired self, a self that one does not wish to be', shame is also associated with distinct physical and facial characteristics, most notably the avoidance of eye contact or lowered head.[7] Though ashamed of his privilege and inability to help, Grass responds not with evasion but with incessant viewing, for he intentionally seeks out the most dreadful places. Using his observations he develops what he calls the '(unwritten) aesthetics of poverty' (SYT, p. 63), implying that the reality of slums is far superior to the flawless decorum of the Deutsche Bank, a rather far-fetched and naïve juxtaposition of antagonistic entities. The more shame and its close companion, guilt, work to overpower him, the more he resorts to constant artistic creativity; only his departure can break this vicious circle and save him from complete engulfment and silence.

In text and images, Show Your Tongue presents Calcutta and India as dark, gloomy and overwhelming, as spaces of abject poverty, hopelessness and incomprehension, 'What is India? An occasion for publishing handsome picture books in color or black and white? The legacy of the British Empire: a great power on crutches? Or the last hope of bankrupt reason? What is there to be revitalized?' (SYT, p. 87). Yet, despite all his attention, the country remains remarkably abstract because his focus is one-sided, and it blends out Indians as individual and diverse subjects. Since almost all encounters and exchanges are placed within the interpretive scheme 'misery', they become repetitive and predictable, and they implicate Grass in the very discourse he critiques. However, Grass tries to break with this approach in his surrealistic treatment of the goddess Kali and in accounts of his wife's experiences. Though Ute suffered considerably under the heat and the physical and emotional hardships of their stay, Grass portrays her as far more engaged with Indian neighbours or acquaintances. He also assigns her the nineteenth-century German Theodor Fontane as fictive companion, thus slipping in intertextual references to Fontane's oeuvre, such as playful allusions to *Effi Briest*'s triangular relationships. Engaging Fontane as Ute's confidant, expert on nineteenth-century British, Indian and German history and astute interlocutor, yields an additional perspective on India that highlights Grass's and Ute's divergent approaches. Fontane's importance is also highlighted in the narrative's final sentence, which possibly also foreshadows his comeback in *Too Far Afield* (1995), 'If we ever come back here, we'll take Fontane with us again . . .' (*SYT*, p. 97).

Dead Wood: An Epitaph

In 1990 Grass published the mixed-media work *Dead Wood: An Epitaph*, a series of black and white lithographs accompanied by subtitle-like messages and a short essay detailing the so-called 'Waldsterben' (dying forests) in West and East Germany as well as neighbouring countries. Just as in previous works of this decade, environmental abuse is depicted in both local and global contexts, but forests, particularly in Germany, are also associated with national identity. As one of the prime tropes of national and cultural (self-)identification, forests have long held a distinctive place in Germany's cultural memory. They act as powerful landscape metaphors in which a plethora of myths, memories and artistic inscriptions coalesce, most of which centre on the themes of memory and loss. Grass is steeped in this tradition and *Dead Wood* goes well beyond recording ecological awareness, showing the author instead in the role of surveillant and interpreter of Germany's sylvan imaginary and warning again that ecological and cultural destruction go hand in hand.

Dedicated to the Brothers Grimm, *Dead Wood: An Epitaph* establishes from the beginning a close link to the Romantic predecessors. Grass couples mournful remembrance with thought-provoking tribute, a tension that structures most of the work and that contrasts Romantic fairy tale forests with today's dead wood. Like the abject poverty of Calcutta, dead wood leaves the author at a loss for words: 'Too lazy to speak I drew on the spot. Subtitles at most, more shorter than longer ones dropped off. Trees that show their roots make me speechless.'[8] The complete destruction of habitats, be they natural or urban, transcends the capacity for verbal expression, thus endangering the poet's imagination and threatening to make his work as obsolete as the trees. Grass tries to fill this linguistic void by turning to his other medium, visual art. Yet, even as 'draftsman', the role in which he presents himself for the most part, he feels overwhelmed and immobilised by the death he forces himself to document.

Interestingly, Grass does not use the well-known term 'dying forest' but 'dead wood', thus shifting the emphasis from a process of dying, to its final results. Not only are forests dead, but their very material, wood, has died and it can now only be eulogised. The drawings depict single trees or groups of them, but they do not show forests, for those are extinct and a panoramic view is no longer possible. Grass also focuses his audience's attention on the extent of destruction by presenting shattered branches, trunks or roots, and he is particularly horrified by the conditions of the roots which he associates with shame. One subtitle reads, 'exhibitionists among themselves: shamelessly showing their roots' (*DW*, p. 42). Similar to *Show Your Tongue*, the key concept of shame is called upon to denote the observer's response to a system that has lost stability and meaningful bonds. The brief narrative passages mirror this incoherence. Sentences are often choppy and incomplete, and clearing happens not only in the woods but also in minds and language.

Against this 'Clearing in our heads' (*DW*, p. 106) Grass sets his eulogy, memorialising a German cultural icon and confronting us with the responsibility for its demise which he locates in boundless greed and expansion. Grass's anti-capitalist stance seems to suggest that in the past forests were ecologically and culturally intact areas. Yet it is well known that Ernst Moritz Arndt (1769–1860), professor at the University of Greifswald and a contemporary of the Grimm brothers, had already deplored heavy deforestation a century earlier, and for Arndt, too, protection of the German forest meant protection of the German nation. The Brothers Grimm shared this sentiment and, so it appears, does Grass. After all, he spent the turbulent months leading up to the fall of the wall in November 1989 in the very realm that represents one of the most ancient icons of German identity. Though *Dead Wood* radiates with Grass's profound aversion to reunification, it strongly links German forests to German people. Thus he proposes an ecological instead of a political reunification, 'starting with glasnost in the forests' (*DW*, p. 89; the word 'glasnost' here refers to Soviet President Mikhail Gorbachev's call from the mid-1980s for the opening up of public discussion in the Soviet Union, a call which was to reverberate in East Germany during the mass protests against the communist state's inflexibility in the course of 1989).

For Grass, the loss of forests also mirrors the loss of political reason. A reunified Germany cannot make up for the breakdown of forests, but by establishing this strong – albeit oppositional – link between forest and people, Grass shows himself most preoccupied by the theme of lost unity which also lay at the heart of the Grimms' forest project. Grass's opposition to a politically reunified nation and his focus on forests again resonate with the idea of Germany as a cultural nation to be grounded in unifying cultural traditions such as scripts and landscapes. Not surprisingly, *Dead Wood* concludes with a nostalgic reference to the famous late eighteenth- and early nineteenth-century Romantic landscape painter Caspar David Friedrich. The visual dissonance between Friedrich's sublime vistas and Grass's ghostly scenery of thin, broken trees is intended as a powerful reminder of the large-scale devastation, yet it also conjoins nature and culture and the different memories buried in the German woodlands. Grass had entered the forests in order to record their destruction and the loss of cultural traditions, but he emerges fearing for Germany's national destiny in a manner that recalls dominant myths. *Dead Wood* reveals that underneath the forests lie elaborate landscape memories that challenge any facile look at trees or history.

Conclusion

With the hindsight of more than twenty years, one could be tempted to write off Grass's apocalyptic fears during the 1980s as unfounded. The atomic meltdown did not happen, India has morphed into a major global player and the German forests have not turned into dead wood. Yet such factual stock-taking would miss the point of Grass's political and literary concerns as well as the innately resilient nature of apocalyptic writing. Grass's work of this decade is informed by a strong moral and didactic impetus, to the extent that he confessed to having lost faith in Enlightenment values. Yet warning against self-destructive growth, he is also forced to appeal to reason and the power of art, a contradiction that is elaborately and often parodistically spun out in these works. The narratives remain anchored in German history and the German present and address a global agenda that today has lost nothing of its urgency, and it would be imprudent to accept Grass's dismissive self-characterisation as 'some crackpot itinerant preacher' (*HB*, p. 14). The interpretive scheme underlying Grass's apocalyptic scenarios of the 1980s – devastation is not a future but a contemporary event – also threatens his mission as author. Abroad in Calcutta and Shanghai and at home in German forests, overwhelmed and angered by the suffering and materialism he is witnessing, Grass responded with fear and a deep sense of shame. This shame, to be understood as a personal and a social gesture, goes to the very heart of his artistic identity and public role.

One could surmise that it also relates to the shame he expressed about his membership as a seventeen-year-old in the Waffen SS as revealed in his autobiography *Peeling the Onion* (2006). In both cases, the shame about individual guilt and the shame about collective failure are perhaps best summed up in Walter Benjamin's assessment of Franz Kafka's *The Trial*: 'It was as if the shame of it was to outlive him.'[9]

Notes

1. Günter Grass, 'Dem Krieg geht die Puste nicht aus', *Die Zeit*, http://zeus.zeit.de/text/2006/22/Grass-Rede_xml (accessed on 10/12/2007). My translation.
2. Günter Grass, *Headbirths or The Germans Are Dying Out*, trans. by Ralph Manheim (New York: Harcourt, 1982), p. 79. Subsequent references appear in the text as *HB* with the page number in brackets.
3. Günter Grass, 'The Destruction of Mankind Has Begun', trans. Ralph Manheim, in *On Writing And Politics 1967–1983* (San Diego: Harcourt Brace Jovanovich), 1985, p. 137.
4. Günter Grass, *The Rat*, trans. by Ralph Manheim (New York: Harcourt, 1987), p. 14. Subsequent references appear in the text as *R* with the page number in brackets.
5. Thomas Kniesche, *Die Genealogie der Post-Apokalypse* (Vienna: Passagen Verlag, 1991), p. 57.
6. Günter Grass, *Show Your Tongue*, trans. by John E. Woods (New York: Harcourt, 1988), p. 4. Subsequent references appear in the text as *SYT* with the page number in brackets.
7. Paul Gilbert, 'What Is Shame? Some Core Issues and Controversies', in Paul Gilbert and Bernice Andrews (eds.), *Shame: Interpersonal Behavior, Psychopathology, and Culture* (Oxford: Oxford University Press, 1998), p. 22 and p. 14.
8. Günter Grass, *Totes Holz: Ein Nachruf* (Göttingen: Steidl, 1990), p. 104. Subsequent references appear in the text as *DW* with the page number in brackets. All translations are mine.
9. Cited in Elspeth Probyn, *Blush: Faces of Shame* (Minneapolis and London: University of Minnesota Press, 2005), p. 41.

9

STEPHEN BROCKMANN

Günter Grass and German unification

Günter Grass was the most prominent German critic of the unification of the two German states that took place on 3 October 1990. In a series of blistering speeches and articles throughout the year, he argued that by perpetrating the crimes against humanity for which Auschwitz has become a synecdoche, Germany had forfeited any right to existence as a unified nation state. He also predicted that unification would precipitate massive unemployment and economic and social displacement in the former German Democratic Republic (GDR, or East Germany), as well as a rise in racist and xenophobic violence. Other leading intellectuals joined Grass in criticising the precise legal or economic means of achieving unification, but only Grass prominently and insistently rejected the whole project.

By the first months of 1990 the energy generated among dissident East German intellectuals by dreams of transforming the economically and politically bankrupt GDR into a socialist utopia had largely dissipated, as it became increasingly clear that the very *Volk* (people), for whom these intellectuals had once believed themselves to be speaking, wanted not a second chance at a socialist experiment or an opportunity to return to the 'antifascist and humanistic ideals from which we proceeded long ago', as Christa Wolf's proclamation 'For Our Country' put it in December of 1989,[1] but rather immediate and unconditional unification with the real, existing Federal Republic in a capitalist, not a socialist, economic system. If there had ever been any doubts about the people's actual wishes, the first truly democratic parliamentary election in the GDR on 18 March 1990 put such doubts to rest, giving the conservative 'Alliance for Germany', led by West German chancellor Helmut Kohl's Christian Democratic Union, almost half of the votes and parliamentary seats and a clear mandate for speedy reunification.

Both in the run-up to and, even more so, in the wake of what Grass later called 'the election disaster',[2] East German dissident intellectuals became silent or could no longer make themselves heard, and Grass, as Germany's most prominent literary intellectual, became the primary and most easily heard critic of unification, attempting to speak for both the East and West German left. The fact that the leading critic of the disappearance of the GDR was a West German (albeit one originally from the eastern territories lost by Germany at the end of the Second World War) spoke volumes about the structural and ideological weakness of the GDR in the run-up to unification: it was not just German unification but also the criticism of it that was being organised primarily in the West. That the leading critic of German unification was also the nation's most famous writer likewise revealed much about the structural function of literature and literary intellectuals in both German states, and in the nascent reunified state: literature, and the literary intellectual, could express prominent and public disagreement with the course of political affairs, even if such disagreement was destined to prove politically fruitless, at least in the short term. Finally, the fact that of all of Germany's literary intellectuals it was Grass who took up the cause of opposing German unification, for the most part *after* unification had essentially already become a foregone conclusion, reveals a great deal about Grass's vision of himself as a champion of lost causes.

In *My Century* (1999), Grass relates how he experienced the March 1990 East German parliamentary elections in Leipzig, the home of the GDR revolution of October 1989, together with various citizen activists and proponents of a 'third path' toward democratic socialism – i.e. a path that avoided both the Scylla of western capitalism and the Charybdis of authoritarian Eastern bloc communism. Grass writes that the photographs taken on that evening by Leonore Suhl, the wife of his friend Jakob Suhl, a Jewish emigré who had fled Hitler's Third Reich many decades earlier – Grass dedicated the book to Suhl, whose mother was murdered in the Holocaust – show these East German idealists' 'mute horror' at the election results: 'a young woman is covering her face. It was obvious to all that the Christian Democratic Union was in for a devastating victory. "But that's how democracy works", said Jakob' (*MC*, p. 244).

For Grass this is the moment of truth, the moment when East German intellectuals suddenly and painfully realise that their struggle for democratic socialism in the GDR has in fact led only to an expanded German capitalist state, and that their dreams *for* the people are not the dreams *of* the people. In a 1990 essay Grass recounted how, after the election débâcle of 18 March 1990, he went to Leipzig's Nikolai church, the epicentre of the East German revolution, and found an imitation street sign proclaiming the square from which the revolution had started in the autumn of 1989 to be 'Suckers Square'.[3] The same anecdote found its way into *My Century* in

1999: 'The next day we found a sign on a corrugated iron fence in front of the side entrance to the Nikolai Church, the center of the Monday demonstrations in the autumn of the previous year. The blue lettering, to make it look like a street sign, said, "Suckers Square" and then, underneath, in small print, "Regards from October's children. Yes, we're still here"' (*MC*, p. 245).

The prominence of the word 'Suckers', and of the anecdote in which it plays a role, in Grass's fictional and non-fictional criticisms of the unification process suggest that the author was motivated at least in part by a desire to make visible the 'October children', so quickly silenced in the months following the opening of the Berlin Wall on 9 November 1989: to reveal the very people pictured in the photographs by Leonore Suhl. For Grass the seemingly invisible 'October children' were those who had actually brought about the end of the GDR regime and dreamed, even if only briefly, of a democratic socialist Germany. These 'October children' do not actually play a prominent role in Grass's fiction of the 1990s, either as heroes or as victims. However, Grass does render their absence from the public eye visible, as in the anecdote about 'Suckers Square' in Leipzig. The author publicly proclaimed his sympathies with the idea of democratic socialism, and in December 1989 he urged his fellow Social Democrats to seize the opportunity to learn about peaceful democratic revolution from the GDR's dissidents: 'Let us learn . . . from our fellow countrymen in the GDR, who, unlike the citizens of the Federal Republic, did not have freedom handed to them, but rather had to wrest it from an all-encompassing system – an accomplishment that makes us, rolling in wealth, look poor by comparison.'[4]

The parliamentary elections in the GDR on 18 March 1990 play a relatively minor role in the two major fictional works that Grass published in the 1990s, the novels *The Call of the Toad* (1992) and *Too Far Afield* (1995). In *The Call of the Toad*, the main character, Alexander Reschke, writes a brief note about the election results, which he calls a 'Pyrrhic victory for the coalition parties'.[5] A Pyrrhic victory is an apparent victory that ultimately leads to a more far-reaching defeat, and it is precisely that far-reaching defeat against which Grass warned throughout the 1990s. The fictional Alexander Reschke therefore has similar political views to the real Günter Grass. In the same chapter the novel's narrator, a semi-autobiographical figure who, like Reschke himself, grew up and went to school in Danzig, complains that Reschke and his Polish companion Alexandra Piatkowska were so wrapped up in their own romantic idyll that they ignored the unpleasant political and social situation in Germany – a particular problem because, as the narrator notes, in March of 1990 xenophobia, particularly by Germans against Poles, has become an acute problem (*CotT*, p. 90). The story's narrator here comes very close to the political concerns of the real Günter Grass, who is well known for his friendliness to Poland and his hatred of xenophobia.

In *Too Far Afield*, the March 1990 elections and their results are mentioned before and after the fact but not actually depicted. The novel's protagonist Theo Wuttke (Fonty), a contemporary reincarnation of the nineteenth-century German writer Theodor Fontane, engages in conversation with his Stasi shadow and spy, Hoftaller, who informs him, several weeks before the actual election, that 'because the Modrow government can't last . . . [we are] supposed to have early elections, by mid-March'.[6] Hoftaller's comment on the election is both critical and dismissive: 'They're in such a hurry, those fellows. Instant unification! But elections mean nothing to us, right Fonty? Elections don't change a thing, at least not in theory' (*TFA*, p. 66). Hoftaller's words point to a number of the novel's main themes, including the critique of a unification perceived as over-hasty, the concept that fundamental power structures in Germany and elsewhere are essentially impervious to real change of any sort, including election results, and, in the word 'us', a grammatical hint that writers and their secret service overseers are united in a common project that is in some way connected to these fundamental power structures.

The next time that the election results of March 1990 are mentioned in *Too Far Afield*, the election itself has already occurred, and Hoftaller and Fonty are sitting in either the attic or the basement of the GDR's House of Ministries, the former Nazi Aviation Ministry, on a couch stuffed with shredded documents belonging to the State Security Services (Staatssicherheitsdienst, or Stasi). Now Hoftaller mocks the West German power elite for its rush to destroy potentially incriminating Stasi files. The novel's narrator, who works at the Fontane archive in Potsdam – and is thus also in the business of studying and providing intelligence on writers – notes that via these documents 'the crumbling of the state in the east did not reveal only its own secrets; it uncovered another, previously hidden, inner life whose branching highways and byways eventually led to the state in the west' (*TFA*, p. 69). The implication is that from the very beginning the East German regime had been cooperating with the West German political elite, and vice versa, and that therefore the collapse of the GDR and the ultimate unification of Germany are merely a cosmetic change that will have no impact on fundamental structures; the West wants to destroy the records that prove its own complicity in the East German system, thus making it recognisable for what it is: just another system of domination passing itself off as something better.

History as eternal recurrence

The critique of German unification that is outlined in each of these works is closely connected to two literary and philosophical predecessors of Grass: Friedrich Nietzsche and Bertolt Brecht. From Nietzsche Grass gets the notion of eternal recurrence that he embodies symbolically in the image of the paternoster where Fonty and Hoftaller have many of their conversations, and where both Fonty and the novel's readers encounter various leading figures from German history. The paternoster is a mode of transportation within buildings that constitutes an endless loop around and around and up and down (unlike an elevator, which moves in a straight line either up or down), and it is an appropriate symbol for eternal recurrence. For Grass, the 'will to power' (Nietzsche) is political and permeates everything from the second German Reich through the Weimar Republic, Hitler's Third Reich and the divided Germany from 1949–1990, to the reunified Germany of the 1990s (*TFA*, p. 463). The building in which Grass's literary paternoster is located is itself a symbol of continuity in the midst of change, since it once housed Hermann Göring's Aviation Ministry and now (in much of the narrative present of *Too Far Afield*) houses the post-unification trustee agency (*Treuhandanstalt*, called 'handover trust' in the English translation; *TFA*, p. 460) responsible for privatising East German industry and, in the eyes of many Germans in the 'new Federal states' (*Neue Länder*), a symbol of West Germany's 'colonisation' of the former GDR after 1990.

It was Nietzsche who had argued that Prussia's victory in the 1870 war against France, together with the foundation of the Prussian-led Reich in January 1871, represented a danger to Germany's cultural existence. He had believed that Germany's military victory might ultimately lead to a political and cultural smugness that would inaugurate a long-term defeat for the German spirit. Grass's 1990 fears about German cultural unity being supplanted by the overwhelming power of the D-Mark (the West German currency before it was replaced by the Euro in 1999) echoed this Nietzschean warning, with a slight twist: for Grass, military invasion is supplanted by economic invasion, as the West German currency takes the place of German troops. Grass has Fonty – drawing on the experience of his 'previous self', the nineteenth-century Fontane – declare to his Stasi shadow Hoftaller: 'No victory goes unpunished. Was no different in '71. German unification is always the unification of the Parvenooskis and Nogoodniks' (*TFA*, p. 343). Somewhat earlier Fonty simply declares to Hoftaller: 'victory spawns stupidity!' (*TFA*, p. 49).

Grass's fears about economic imperialism find further literary expression in *The Call of the Toad*, a novel that depicts the way that economic

motivations ultimately displace originally idealistic desires for reconciliation between the Germans and the Poles, and in which the D-Mark rapidly
makes its move beyond the former GDR and into the city of Grass's birth,
Danzig – now the Polish Gdańsk. Economic 'soft power' has replaced
military 'hard power'. Alexander Reschke ultimately resigns from his position as chairman of the board of the 'German-Polish Cemetery Society', an
organisation which springs up in the wake of unification to facilitate the
'return' of deceased Germans to what is now western Poland to be reburied
in the lands from which they were expelled in 1945, arguing that 'what was
lost in the war is being retaken by economic power. True, it's being done
peacefully. No tanks, no dive bombers. No dictator rules, only the free
market' (*CotT*, p. 204). Here once again, Reschke is echoing the real-life
sentiments of Grass himself, who, in February of 1990, had warned: 'Eventually, because enough is never enough, we'll succeed, with our strong
currency and after formal recognition of Poland's western border, in subju-
gating economically a large chunk of Silesia and a small chunk of Pomer-
ania' (*TSON*, p. 3). Like the GDR's 'October children', Reschke is a sucker.
The 'October children' discovered in March of 1990 that their idealistic
revolution had ultimately paved the way for the triumph of West German
capitalism; Reschke, a year later, must face the bitter realisation that his
hopes and plans for German–Polish reconciliation in the cemetery society
have simply made possible the invasion of Poland by West German capital.

The same fundamental criticism of economic power in the face of cultural
and moral bankruptcy features in *Too Far Afield*, whose narrator, much like
Grass himself in 1990, explains the monetary union between the GDR and
the FRG (Federal Republic of Germany, or West Germany) by noting that
money is intended as a surrogate for actual ideas and feelings of unity:
'Because the ruling mass [Helmut Kohl] could think of no other way to
shoulder the national burden and achieve a unified balance of effort, money
had to compensate for the dearth of ideas' (*TFA*, p. 123). But the East
Germans who are longing for the hard West German currency ultimately
discover that their fairy tale dreams of fantastic wealth – 'Once upon a time'
(*TFA*, p. 123) – must be disappointed: 'All that money, and even more
money – yes, there was money, and plenty of it, in fact, only money – didn't
produce the desired prosperity. Having quickly slaked some of the thirst for
consumption, it hustled back to the West' (*TFA*, p. 124).

Two poems by Brecht (who makes a brief appearance in *My Century*, in
the chapter devoted to 1956, the year of his death) are particularly apposite
to Grass's literary critique of German history in general and German reunification in particular: 'Ballad of the Waterwheel' and 'Questions from a
Worker Who Reads'. 'Ballad of the Waterwheel' is a poetic invocation of

the circularity of history, but from a left-wing rather than a right-wing perspective. In Brecht's poem, the water wheel of history is constantly turning, but the fact that 'what's on top is bound to fall' is hardly a source of consolation for the labouring proletariat, represented by the water that turns the wheel, which, no matter how often or how quickly the wheel turns, always remains beneath the wheel.[7] Grass's paternoster is a literary echo of Brecht's water wheel. Fonty sees Detlev Rohwedder, the first head of the trustee agency, going down in the paternoster – 'A person who radiated strength of will. A person to whom success seemed custom-fitted, like his jacket and his trousers. A fine figure of a man, so to speak' (*TFA*, p. 474) – and is immediately transported fifty years into the past, when, as a young soldier, he once saw the Nazi leader Hermann Göring, the so-called 'Reichsmarshall', going down in the same paternoster. In Fonty's imagination Göring is followed, in rapid succession, by Walter Ulbricht, the first leader of the GDR, and then by Ulbricht's successor Erich Honecker (*TFA*, pp. 475–76). The presence of all these figures in the paternoster suggests a kind of sameness in the midst of seeming change, just as the paternoster's movement, while continuous, is always the same.

In Brecht's poem the longed-for socialist revolution may one day put an end to the endless spinning of the water wheel. Grass, who is writing about precisely the failure of the dream of German socialism, is not as hopeful as Brecht. For him, East German socialism itself was just another turn of the paternoster, and the GDR's socialist leaders Ulbricht and Honecker are not significantly different from Göring before them or Rohwedder after them. Moreover, whereas Brecht had at least some faith that the German proletariat would follow its own self-interests, Grass's Fonty no longer believes in the working class; referring to the first German unification of 1871, he declares that 'in those days there was the fourth estate, the working class. There was still some hope there. At least it looked that way' (*TFA*, p. 343). The clear implication is that the hopes of 1871 were merely an illusion, and that at any rate there is no hope now: well over a century after the first German unification, the proletariat as the revolutionary subject of history has disappeared. In the course of *Too Far Afield* (as in reality) Rohwedder is assassinated, only to be replaced by yet another, more successful and ruthless leader, this time a woman – although the name of the woman (in reality, Rohwedder's successor, Birgit Breuel) is, like the name of Rohwedder, never mentioned in the novel. The assassinated Rohwedder, meanwhile, lives on (in Grass's novel and also in reality) in the name of the building that houses Fonty's paternoster: 'in future the building on the former Wilhelmstrasse would bear the name of this extraordinary public servant' (*TFA*, p. 535).

Breuel makes an appearance at the end of *Too Far Afield* – at least in a speech Fonty gives – as a contemporary reincarnation of Theodor Fontane's materialistic heroine Jenny Treibel (from Fontane's 1892 novel *Frau Jenny Treibel*) at a costume party to celebrate Treuhand's closing of the thousandth GDR company (*TFA*, pp. 634–38). Breuel also puts in an appearance in *My Century* under the rubric 1994 (the year the trustee agency's operations ceased), where (although she is still not named) she defends her handling of the the privatisation of ex-GDR concerns and even criticises Grass himself (whom she likewise refuses to name, calling him instead 'the man who is putting me down on paper here and thinks he can give me a grade', *MC*, p. 255) for the depiction of her that he plans to publish a year later in *Too Far Afield*: 'the man I refer to above . . . think[s] of writing one of his usual overblown novels to compare me to a character from the work of Fontane because a certain Frau Jenny Treibel was as good as I am at combining business and poetry' (*MC*, p. 256).

In *Too Far Afield* Fonty condemns Breuel and the other movers and shakers of the unified Germany, disguised as figures from novels by Fontane, 'to ride . . . up and down for all eternity' (*TFA*, p. 637). The resemblance of Breuel and others to figures from novels by Fontane allows Fonty (and Grass) to conceive of Kohl's second German unification as a pale shadow of Otto von Bismarck's first unification, even if, as Fonty argues, all comparisons between Bismarck and Kohl are inadequate because Kohl does not have the larger-than-life aura accorded to Bismarck: 'He lacks the necessary grandeur, no matter how much he inflates himself. For that reason alone, any comparison with Bismarck is off the mark' (*TFA*, p. 524). The refusal to give names to such political figures from the novel's narrative present suggests that it is they, and not Fontane's or Grass's literary figures, who are the real shadow figures, somehow unreal und indistinct. The German past represented by Bismarck may have been oppressive, but at least it had some dignity and grandeur. In contrast, the German present has no name and seems to be characterised primarily by mediocrity: 'Everything that calls itself German is ruled by mediocrity, which finds its most stifling expression in "his" [Kohl's] ostentatious complacency' (*TFA*, p. 525).

The circular motion of Fonty's paternoster is ultimately brought to an end not by Brecht's water but by Fontane's fire when someone launches an arson attack on the trustee agency's headquarters, while Fonty himself proceeds to expatiate on the significance of fire in Fontane's works before a large and enthusiastic audience. In this passage it is as if Fonty himself, by describing Fontane's fictional fires, has willed a real fire to occur in the Detlev Rohwedder building. In the middle of Fonty's speech someone shouts into the crowd: 'It had to happen. The Handover Trust's burning!'

(*TFA*, p. 639). In *Too Far Afield* it is not fiction that imitates reality but rather reality that imitates fiction.

The end of the paternoster, caused by the fire, does not indicate an end to the circular motion of history, however. It just means that a particular metaphor for that circular motion has come to an end, possibly making it more difficult to understand and therefore rendering the FRG (the name of the German state inherited by a united Germany from West Germany) and its real structures less understandable. In place of the paternoster there will now be a fast modern elevator to take Germany's movers and shakers where they need to go. However, history itself, and its endless repetition, have not fundamentally changed.

Brecht's poem 'Questions from a Worker Who Reads' lists the great men of history and the deeds that they supposedly accomplished all on their own. The history books, Brecht and his literate labourer tell us, are full of these great men and their victories, but there is much that the history books leave out (particularly the role of workers in history): 'So many reports./So many questions'.[8] Grass echoes Brecht's syntax in describing the endless motion of the paternoster. Fonty 'grasped the changeover mechanism in the guise of a tirelessly obliging' paternoster. 'So much greatness. So many descents. So many endings and beginnings' (*TFA*, p. 476).

The use of the word *Wende* here, translated in this instance as 'change-over mechanism', is anything but innocent, since this is the word generally used in German to refer to the collapse of the GDR and the unification of Germany. For Grass, the word specifically means the points at the bottom and top of its run where a cabin in the paternoster makes a lateral motion and then begins to move in a different direction. These are, in essence, the points that make a paternoster circular and not linear. While the use of the word *Wende* to refer to the political events of 1989–1990 generally suggests a decisive and positive change for the better (i.e. linearity), the use of the same word in Grass's language suggests merely more of the same, with a twist. (Leaders who once called themselves followers of the Kaiser now call themselves Nazis; leaders who once called themselves Nazis now call them-selves socialists; leaders who once called themselves socialists now call themselves democrats, etc.). Whereas the water in Brecht's poem 'Ballad of the Waterwheel' is at least potentially capable of action that would finally put an end to the repetition of an oppressive history, Grass's fire does not have this potentially liberating power. It merely forces the replacement of the paternoster with a new, safer, and more efficient method of transporting the high and mighty. And whereas Brecht's literate labourer poses questions, Grass's Fonty does not, since he already seems to know the answers. At any rate, all the answers seem preordained. There is no escape from the circularity of German history, except to leave it. And leave Germany is precisely what Fonty does at the end of *Too Far Afield*.

Gardens of peace

Like Fonty, Alexander Reschke and Alexandra Piatkowska, the hero and heroine of *The Call of the Toad*, ultimately leave Germany. Fonty makes his way to France, while Alexander and Alexandra die in a car crash somewhere on the road between Rome and Naples, where they are buried in a village that the narrator chooses not to name. Since the entire novel deals with the creation, destruction, and use of graveyards, it is fitting that it ends with its main characters lying peacefully in a double grave. The irony, however, is that Alexander and Alexandra, a German-Polish couple who have dedicated their lives to the creation of a German-Polish graveyard in Danzig/Gdańsk, end up not in their own graveyard but in an anonymous Italian one.

The Call of the Toad begins on All Souls Day, 2 November 1989, when Alexander and Alexandra meet each other at an outdoor market in Danzig, where both are looking for flowers to place on the graves of the dead. The fate of Alexander's parents, who were forced to flee their hometown of Danzig at the end of the Second World War, resembles the fate of Alexandra's parents, who were forced to flee Vilnius. Both sets of parents, readers learn, always longed to return to their original home, even if only after death. The idea for the 'German-Polish Cemetery Society' whose fictive history forms the core of *The Call of the Toad*, comes precisely from these parental wishes. Alexander and Alexandra's creation makes it possible for elderly German refugees from Danzig and other now Polish cities to be buried in their hometowns. Even if they could not return home in life, they can return in death. The two protagonists, widow and widower, are in agreement 'that politics was a curse and had to stop somewhere, and that it was most certainly out of place in cemeteries' (*CotT*, p. 17).

This fictional construction resonates with Grass's own work as a craftsman making statues for graveyards in Düsseldorf after the end of the Second World War, an activity that he was later to describe in his controversial memoir *Peeling The Onion* (2006), and of which he had already given a fictional account in *The Tin Drum* almost half a century earlier, where Oskar Matzerath has the same job. Far from being deadly serious or lugubrious, however, *The Call of the Toad* is filled with black humour and satire. Alexander and Alexandra's idealistic plan ultimately fails due to the covetousness of German capitalists and the Poles who are determined to woo them, but Grass displaces the concerns of the German-Polish present by introducing various destabilising elements, almost Brechtian alienation effects. In particular, there is Mr Chatterjee, the Indian rickshaw capitalist who introduces bicycle rickshaws to Gdańsk and other European cities, and who becomes an investor in the cemetery society. Chatterjee is a messenger from a European future that will look less white and more global; in the face of that future, present-day German-German and German-Polish concerns pale in significance.

The graveyards in *The Call of the Toad* tellingly parallel the role of graves and graveyards in *Too Far Afield*. Of particular importance in the latter novel is the grave of Fontane himself, near the former Berlin Wall, which Fonty visits more than once. Almost as important is the grave of the famous German dramatist Gerhart Hauptmann on the Baltic island of Hiddensee. Hauptmann, from the eastern German province of Silesia, had died in June of 1946, one year after the end of the Second World War, and because Silesia became part of Poland after the end of the war his body was transported to Hiddensee for burial, along with portions of Silesian earth to be buried with him (*TFA*, p. 300). Another key burial in *Too Far Afield* is the reburial of Frederick the Great at the palace of Sans Souci in Potsdam, which occurred in the summer of 1991, and to which the novel's narrator devotes almost a chapter. Frederick the Great's remains had been removed from Sans Souci at the end of the war in order to prevent Russians or communists from desecrating them, and it was only after the collapse of the GDR regime that the remains were returned, with full pomp and ceremony, to Potsdam. The return of Frederick the Great to Sans Souci allowed Helmut Kohl and the unified Germany to publicly proclaim a connection to a supposedly noble Prussian tradition. Fonty cuts against the grain of this narrative by first stopping at the Wannsee grave of the literary suicide Heinrich von Kleist, one of Germany's most important writers of the early nineteenth century, whom Fonty calls the 'better kind of Prussian' because of his celebration of insubordination and even tyrannicide (*TFA*, p. 613). Secondly, Fonty and a troupe of Polish mimes relate the story of Frederick the Great's own insubordination against his father Frederick William and the execution of Frederick's friend Katte, whom Frederick William ordered decapitated in the presence of Frederick himself. Fonty even tells his companions the story of the removal of Katte's remains to the family estate in Wust: 'Even in those times, mortal remains were moved. Upon the family's petition, the coffin with Katte's head and body was dug up in Küstrin and hauled along miles of sandy roads on a narrow wooden cart pulled by two scrawny horses, all the way to his father's manor' (*TFA*, p. 618). He also tells of Fontane's and his own visits to that grave, where 'grave-robbing souvenir-seekers – for instance, a traveling Englishman – had stolen the vertebra severed by the executioner's sword, while others had pulled out the dead man's teeth' (*TFA*, p. 618).

Exactly why do graves and graveyards play such a significant role in both *The Call of the Toad* and *Too Far Afield*? The answer is that both novels are about the connection between the living and the dead, and it is precisely at graveyards that this connection is most prominent. In both of these novels the dead are not really dead – they are the undead, or revenants. They are constantly emerging from their graves to visit the living, and likewise the living are constantly descending into the grave to visit them. Graveyards are supposed to be places of rest and peace, but that is precisely what they are not in either of these novels. In *The Call of the Toad* entire cemeteries are flattened or constructed, and those who have already been buried emerge from their graves in Germany to return to Polish earth. Both of the main characters in *The Call of the Toad* are professionally and personally interested in graves and graveyards, and both visit them frequently, establishing a connection between themselves and the dead whom they ultimately join. Fonty, in *Too Far Afield*, not only visits and communes with the dead but is actually their representative in contemporary Germany: he is a reincarnation of Fontane. Hoftaller, Fonty's Stasi shadow and spy, is also undead: Grass has resurrected him from a 1986 novel by Hans Joachim Schädlich, in which the eponymous character Tallhover ultimately commits suicide. But in the view of Grass's narrator, neither of these figures, neither the compromised writer nor the spy, is really capable of dying. (A central strand of the novel is its reflection on the compromised writer in both the past and the present – the 'real' Fontane was involved in the 1848 revolution against the reactionary Prussian state and composed a number of radical pamphlets, yet only a few years later he worked as an agent of Prussia in England and began writing for conservative newspapers.) As Hoftaller declares to Fonty in a chapter entitled 'The Double Grave', 'for us there is no end. Blow us away, and we're back in a flash' (*TFA*, p. 112). Throughout *Too Far Afield* Fontane is referred to as 'der Unsterbliche', i.e. 'the immortal one', but literally what this means is 'the undying one'.

The prominent presence of graveyards and graves in both *The Call of the Toad* and *Too Far Afield* suggests a world in which the dead are not really completely dead but rather exist in communion with the living. All Souls Day, on which day the action of *The Call of the Toad* begins, is a day set aside for precisely such communion between the living and the dead, but in both novels this communion is a constant occurrence. Likewise a graveyard may be a place set aside for communion between the living and the dead, but in both novels this communion occurs not just at graveyards but throughout Germany, which in a sense becomes a massive graveyard and monument to its own past.

Dead letters

The significance of literature, and the reason for its power, in Grass's conception, is that the writer is quite specifically the person who channels the words and energies of the dead, and it is the writer who exercises power over the living. The narrator of *The Call of the Toad* channels the words of the novel's protagonists, who are now dead, but whose impact on the German present can still be felt in the novel's narrative. The narrator of *Too Far Afield* – a woman who works at the Fontane archive in Potsdam – channels the words not only of Fontane himself but also of Fonty and Hoftaller, all of them undead or undying. In *My Century*, Grass makes the role of the writer as medium for the dead explicit, declaring in the book's opening sentence: 'I, trading places with myself, was in the thick of things, year in and year out' (*MC*, p. 1). Not only is the writer capable of time travel, of being 'in the thick of things' every year, but he is also capable of a kind of transubstantiation indicated by the words 'trading places with myself'. The writer not only gives voice to but also in a sense *becomes* the characters about whom he is writing. At the end of *My Century* Grass channels the voice of his own mother from beyond the grave: 'He didn't force me into it, he talked me into it, the rascal. He was always good at that. I always said yes in the end. So now he's brought me back to life supposedly: I'm over a hundred and in decent health because he wills it' (*MC*, p. 272). And just as Grass's Birgit Breuel had commented on the author himself, so too Grass's mother cannot resist a comment about Grass's own old age: 'He's over seventy, the boy, and he's made quite a name for himself. Still can't stop telling his stories, though' (*MC*, p. 276).

In all of these works Grass channels the voices of the dead and the living – from writers like Fontane, Brecht, Hauptmann, and Kleist through political figures like Frederick the Great, Hans Detlev Rohwedder, Birgit Breuel, and Helmut Kohl to more private figures like Grass's mother and his friend Jakob Suhl. In all of these works the world – perhaps because of the failure of the living to accurately heed the warnings of the dead, those 'toad calls' which give their name to one of the novels – is out of order and does not seem capable of ordering itself. Grass confessed in February of 1991: 'I am not one of those people who believe that our world can be cured.'[9] The horror of history cannot come to an end, and there is no resurrection from death because there is no real death. However, the world's habitation by the undead is not simply negative for Grass. It is not just that Bismarck and Göring and Ulbricht are not really dead; it is also that all of their opponents, those 'suckers' who naïvely fought for a better world, are also still very much alive, even if they usually cannot be seen. The rhetoric that Grass used in his unsuccessful battle against German unification reveals much about his conception of history: it was true, he conceded, that the train had left the station, but there were various points at which it could stop before it experienced a complete wreck. 'The train has left, but the signals to bring it onto the right track . . . are still working' (*GvZ*, p. 76). Grass does not believe that human beings will reach a utopia of freedom and prosperity, but he senses that complete catastrophe can be avoided. And it is precisely those signals that he, with his literary works, wants to give.

Notes

1. Cited in Stephen Brockmann, *Literature and German Reunification* (Cambridge: Cambridge University Press, 1999), p. 52.
2. Günter Grass, *My Century*, trans. by Michael Henry Heim, New York, Harcourt, 1999, p. 244. Subsequent references appear in the text as *MC* with the page number in brackets.
3. Günter Grass, 'What Am I Talking For? Is Anybody Still Listening?', trans. by Stephen Brockmann, *New German Critique* 52 (1991), 66–72, at p. 67.
4. Günter Grass, *Two States – One Nation*, trans. by Krishna Winston with A. S. Wensinger (San Diego: Harcourt Brace Jovanovich, 1990), p. 10. Subsequent references appear in the text as *TSON* with the page number in brackets.
5. Günter Grass, *The Call of the Toad*, trans. by Ralph Manheim (New York: Harcourt, 1992), p. 92. Subsequent references appear in the text as *CotT* with the page number in brackets.
6. Günter Grass, *Too Far Afield*, trans. by Krishna Winston (New York: Harcourt, 2000), pp. 65–6. Subsequent references appear in the text as *TFA* with the page number in brackets.
7. Bertolt Brecht, 'Ballad of the Waterwheel', trans. by John Willett, in *Poems and Songs from the Plays*, ed. by John Willett (London: Methuen, 1990), 127–8, at p. 127.
8. Bertolt Brecht, 'Questions from a Worker Who Reads', trans. by Michael Hamburger, in *Poems 1913–1956* (New York: Routledge, 1979), 252–3, at p. 253.
9. Günter Grass, *Gegen die verstreichende Zeit: Reden, Aufsätze und Gespräche, 1989–1991* (Hamburg: Luchterhand, 1991), p. 124. *GvZ* in text; citations from this source are translated by Stephen Brockmann.

10

STUART TABERNER

Günter Grass's *Peeling the Onion*[1]

In an interview published in the *Frankfurter Allgemeine Zeitung* (*FAZ*) on 12 August 2006 in advance of his new book *Peeling the Onion*, Günter Grass divulged that he had served with the Waffen SS from late 1944 until his capture by American forces on 8 May 1945. In the weeks that followed, writers, literary critics, historians and politicians disagreed on whether this belated confession had enhanced the Nobel-prize-winning author's moral authority or rather undermined his insistence over almost sixty years on the need to confront the Nazi past. Grass's biographer Michael Jürgs, for example, asked in the weekly news magazine *Der Spiegel* whether the affair denoted the 'end of a moral authority' (12 August). The more acerbic conservative journalist, editor and Hitler biographer Joachim Fest seized the opportunity to condemn a longtime political opponent, writing in the popular daily tabloid *Bild*: 'I'd no longer even buy a used car from this man' (13 August).

In this chapter, I am concerned less with the furore caused in Germany and abroad by the more or less incidental confession made by Grass in his *FAZ* interview than with the literary text within which this confession is elaborated.[2] I argue that there are (at least) two approaches that may be taken to *Peeling the Onion*. In the first half of the chapter, correspondingly I look at Grass's presentation of his wartime experiences and at the manner in which he establishes his biography as 'exemplary', in the sense of 'typical' but also in the sense of an 'example to be followed'. This process allows him to transform his youthful error into a positive: his seduction by National Socialism and subsequent, postwar working-through of this (self-)delusion in his literary fiction and political engagement places him in a position of some moral authority. In the second half of the chapter, I take a quite different tack, in order both to demonstrate the polyvalence of Grass's literary fiction and to offer a reading of the novel which emphasises the personal rather than the political. Grass's *Peeling the Onion*, I argue, can be interpreted not just as a 'political intervention' but also as an elderly author's reflections on the agonies and uncertainies of growing old.

Peeling the Onion claims the status of autobiography: we are presented with the author's account of his adolescence, relationship with his parents, growing obsession with the opposite sex, and experiences at school, for example. Later, we are told of his time spent manning an anti-aircraft battery, attempt to volunteer for the submarine corps, and induction into the military and eventual deployment as a member of the Waffen SS 10th Tank Division Frundsberg, and of how he was wounded during shelling by Red Army artillery, managed to return to his own lines whilst avoiding the *Kettenhunde* – German units scouring the countryside for deserters – and was captured by the American army in a military hospital in Marienbad. In the aftermath of the German defeat, we subsequently read, Grass was interned in prisoner-of-war camps in Bavaria, where he took a cookery course using ingredients available only in the imagination of the partici-pants, and, after his release, lost his virginity, began a career as a sculptor working on tombstones, travelled to Italy, met his future wife Anna, moved to Berlin and then Paris, and, in 1959, published *The Tin Drum*, the literary work for which he remains best known.

At the same time, *Peeling the Onion* is also a *Künstlerroman* – an 'artist novel'. It tells the tale of how Grass became fascinated as young boy with the reproductions of famous paintings distributed with cigarettes in the 1930s, recounts how he entered a writing competition organised by the Nazi school newspaper *Hilf mit!* (Get Involved!) but – in retrospect, happily – won nothing, and narrates his efforts as a sculptor and his first successes as a writer, including the invitation extended by Hans Werner Richter, postwar author and key shaper of West Germany's emerging literary culture, to read at a meeting of the Group 47, the loose consortium of West German writers which emerged in the postwar period, many of whom later became famous for their political engagement. As if this were not enough, Grass's text is also a historical novel. Thus a vivid sketch of the Nazi period and the war is followed by a recreation of postwar life in the era of the 1948 currency reform – the introduction of the German Mark in the American, British and French occupation zones in 1949 which relaunched the economy in western Germany – and the 'economic miracle' of the 1950s. And finally, *Peeling the Onion* is a philosophical rumination on memory in which, on the one hand, the metaphor of the onion is used to describe the peeling away of layers of the past, a process which can never reveal the core, and, on the other hand, references to key moments as if suspended in amber appear to suggest that certain events will forever remain fixed and in sharp focus.

In answer to the question he himself has just framed as to why he has chosen to write the story of his life, and why at this particular moment, the narrator of *Peeling the Onion*, Günter Grass, elaborates:

Because something flagrantly significant could be missing. Because certain things at certain times fell into the well before the lid went on: the holes I left uncovered until later, growth I could not halt, the linguistic give-and-take I had with lost objects. And let this, too, be said: because I want to have the last word.[3]

This short passage highlights a number of motives which will be key to our understanding of the text. The references to something missing from the public record of his life, to falling 'into the well' (no doubt an allusion to Germans' susceptibility to Nazism), his (postwar) attempts to conceal the ruptures in his story, his artistic development (in contrast to the stunted growth of his most famous character, Oskar) and his 'linguistic give-and-take' with the lost objects of the past, reinforce this interplay of meanings and create a progression from repression to revelation to recovery and redemption. Above and beyond this, however, his aim is also to 'manage' the interpretation of his biography: 'because I want to have the last word'.

Indeed, Grass ensures the investment and acquiescence of his audience in a variety of ways. First, he introduces a form of theatricalised self-doubt which induces the implied reader to adopt a position of empathetic understanding less harsh than the author's own insistent self-questioning. Second, he moves away from autobiography into a *Künstlerroman* and thereby shifts the emphasis away from private failings *per se* onto the transformation of these private failings into literary achievement. Third, the author/narrator accentuates the exemplary, that is, representative and salutary, sacrifice made by the public figure who offers up his own biography as an object-lesson in self-deception and a guide to personal and political rehabilitation.

The sections of the book dealing with Grass's early adolescence through to his time served in the German armed forces are thus structured by a series of insistently self-critical questions posed by the author in respect of his former self. The process of asking questions is itself emphasised as a vital duty incumbent upon the engaged citizen, insofar as Grass's self-examination relates to questions he *failed* to ask as an adolescent and young man. Why did he not ask about the German assault on Poland of September 1939 (O, p. 10)? Why did he not ask about the fate of a classmate who was suddenly absent following his startling revelations of German naval defeats (O, p. 15)? Why did he not ask what happened to the Latin teacher who 'disappeared' (O, p. 37)? And, just one more example of many similarly omitted questions: why did he not wonder whether the young fellow recruit, most likely a Jehovah's Witness, who refused to take up his weapon during training, comically named by his peers 'Wedontdothat' (*Wirtunsowasnicht*) on account of his repetition of this mantra, might provide an example for *him* of the possibility of at least passive resistance? (*O*, p. 93). For Grass aged seventeen, of course, resistance was an alien concept.

The question asked by the suitably sympathetic reader, however, might not be concerned with Grass's failure as an adolescent to find out what had befallen those at odds with a regime with which he had grown up but rather with the more general issue of whether he might in fact reasonably be expected, at such a tender age, to have demonstrated such insight in any case – 'Wedontdothat' was exceptional, Grass the representative 'norm'. This question may edge out the larger question, quickly resolved in the text via the perhaps opportune literary conceit of the onion from which the skins of memory must be peeled away, of why the author did not reveal his service with the SS at an earlier point in time. Indeed, it seems unlikely that the present-day reader, conscious that so many 'ordinary' Germans failed to ask the 'right' questions, would rush to condemn this one individual and take no account of mitigating circumstances. And just such a mitigating circumstance is offered to the reader, albeit indirectly, perhaps even covertly, in the form of a defence initiated, intriguingly, by the onion but initially rejected by the author/narrator, who, it would appear, is resolutely determined to confront his past errors. The onion's plea that Grass was 'foolish boy' (*O*, p. 36) is thus rebuffed, as is the later suggestion that his youth might excuse his rush to volunteer for active service: 'What I did cannot be put down to youthful folly' (*O*, p. 64). Yet precisely this manner of mitigation is subsequently reintroduced, by Grass, as he speaks of how the prospect of military service promised escape from the 'cramped feeling' (*O*, p. 66) of his petit-bourgeois home and success with girls, and, most significant of all, refers to 'the stupid pride of youth' (*O*, p. 110). The plea for mitigation, once rejected, is now adopted by Grass, and the reader may well feel that the author has committed only a minor sin of omission in remaining silent for so long about his foolish youthful pride.

Convinced of the author's readiness to confront his past, the reader is most likely inclined to accept what was in any case all along the most credible explanation for the young Grass's eagerness to serve the Third Reich: adolescent pride, a juvenile glorification of combat, and an immature craving to impress (especially the opposite sex). As such, the reader may be receptive to the certainly more circumscribed, but also more plausible admission of culpability and collusion that follows the occasionally somewhat formulaic self-questioning described above:

> But the ignorance I claim could not blind me to the fact that I had been incorpor-
> ated into a system that had planned, organized, and carried out the extermination
> of millions of people. Even if I could not be accused of active complicity, there

remains to this day a residue that is all too commonly called joint responsibility.
I will have to live with it for the rest of my life.   (O, p. 111)

The key word here is 'joint responsibility' (*Mitverantwortung* in the
German text). The phrase may, the author claims, be 'all too commonly'
used, but it does nonetheless describe the extent of his complicity: he was
part of a system which carried out mass murder even if he himself was not
directly involved. At the same time, the prefix *Mit* ('joint') in combination
with *Verantwortung* ('responsibility'), denoting collective responsibility
rather than individual guilt (or, indeed, collective guilt), integrates the one
aspect of Grass's biography which might have been seen as exceptional, as
requiring specific explanation, into a more generalised liability borne by all
manner of 'ordinary' Germans for a range of forms of moral blindness.
Simple membership of the Waffen SS no longer appears as an egregious
crime in itself, as proof positive, then, of a fanatical mindset or of murderous intent.

The assertion that he is an 'ordinary' German has been deployed by Grass
throughout his career to legitimise his political engagement. As such, his
wartime biography is generalised as the 'lived experience' of millions of
'ordinary' Germans, and his subsequent coming to terms with his own
errors offered as a positive example to be followed. What Grass saw, felt
and did – and failed to do – is thus repackaged for public consumption: the
citizen is offered an opportunity to identify with the public celebrity, an
invitation to participate in an avowedly democratic construction of a collective history, and, most important of all, a lesson in how to acknowledge one's
own part in, or, for later generations, relationship to, the catastrophe at the
core of Germany's recent past. Within this stylisation of biography, historical
accuracy is necessarily subordinate to the transformative power of art.

This reading makes it possible to explain the rather curious sub-narrative
relating to Grass's time in the POW camp Bad Aibling when he claims to
have played dice with a fellow captive, Joseph, who was 'so single-mindedly
catholic' that he desired nothing more than to become a 'priest, a bishop,
maybe even a cardinal' (O, p. 137). Assuming the rather implausible claim
that the young Grass befriended the future 'German' Pope Joseph Ratzinger,
elected in 2005, is accepted, this episode contrasts the public personae
of Günter Grass, politically engaged writer and intellectual, and the Bishop
of Rome, head of the Catholic Church. Grass's transformation of his life-
story, including, and perhaps now even emphasising, his short period in the
SS, into an exemplary demonstration of how dogmatic certainties are to be
rejected in favour of a democratic scepticism, is thus implicitly contrasted
with the young man he once knew, 'whose faith was as securely bunkered as

the Atlantic Wall once was' (O, p. 373; the Atlantic Wall was built as Hitler's supposedly impregnable fortifications against the successful Allied invasion which finally came in June 1944). Like Grass a former servant of the Nazis, this young man (and the author playfully insists that his recollections do in fact concern Ratzinger) seems – now unlike Grass – not to have grasped that scepticism is the only defence against blind faith and self-delusion. Grass may once have been 'incorrigible' (O, p. 382) but has, even so, learnt from his experiences, whereas Ratzinger – the former follower of Hitler 'who today as pope claims infallibility' (O, p. 420) – has learnt nothing, and, as a consequence, deserves no absolution for his youthful sins of moral blindness, submission and unquestioning conformity.

Thus it is possible to argue that Grass's *Peeling the Onion* is not so much a belated confession of the author's SS service as an attempt to incorporate this episode into his public persona and to put it to some use. Grass's 'real-life' story, I suggest, is transformed into a 'usable past', to cite an oft-cited but here entirely appropriate term.[4] At the same time, a resolute defence is mounted of the author's career as a politically engaged artist in a legitimate attempt to redeem the failings of his youth. Grass as a young man was certainly misguided, but he offers himself now to his peers as an example of how their own youthful follies may be compensated by an unwavering commitment to democratic principles in the present and, to subsequent generations, of the need to be on the lookout for the first signs of extremism.

In itself, of course, Grass's plea for mitigation may be justified: the sincerity of the author's determination over five decades to help forge a more complete public reckoning with the Nazi past can hardly be contested, and the fact that this may, in part, be prompted by a desire to enact a kind of personal atonement need not necessarily undermine that record. Whether this represents a genuine engagement with the author's own biography, and in particular with his membership of the SS, however, is doubtful. Quite apart from the fact that Grass intimates that *Peeling the Onion* may be motivated by a desire to counter his critics and shape his own public image – 'because I want to have the last word' (O, p. 2) – the fact that the various strands in the text combine to lead, seemingly inexorably, to the composition of *The Tin Drum* might be read as implying a certain teleology within the author's account. Towards the end of *Peeling the Onion*, accordingly, we learn of how Grass struggled in Paris to find the first line of what would become his most famous work, and his best-known contribution to the task of confronting the German past. It was only following his realisation, at the height of France's war in Algeria and in the aftermath of the Soviet suppression of the Hungarian uprising, that writing about the past is inextricably linked to political engagement in the present, that he was able, he claims, to begin his investigation of the origins of Nazism: 'Granted: I am an inmate at a mental institution' (O, p. 421). It is surely significant that Grass's most famous protagonist Oskar is an unreliable narrator who takes the greatest liberties with his own life-story for the purposes of revealing more general principles to his reader.

A portrait of the artist as an old man

As the chapters in this volume have amply demonstrated, the one constant within an oeuvre that spans media, genres and almost sixty years of postwar German history is the polyvalency of Grass's output; all of Grass's literary texts, other artistic endeavours, essays and speeches are capable of many different approaches and interpretations. Here, *Peeling the Onion* is no exception. The reading offered above, then, is a determinedly 'political' understanding, which analyses Grass's most overtly autobiographical work in relation to the link between his biography and tireless social activism and public labours to encourage Germans to confront their country's Nazi past. Such a reading tends to be a 'critical reading', insofar as it sets out to explore the author's strategies, and evasions, in his use of his life history to both further his political programme and to justify his career as a politically engaged artist.

A quite different interpretation, however, might focus more explicitly on what might well have been received as the most striking aspect of the text if it were not for the episode, in fact a rather short section of the book, in which it is revealed that Grass had been a member of a Waffen SS tank division: the text's function as a vehicle for the author's ruminations on his advancing years. (Indeed, it is important to note in this context that he belonged to a *combat* unit of the SS – denoted by the prefix 'Waffen' (armed) – rather than the more familiar SS, without the prefix, deployed to control and terrorise civilian populations and persecute Jews.) *Peeling the Onion*, therefore, released in September 2006 (a few weeks before the planned date following the media furore surrounding his *FAZ* interview), a year before he would turn eighty (on October 16 2007), extends a process of reflection on his continued relevance, or otherwise, begun in his 2002 literary text *Crabwalk*. There, the authorial alter-ego, who appears in the text as the much younger narrator's 'taskmaster' and instructs him to relate the tale of the sinking of the German refugee ship *Wilhelm Gustloff* by the Russians in 1945 for a modern-day audience, is repeatedly alluded to as the 'the old man', prompting the reader to ask whether Grass's commitment to socially engaged storytelling can be sustained by subsequent generations of narrators. In *Peeling the Onion*, alternatively, the emphasis may be less on his *legacy* – although the lengthy sections tracing the genesis of his literary texts certainly imply his claim to have had a lasting impact on culture and politics in the Federal Republic – and more on the *sacrifice* of his individual life-story to: first, the all-obliterating maelstrom of German history in the twentieth century; second, his representative status as both personification and biographer of the 'ordinary German' and spokesman for his compatriots' efforts to come-to-terms with Nazism; and, third, the sudden fame thrust upon him at the tender age of thirty-two following the publication of *The Tin Drum* in 1959.

Grass's childhood, he tells us in the second paragraph of the text, was ended on the day war broke out on 1 September 1939, at the border between Poland and the German Reich, but also closer to home with fighter planes screaming overhead to attack Polish targets and at the Polish Post Office located within the Danzig Free State. (Grass's uncle Franciszek Krauze, from the Kashubian side of his family, was killed while defending the Post Office and that Grass's 'German' family broke off contact with their 'Polish' relatives in the first weeks of the conflict.) For the soon-to-be octogenarian author narrating his twelve-year-old self, the most vivid memory of the day that his youth was so abruptly curtailed relates to the accompanying radio commentary: 'Thus the end of my childhood was proclaimed with words of iron, in a ground-floor flat of a three-storey building on Labesweg, in Langfuhr' (O, p. 7).

Even at the very beginning of *Peeling the Onion*, Grass implies the annihilation of his private self by the overwhelming, destructive power of German history. The story that might have been told of the author's early years, the story of an idyllic childhood, will be subordinated to the chronicle of the way a young German from Danzig came to be swept up by global upheavals and epoch-making conflicts and be fashioned by a series of dates which, for his readers in the present, resonate with world-historical importance: the anti-Jewish pogrom of 9 November 1938, the outbreak of war on 1 September 1939, the German defeat at Stalingrad in February 1943, Germany's unconditional surrender on 8 May 1945, the currency reform of 20 June 1948, and the uprising in East Berlin against the Soviet authorities in the German Democratic Republic of 17 June 1953. The German teenager, SS recruit, POW and postwar citizen Günter Grass features in the text as a witness to these events, but also increasingly appears to be a product of them, a construct, so to speak, of the larger history of which he was an insignificant part.

Grass's biography thus occasionally seems curiously one-dimensional, flat even, and as if collapsed in on itself, or, more accurately, collapsed into German history. What is missing, it might be argued, is any real sense of the *uniqueness* of his story, or, just as damaging, the lack of an emotional connection to his childhood, so overpowering is the narrator's sensation that his younger years were subsumed by larger events. Even in retrospect, the narrator is debarred from filling in the gaps with invention or imagination; the spectre of Nazi horrors requires him constantly to invoke what he knows about the period 1933–45 as a restraint on his natural urge, towards the end of his life, to imagine childhood as a time of innocence.

Consequently, the relationship of subjective, 'felt' memory (that is, the way in which the individual recalls, often with embellishment or even fabrication, moments of importance to his or her sense of self) to collective memory (that is, the memorialisation of a nation's past, shaped and shared by many people in interaction with social narratives, public exposition, and formal remembrance) is experienced by the narrator as a contradiction, even as conflict. This is the distinction in German between *Erinnerung* (the individual's emotional processing of particular events significant to him or her) and *Gedächtnis* (the storing of records of the past more broadly), which is lost in Michael Henry Heim's (excellent) English-language version of Grass's text, and so is reproduced here in a more literal translation:

> [Die Erinnerung liebt das Versteckspiel der Kinder. Sie verkriecht sich. Zum Schönreden neigt sie und schmückt gerne, oft ohne Not. Sie widerspricht dem Gedächtnis, das sich pedantisch gibt und zänkisch rechthaben will.][5]

> Subjective memory [*Erinnerung*] likes to play hide-and-seek, to crawl away. It tends to beautify and embellish, often needlessly. Subjective memory often contradicts our store of knowledge about the past in general [*Gedächtnis*], which often appears pedantic and irritatingly insistent that it knows better.[6]

It is a function of subjective memory, of course, that it should fade and become increasingly unreliable. In the narrator's case, however, any desire to be allowed to indulge this natural forgetfulness and enjoy the game of hide-and-seek that memory plays, to imagine what he can no longer recall, is blocked by his awareness that his telling of his story, in this text and in others across a timespan of fifty years, is largely *functional*: his story is to be representative, a real-life instance of the abstractions of the collective memory of the Nazi era, rather than a journey of self-discovery.

Indeed, only a very few episodes can truly be considered to offer a glimpse of a more intimate self. Only a very few moments may be considered 'authentic' (authentic, that is, to the extent that the narrator is free to recall them as he wishes) rather than merely representative, for example, when the narrator is able to attach a memory to an object, something 'real' that his 'knees bump into' (O, p. 4), or when he recounts his sexual initiation in a haystack just after he is released from the POW camp. When he attempts to reconstruct this occasion, revealingly, he is scarcely interested in picturing the woman with whom he begins his postwar euphoria of sex, jazz and dancing, but is 'in search of self, the vanished I of earlier years' (O, p. 214).

Throughout, Grass experiences himself as split between an 'I' who writes in the present and the 'he' inhabited by the young man he once was. Paradoxically, however, this 'he' may be closer to the 'real' Grass, that is, the individual who as a seventeen-year-old joined the Waffen SS, who survived the war as a POW in Marienbad, and who first had sex in a haystack – the 'I', it is implied at various points in the text, may be a construct of sorts, shaped by the media, scholars, readers and critics. The 'I' who narrates, then, may be the 'representative Günter Grass', the Grass whose early success led to an unexpected and all-encompassing fame but whose biography, subsequently, has been stylised, shaped and sacrificed within public discourse (both by the author himself, it must be said, and by others who support or decry his political and literary interventions). Indeed, since the publication of *The Tin Drum* in 1959, the narrator declares in the text's closing paragraph, he has existed only 'from page to page and between book and book' (O, p. 425). This lament, in fact, arcs back to the very beginning of his account, when he laments in the opening pages:

> Everything that happened to me between milk teeth and permanent ones – my first day at school, scraped knees, marbles, the earliest secrets of the confessional and later agonies of faith – all merged in the jumble of jottings that has since been associated with a person who, no sooner had he been put down on paper, refused to grow and shattered all manner of glass with his song, and thanks to a tin drum made a name for himself that thereafter existed in quotable form between book covers and claims immortality in heaven knows how many languages . . . (O, p. 2)

In this passage, the narrator is more specific about the manner in which his 'I' came to be detached from the boy he once was, the 'he' to whom he has such limited access. Not only has the overwhelming force of German history squeezed out all individual content from his biography and replaced it with representative experience, but his more intimate experiences, those moments of anxiety, physical pain and existential doubt which typically infuse an individual's sense of self and provide the basis for identity and self-knowledge, have, ever since the publication of *The Tin Drum*, been appropriated by, or attributed to, his most famous character: Oskar.

To some extent, at least, Grass's *Peeling the Onion* may thus be read as an attempt, doomed from the outset, to recover a self that has been pushed to the margins, first, by the events that the author lived through as a young man, and, second, by his own postwar success and emergence as a representative figure in the campaign to educate Germans about their country's Nazi past. So deeply troubled is the author by his youthful enthusiasm for National Socialism, by the way in which he *allowed* himself to be subsumed by German history rather than resisting it, that he cannot reconnect with the boy and adolescent he once was; so profoundly aware is he of the way in which he has been identified with Oskar that he feels scarcely able to claim his biography from the uses to which his most enduring, versatile and irrepressible protagonist has put it. All that is left to him – and this he does throughout the text – is to recover the real-life biographies of the panoply of other real people whose stories he has, over the years, incorporated into characters who appear in his literary works, thereby honouring them and giving them what he cannot have: a unique rather a merely representative existence. They, of course, were unique to begin with: they stood out for their opposition to the Nazis, or for their willingness to be different, or for their determination to think for themselves. We are told, for instance, of how Uncle Franz, executed by the Germans for his part in the futile defence of the Polish Post Office in Danzig, would later appear in *The Tin Drum* as an example of courageous defiance (O, pp. 10–11). The recruit who refuses to pick up his rifle, 'Wedontdothat', we are later informed, was transformed into Joachim Mahlke' (O, p. 88) in *Cat and Mouse* (1963). Elsewhere, the Latin teacher whose disappearance the young Grass 'neglected' to question, appears in *The Flounder* (1977), a testament, without a doubt, to his courage in refusing to bend to the Nazis (O, p. 38).

At best, Grass can only recover his life-story as a pale, inverted image of the biographies of those he has known who set themselves against the Nazis – their defiance allows them an individuality that he, representative of so many millions who followed blindly, is denied. His work as a writer and a public figure, therefore, is an essentially humanist endeavour – to give value to the stories of those few who displayed common human decency when so many allowed themselves to be misled – but it demands of him the sacrifice of his own truly authentic sense of self. This, it might be argued, is the price that Grass continues to pay for his youthful enthusiasm for National Socialism and his complicity, relatively insignificant, including his service in the Waffen SS, in the criminal structures of the Hitler regime.

In conclusion, I have tried to demonstrate that Grass's *Peeling the Onion* can be read in at least two quite different, though not entirely unrelated, ways. On the one hand, a more obviously 'political' reading of the text might thus challenge the narrator's efforts to suggest that more than half a century of literary and social engagement allows him to evade individual responsibility, if not for his time in the Waffen SS then at least for the decades of delay in revealing this error. A more sympathetic appreciation of the book, on the other hand, attentive to the interplay of autobiographical fiction and the almost eighty-year-old author both within and without the text, might see Grass's narrative as a reflection on a life, and a life's work, defined by the errors of his youth and subsequently (and literally) writ large as representative of an entire nation's folly, and as a reflection on the personal cost of this. As with all of Grass's work, and testament to the essentially democratic tenor of his literary texts, artistic endeavours, essays and speeches, *Peeling the Onion* tenders an invitation to its reader to think in shades of grey rather than in black and white: nothing is straightforward, nothing is entirely certain, and there are always alternative understandings.

Notes

1. Parts of this chapter appear in *The Modern Language Review* (103 [2008]). I am grateful to the editors for permission to reuse material here. The chapter has been rewritten and significantly extended for publication here.
2. For a discussion of the debate, and the text, see Anne Fuchs, ' "Ehrlich, du lügst wie gedruckt": Günter Grass's Autobiographical Confession and the Changing Territory of Germany's Memory Culture', *German Life and Letters*, 60:2 (2007), 261–75.
3. Günter Grass, *Peeling the Onion* (London: Harvill Secker, 2007), p. 8. Subsequent references appear in the text as O with the page number in brackets.
4. See Robert G. Moeller's excellent *War Stories: The Search for a Usable Past in the Federal Republic of Germany* (Berkeley: University of California Press, 2001).
5. Günter Grass, *Beim Häuten der Zwiebel* (Göttingen: Steidl Verlag, 2006), p. 8.
6. Heim's translation is: 'MEMORY likes to play hide-and-seek, to crawl away. It tends to hold forth, to dress up, often needlessly. Memory contradicts itself; pedant that it is, it will have its way', p. 3.

11

KAREN LEEDER

Günter Grass as poet

The place of poetry in Grass's work

Grass's first book was a collection of poems, with graphics of his own.[1] Poetry first brought him to the attention of the Group 47, the loose gathering of West German writers which emerged in the immediate post-war period, many of whom later became famous for their political engagement; and his poems were explicitly cited in his commendation for the Büchner Prize in 1965. Throughout his career, he has always returned to this first literary medium, very often in conjunction with his skills as draughtsman, etcher and water-colourist, for which he trained at art school. Collections of poems and limited editions have continued to appear throughout his career, right up to the 650-page volume of *Sämtliche Gedichte* (*Collected Poems*) published in 2007. Over the years, he has come back to the subject of poetry repeatedly in essays and interviews: 'Everything I have written up until now is the result of lyric impulses, sometimes extended over 700 sides.'[2] Along with his graphic work, poetry is undoubtedly a kind of seedbed for ideas, which will sometimes emerge in other genres years, even decades, later. Indeed, a key topos of critical engagement with Grass's poetry is that his lyric work offers early, abbreviated versions of his prose or dramatic work. Grass has supported this line of interpretation and given a number of examples: pointing to his early poems 'Flag of Poland' (*SP*, p. 5) and 'The Scarecrows' (*SP*, pp. 27–9) as condensed versions of *The Tin Drum* and *Dog Years* respectively. In the archive folders associated with his early work on *The Flounder* ideas move quite freely between prose, poetry and drawings, constantly circling the central themes and giving an illuminating insight into Grass's processes of composition. There is even a suggestion that Grass thinks of poems as a way of navigating, measuring and marking out this creative landscape, like 'surveyors' markers in a desolate rubble of material'.[3]

Related to this role is the fact that Grass thinks of poetry as the most direct and intimate form of writing. 'For me poetry, the poem, has always been the most precise instrument for getting to know myself and surveying myself anew.'[4] This might have to do with poetry's ability, like drawing, to reflect the author back to himself, rather than facing outwards towards an audience in a communicative gesture. Certainly, Grass uses poetry to pinpoint moments of self-reflection, as in the fine autobiographical poem 'Kleckerburg' (*SG*, p. 196), or the portrait poems 'How I see myself' (*SG*, p. 226), and 'What I write about' (*SG*, p. 215; both of these poems also appear in the 1977 novel *The Flounder*). There have even been claims that poetry is the only genre in which Grass truly reveals himself. Nevertheless, one should probably not exaggerate this aspect. On the one hand, Grass has always emphasised the communicative, even dialogic, aspect of his poetry and, on the other, Grass is arguably always engaged in a self-conscious staging of self that operates across all genres.

If verse is the genre in which Grass can test himself, it also functions as a refuge, a place to gather himself. Indeed, he often returns to poetry after a major excursion into prose, or a particular trauma, as a kind of breathing space; and that lyric work, along with the visual work with which it is so often associated, acts in turn as an inspiration for future projects. However, Grass's predilection for poetry as a first and intimate reflection and its function as a kind of private workshop for ideas does mean that it can be difficult to understand and interpret. A case in point is the 1956 poem 'Lamento bei Glatteis' ('Lament on black ice') (*SG*, p. 35) containing a covert reference to prussic acid that was not made evident, along with a cryptic biblical citation, until the publication of *From the Diary of a Snail* sixteen years later (1972). Less acutely perhaps, a poem like 'Racine läßt sein Wappen ändern' ('Racine has his coat of arms changed') (*SG*, pp. 91–2), could certainly be read allegorically on publication in 1960, but its full range and depth of meaning could not be fathomed until the publication of *The Rat* some twenty-five years later (1986). The easiest way of visualising the process is to imagine the Chinese paper flowers that expand on contact with water to reveal their intricate form and colours, but only become recognisable as flowers when they have opened. What might appear to be heretic, arbitrary, or purely personal imagery in Grass's poems must sometimes wait for decades before being elucidated in the context of a novel, just as the paper flowers when dry are impenetrable, with no indication as to what they will reveal. Dieter Stolz has offered the most in-depth unfolding of Grass's imagery so far (1994). However, more important than the weight of individual metaphors are the questions raised more generally about the independent value of the poems, but also about the relation of Grass's poetry to his work in other genres.

Even in his earliest prose works Grass wrote with a poetically heightened tone and passages in early works like *The Plebeians Rehearse the Uprising* (1965/6), *The Tin Drum* (1959) or *Dog Years* (1963) appear in poetically patterned and rhythmic language. Occasional poems appear in early dramas (*Flood, Only Ten Minutes to Buffalo*, from 1955 and 1957 respectively) as well as in the *Tin Drum*, and *From the Diary of a Snail*. In these works, one is dealing with a kind of lyric 'Engführung' (IV, p. 287). This term comes from music and is translated as 'stretto' or 'straitening'. In using it Grass is doubtless aware of the Jewish poet Paul Celan's famous poem of the same name. Indeed comparisons have been drawn between Celan and Grass's early work.

The last seven lines of Oskar's account of his life story in the *Tin Drum* reappear, with new line divisions, as the poem 'Die schwarze Köchin' ('The black witch') (*SG*, p. 436) and the 1975 poem 'Federn blasen' ('Blowing feathers') (*SG*, p. 276) returns unaltered as prose in the seventh month of *The Flounder*. Significantly too, several of the later novels include poems that are integral parts of their imaginative and thematic structure, yet remarkable enough to stand independently when removed from that context. The forty-six poems that appear in *The Flounder* for example, are largely independent from the prose text, offering condensed and self-contained reflections on the same themes. Indeed, along with the etchings from this period, they appeared as an independent cycle in the 1983 volume *Ach Butt, dein Märchen geht böse aus* (*Ah Flounder, your fairy-tale will end badly*).[5]

An important aspect of Grass's lyric work is the intimate connection with the visual arts. Even while he was studying at the Düsseldorf Academy of Art, Grass was also writing poetry. Then he was seen first and foremost as 'a sculptor who wrote beautiful poems', according to the German thinker Hans Mayer, though Grass self-deprecatingly recalls sending poems to the famous poet Gottfried Benn, only to receive the tart rejoinder: 'interesting, interesting, this man will one day write prose'.[6] Although his twin passions for the visual arts and poetry might have seemed to strain in different directions, he nevertheless insisted that 'they lived from the same ink'.[7] Grass's essays often range across the two genres (XV, p. 499) and he has insisted on the interrelation between different aspects of his life and work: 'encounters between different disciplines: drawing, writing, reading, cooking, doing nothing' (X, p. 30). This kind of approach intensifies in his works of the period 1988–91: a prime example being the 1988 volume *Show Your Tongue*, in which a prose text, a long poem and drawings offer a threefold perspective on Grass's Calcutta experience and open up a unique intertextual dialogue. Sometimes, and increasingly in the later works, texts are taken up into the images themselves, to become part of an integral whole.

Grass has often commented on the particular significance of drawing in his creative process. This lies in its power to test, survey, and take the measure of his ideas; the word 'vermessen' (survey) appears regularly in this context, as in the examples above. For him graphic art is simply more exact (XV, p. 499). He warns: 'A written metaphor sometimes arrives on paper too easily; it is only when I test it out in a visual form that I can see whether it is going to work or needs to be corrected.'[8] Poetry seems to occupy a similar function in relation to his prose works. The precision and constraint of a poem, offering precious little room for manoeuvre, gives the opportunity to test the rhetorical flourish of a seductive phrase, rendering it much more naked, much more open to question than a prose form might.

The poetry

While Grass was still struggling with the problem of how to begin his literary career, the two most prominent poets of the older generation were approaching the end of theirs. Gottfried Benn and Bertolt Brecht represented the twin poles of artistic practice. Benn saw poetry as the articulation of a privileged inwardness; Brecht measured it by its social and political usefulness. Benn strove for what he saw as 'absolute poetry' that had little truck with the indignities of the real; Brecht sought a profoundly communicative poetry that responded precisely to the exigencies of the everyday. Both poets died in 1956, in their different sectors of Berlin, as unrepentant champions of their quite different understandings of poetry. What made Grass's *Die Vorzüge der Wind-hühner* (*The Merits of Windfowl*), published in that same year (1956), and the subsequent collection, *Gleisdreieck* (1960; referring to the place in Berlin, literally 'Railroad Triangle') so memorable, was his determination to strike a peculiar balance between these two modes: between the usually irreconcilable extremes of personal almost obsessive idiosyncrasy on the one hand, and of social conscience and social vision on the other.

This determination can be traced to three of his earliest prose pieces, which appeared later as 'Der Inhalt als Widerstand' ('Content as Resistance') (XIV, pp. 16–22), in which imagination and verisimilitude, fantasy and realism, are treated not as alternatives but as generators of a particular and necessary tension. The middle essay, a brief dramatic account of a walk taken by two poets, Pempelfort and Krudewil, presents the extreme alternatives available to the contemporary writer. It has often been misunderstood: critics reading Krudewil's desire to 'knit a new Muse' who is 'grey, mistrustful . . . and totally dreamless, . . . a meticulous housewife' (XIV, p. 20) as Grass's own. The piece should rather be understood as a genuine dialogue between the positions articulated by Benn and Brecht, even in the ironic and grotesquely pantomime form they appear here. This is after all an equivocation which will preoccupy Grass throughout his career in different forms; and indeed an imaginary meeting between Brecht and Benn appears once again as the entry for 1956 in Grass's 1999 *My Century*.

In fact, Grass's beginnings are closer to Benn, even to Surrealism, and Dada, than to his grey, committed muse, although implicit social and political concerns are never far from the surface. *The Merits of Windfowl* is subtitled 'poems and drawings', and gives as much space to Grass's fantastical line drawings of beasts, birds and objects as to the poems. Objects proliferate in the verse too: a collection of the spoons, birds, scarecrows, nuns, cooks, fingers, scissors, musical instruments and dolls, which will also emerge in *The Tin Drum* and *Dog Years*. The surrealist element comes from the sense of the random encounter of found objects in unexpected ways, but the poems also operate with a sustained tension between these and a colourful fantasy life fed by nursery rhymes and childhood fairytale. Compare 'Musik im Freien' ('Open air concert') (*SG*, p. 20):

> When the yellow dog ran over the meadow
> the concert expired.
> Later the bone could not be found.
> The scores lay under the chairs,
> the conductor seized his airgun
> and shot all the blackbirds.

Objects are viewed through the lens of the 'exaggeratedly pointed realism', celebrated in Grass's 1958 essay 'On the writing of poems' (XIV, p. 23), which generates a precise but distorted perspective. This is exacerbated by the lack of causality or connection between images, which then seem to gesture towards an absurd cosmos without meaning, or at least a meaning concealed from our comprehension. What prevents the poems from disintegrating into arbitrariness is the scaffold of syntactic patterns and repetitions, which allow the bold metaphors to stand out even more. Out of this sense of disproportion comes the tone of grim portent. Poems like 'Prophets' Fare' (*SP*, p. 7) exploit political fairytale or biblical parable. Threat seems to be everywhere. In 'Open Wardrobe' (*SP*, p. 3) the contents of the wardrobe take on a closely observed but sinister life of their own, for example. Many of the poems operate with a private catalogue of motifs, giving the volume the sense of a glimpse into a dark but private mythological universe. Some, however, speak more plainly of time in a way which points forward to later work.

Family Matters

> In our museum – we always go there on Sundays –
> they have opened a new department.
> our aborted children, pale, serious embryos,
> sit there in plain glass jars
> and worry about their parents' future.   (*SP*, p. 13)

Gleisdreieck was published in 1960 after the success of *The Tin Drum*. It shares much in common with the first collection: the mania for objects, the use of fairytale and parable, the concision. Yet it also builds on the strengths of the first collection, and discards some of the most obscure play, giving it a greater focus, bite and existential depth. The collection boasts Grass's famous existential parable 'In the Egg' (*SP*, pp. 21–3), which portrays a blithely chattering and wilfully blind humanity, bolstered by the false consolations of religion or ideology, and refusing to face the existential void. There are also experiments with longer sequences 'From the Daily Life of the Doll Nana' (*SP*, pp. 45–51), or 'My Eraser' (*SP*, pp. 52–5), which cast an ironic light on the creative act. Generally, however, Grass now seems more willing to use readily accessible images, and a clear form. In 'Folding Chairs' (*SP*, p. 19), the ship deck chairs that 'advertise departure' become metonyms of impermanence and exile. 'Saturn' (*SG*, p. 121) is a grim take on the squalor of bachelor living and 'Pan Kiehot' (*SG*, p. 89), on the theme of Polish gallantry, depicts the Polish Don Quixote attacking German tanks near Kutno, as the Polish cavalry did in 1939.

The title of the collection refers to a Berlin underground station where the lines from the two sectors of the city form a triangular junction. A number of poems reflect upon on state of Berlin, including 'The Great Rubblewoman Speaks' (*SP*, pp. 59–67), which conjures up one of Grass's great grotesque creations striding across the blasted city: her lamentations, however, drowned out by the schmalz of a society comfortably reinstalled in its own wilful ignorance. Several of the best poems document unease at the whitewashing of the very real political threats of the time, in particular the danger of totalitarianism. The poem 'Sale' (*SP*, p. 25), for example, uses the surreally tinged image of a house sale to deliver a comment on Grass's own poetic processes, but also a clear political warning:

> While I was selling it all
> five or six streets from here they expropriated
> all the possessive pronouns
> and sawed off the private shadows
> of little innocuous men.

'Nursery Rhyme' (*SP*, p. 15), reportedly Grass's favourite poem, moves in similar territory and is a *tour de force* of technical skill. It consists of five strophes (or verses) of four lines and a regular three-beat rhythm, like a children's rhyme, and each strophe (except one) uses a single recurring rhyme. Each strophe begins with a question: 'Who laughs here?', 'Who weeps here?' But laughing, weeping, talking, keeping silent, playing and dying, the spontaneous and uncalculated actions of essential humanity, all reap a grim rejoinder:

Wer spielt hier, spielt im Sand?	Who plays here, in the sand?
Wer spielt, muß an die Wand	Against the wall we stand
hat sich beim Spiel die Hand	players whose games are banned.
gründlich verspielt, verbrannt	They've lost, thrown in their hand.

What makes this poem so powerful in German – the exploitation of idioms, the permutations of meaning – renders it almost untranslatable. The whole poem exploits variations of the word 'Grund', meaning reason, and the strophe cited here plays on the idiom 'an die Wand gehen' (to go to the wall, but also implying to face a firing squad); 'die Hand verspielen', to play a hand of cards badly or waste an opportunity; and 'die Hand verbrennen' meaning 'to get one's fingers burned'.

Gleisdreieck was successful because of the finely judged balance of political and poetic impulses. Grass's next collection *Ausgefragt* (*Cross-examined*) of 1967 seemed to represent an aggressive departure from that kind of balance. The intervening years had seen the radical politicisation of literature and the renunciation of the extraneously lyrical under the banner of the 'death of literature'. By this time too Grass was committed to the Social Democratic Party (SPD) and actively involved in the election campaigns. He characterised his own function as that of the 'court fool in consideration of nonexistent courts' (XIV, pp. 167–72). It was as a citizen, not as an artist, that Grass could commit himself for a time to party-political electioneering with impassioned speeches.

It is important to remember, however, that Grass believed that his imaginative writing should resist every kind of external pressure that would transform it simply into a vehicle for ideology: 'Poems admit of no compromises; but we live by compromises. Whoever can endure this tension every day of his life is a fool and changes the world' (XIV, p. 172). Nevertheless, references within the collection are more obviously historical, not to say strident (one poem finishes 'I advise you to vote Es-Pe-De', *SG*, p. 189); the illustrations more savagely realistic. Overall there is a move from the proliferation of objects of previous collections to people and inner states and, despite a proclaimed intent to 'hit on the imprecise thing precisely' (*SP*, p. 85), also a loss of economy. There is also a certain amount of political and poetic infighting: the sequence 'ANGER FURY RAGE' is in effect a polemic against the radical left, and poems like 'Powerless, with a Guitar' (*SP*, p. 91) or 'Do Something' (*SP*, pp. 93–101) reflect on the impasse of the political poet. Perhaps the most strikingly original of these is 'The Jellied Pig's Head' (*SP*, pp. 103–9): a metaphor for impotent fury sublimated into cooking. On closer inspection, though, the collection also documents a far more intimate, domestic realm: autobiographical reflection, anxiety, sleeplessness, an acute sense of mortality and transience, the comforts of sex, birth of children and, in deadpan and painful detail, the breakdown of a marriage. Poems like 'Marriage' (*SP*, pp. 69–71), or 'Love' (*SP*, p. 79) chart the brittle antagonism of a relationship on the rocks or the listless disappointments of love and suggest a tone which will dominate in the poems of *The Flounder* and beyond. The poem 'Writing' (*SP*, pp. 83–5) offers a famously urgent injunction to embrace transitoriness for its own sake, as a bulwark against the senselessness of existence:

> Conclude with a colon:
> I'm coming back. I'm coming back.
> Remain cheerful in a vacuum.
> Steal only things of one's own.
> Chaos
>   More skilfully executed.
>   Not adorn – write:

The difficulty of combining explicitly political commitment and poetry left its mark and that poetic colon was to remain unanswered for some time. If *Cross-Examined* responded to the political charge of the late 1960s, Grass's next collection, the first independent poetic publication for twenty-five years, documents the upheaval following German unification. *Novemberland* (1993) comprises thirteen sonnets, interspersed with a matching number of rudimentary sepia drawings, and responds to the events of the preceding November: the killing of three Turkish women in a hostel for asylum-seekers in Mölln. The themes are clear: the perversion of traditional values, political opportunism, the resurgence of the New Right, the cynicism of the media, the ruthless pursuit of profit, and unification itself which 'struck us and proved merciless' (*SP*, p. 153). The cycle has already suffered from its immediate topicality: the rhyme of 'anonym' (anonymous) with 'Minister Blüm' (*SP*, p. 153), or a reference to a xenophobic speech by the Bavarian politician Edmund Stoiber, marked in the use of the word 'durchrassen' (miscegenate) (*SP*, p. 139); even the events in

Mölln would probably already need footnotes. But in describing Germany as 'Fortress Novemberland' (*SP*, p. 147) Grass is referring both to attitudes towards asylum-seekers in contemporary Europe, but also to a larger and more particular historical legacy. By strange coincidence the date 9 November marks Hitler's putsch in 1923, 'Kristallnacht' in 1938 and the fall of the Berlin Wall in 1989.

It is no chance that Grass turns to the great poet of the Thirty Years War, Andreas Gryphius, to find a language to answer this reality, and the cycle is marked both by a debt to the baroque prosody and poetic conceits of Gryphius himself, but also the ingenious and facetious poetic colleague, Peter Rühmkorf, to whom the cycle is dedicated. It is an ambitious experiment: working within a strict sonnet form, containing multiple rhyme and dense alliteration, and also using camouflaged quotation from folksongs, hymns and other *Wende* (turning point = the fall of the Berlin Wall) poems. However, the mixture between savage political attack and whimsical reflection, the rhetorical and the cavalier, or even vulgar, creates an unsettling mood. Some of the political points are overwrought and a number of the rhymes forced – 'unstetig' / 'Ästhetik' (jerkily / aesthetic) (*SP*, pp. 142–3) – or overly drastic: 'ausgeschwitzt' (*SP*, p. 146), for example, means 'sweated out', but also contains within it a reference to Auschwitz. The scansion is regularly distorted by the need to accommodate the rhyme and there are moments of bathos. A charitable account might suggest that Grass was using these deliberate false notes as an aesthetic means to insist on the discord of the united Germany. However, it is clear that this cycle represents some of the difficulties in using poetry as an immediate vehicle for political comment. Later work has generally turned to the politics of the self.

In the last decade or so Grass has turned inwards to fashion a sense of 'lateness' in respect of his own person and this is nowhere clearer than in the poetry volumes *Fundsachen für Nichtleser* (*Found Things for Non-Readers*) (1999), *Letzte Tänze* (*Last Dances*) (2003) and *Dummer August* (*Everyone's Fool*) (2007). Of course other works contribute to this sense: the monumentalism of *My Century* and *Too Far Afield* (1995), or the self-stylisation as 'the old man' in *Crabwalk* (2002). In speeches and interviews too, he describes himself as one of very few still fighting the good fight against the apolitical cynicism of the present: 'The last Mohicans. Three OAP Musketeers. Three dinosaurs, who know no other.'[9] But the poetry volumes insist most powerfully on the themes of age, infirmity and mortality, and explore the responses to them.

In some senses *Found Things for Non-Readers* returns full circle to Grass's early work: the same delight in the occasional poem; the interest in a collection of 'found objects' in their physical reality; a litany of familiar motifs – stones, feathers, mushrooms, rubbers – and a certain whimsical irony. The volume emerged from a retreat to the Baltic island of Møn after the public furore surrounding *Too Far Afield*, during which the book was attacked both as aesthetically flawed and 'soft' on the former GDR, and bears witness to the preoccupations of a simple, rural life with forests, animals, vegetables, fish and seasons prominent among the concerns. The almost epigrammatic poems stand opposite quite brash, explicitly representational, watercolours by Grass, which illustrate the poems directly and contain the text of the poem. In keeping perhaps with the 'non-readers' of the title and the dedication to his 'grandchildren in growing number' the poems are all very short (some three or four lines long) and written in simple, reflective mode. This does not preclude a wry philosophical bent, biting irony, the occasional political aside or some sly word play. What is quite different from the early work is the monumental scale of the volume (some 240 pages in an A4 format with full-colour pictures) which is characteristic of the late work, but also the increased awareness of mortality. Though the images are among Grass's most aesthetically pleasing, and the miniatures are sometimes arresting, these are not Grass's most significant works.

Interestingly, however, images of wintering, dancing, farewell, shards, silence, and marks in the snow will reappear directly in the later collections. One poem, 'Wegzehrung' ('Viaticum') (*SG*, p. 343), in which the lyric subject desires to be buried with a sack of nuts and his newest teeth, reveals, notwithstanding, Grass's characteristic bite:

> And if there's a cracking
> from where I lie
>   it can be safely assumed:
>   its him again
>   he's still at work.

Last Dances is the most persuasive of the three volumes: a collection of love poems of a sort, but also a model lesson in growing old disgracefully, which focuses on war, acrobatic sex, dancing and death. The beginnings of the volume are related in the first poem (*SG*, p. 349), which insists on the collection as 'something cheerful', as an antidote to having condensed 'the sinking of the ship and / the echoing scream' into his book *Crabwalk* (2002). Grass turns to pottery, and the dancing couples Grass began to craft in clay appear in the collection as drawings. Moreover, many of the poems document different dances: from the waltz to the dance of the seven veils, tango and quickstep to ragtime. But the collection announces itself as a repertoire of 'last dances', and the poems document not only the energy of the dance but also decline, loss and approaching death. A good example is 'Einst in der Löwenburg' ('Once in the Löwenburg') (*SG*, pp. 352–3), in which the sensuous vitality of the wartime dancing – 'Rag on steaming soles / our limbs like matchwood / to boiling point and beyond' – gives vitalist proof that the young people have survived the horror. By the end of the poem, we discover that the place where they danced is long gone, as are those who danced there. Only the hammering beat continues, morphed finally into a macabre 'dance of death', with the old bones once more united.

For all the gusto, humour, eroticism and physicality of the poems, they are shot through with mortality and document physical decline, acute vulnerability, dead friends, and memories almost lost. Some of the best poems return to the domestic in a muted but defiant tone. 'Nach Mitternacht' ('After Midnight') (*SG*, p. 361), for example, sees the couple at home and alone in the early hours. After hearing a news bulletin on the radio warning of war, they dance a slow foxtrot, 'brought together' ('zusammengefügt') in a poignant and tender awareness of old age and mortality. But the collection also opens out explicitly to the political realm. In 'Nach alter Melodie' ('After an Old Melody') (*SG*, p. 364), for example, a fiddle-playing figure of death appears coaxing the corpses and scattered limbs from the ground after an American cluster bomb. But this time they refuse to come together into the 'danse macabre' one might traditionally expect of a battlefield poem and the poem mourns the numberless and unidentified dead.

Against what has been lost, however, comes a rowdy and obstinate celebration of the private realm and faculties that remain: the ability to do a headstand to the surprise of the assembled family gathered round to celebrate a seventy-fifth birthday (*SG*, p. 378) or, in a section of short erotic poems, a vivid delight in acrobatic and geriatric sex. Though these poems are not the most lyrically persuasive in the collection, the sentiment they represent echoes through the work: a kind of reprieve of the here and now, found in the couple. And another poem, one of the strongest in the collection, 'Zum Paar gefügt' ('Made into a Pair') (*SG*, p. 363) also makes explicit the desire for union which runs through the work, and is expressed in the pairs dancing or making love, or here, two beech trees grown together and dancing in the breeze.

The collection *Dummer August* (*Everyone's Fool*) continues many of the same concerns, but with one important new frame of reference. It responds directly to the scandal surrounding Grass's autobiography, *Peeling the Onion* (2006), taking inspiration from the aftermath of the publicity campaign against the writer in August 2006. The German title refers both to the month in question, the 'silly season', which arguably allowed the debate to ignite with such vigour, and the figure of 'dumb August' the simpleton

Figure 1. Illustration from the poetry collection *Everyone's Fool* (2007).

clown. A line drawing accompanies the title poem: a self-portrait as a grimacing clown, 'in a pointed hat / made of yesterday's newspaper', and stood before the 'summary court of the just' (*SG*, p. 390) (see Figure 1). The almost uniformly negative critical response to the collection derived primarily from the view that many of the poems were blatant exercises in revenge or self-exculpation. A tone perceived as a mixture of disingenuous naïvety, coarseness and self-pity won few fans; and particular exception was taken to the implied comparison of Grass's own situation with that of Goethe who accepted a decoration from Napoleon, which he wore proudly even after the political climate had changed. Grass writes a response to Goethe's poem 'Wanderers Gemütsruhe' ('Wayfarer's Equanimity') turning his scorn on his newspaper critics, 'where – in Frankfurt am Main / baseness as might / enjoys good profits / and stirs old shit' (SG, p. 427).

Certainly some of the poems appear simply too raw and unprocessed an emotional response to Grass's situation. But aside from the polemical poems, there are moments of much quieter and more complex reflection on memory, stigma and shame, such as the poem 'Mein Makel' (My Blemish) (SG, p. 417). These, along with a sequence of epigrammatic meditations on food and cookery, a celebration of 'earthly pleasure' (the title of one poem, SG, p. 392) that would not have been out of place in the 1999 volume, will perhaps only be appreciated when the political contro- versy has died down. The centre of the collection is quite different: a long- lined, rollicking take on Laurence Sterne's *Tristram Shandy*, 'Ich lese' ('I read') (SG, pp. 407–9), which seems to come from a quite different mood and significantly continues Grass's interest in self-invention. However, per- haps the dominant tone is one of melancholy transience: marked by trem- bling hands, dead friends, the new boots that 'squeak self-confidently', as if they wanted to outlive the wearer (SG, p. 412). The response is a character- istic and truculent determination to endure: 'For still / the last word has not been said' (SG, p. 387).

Grass's place as a poet

Early critics of Grass's work reckoned his lyric output too slim to be of great significance in assessing his *oeuvre* or overall standing. The number of poems now published individually and in collections is certainly large enough to bear comparison with many key figures in modern German poetry. A handful of poems, especially from the early years, where his work burst on the predictable postwar poetry world as a kind of explosion, will certainly continue to be anthologised. Despite having produced in the intervening years a very substantial body of poetry, Günter Grass as a poet remains, however, largely unrecognised. The majority of his poetry has not been translated and is generally little known or appreciated in critical literature. This derives partly perhaps from the curious embarrassment that surrounds the poet-novelist figure in general, but also, paradoxically, from the fact that Grass has remained out of step with movements or tendencies. For the experimentally minded of the 1960s Grass's poetry lacked the necessary level of linguistic self-reflexiveness, and for those on the left it lacked a proper left-wing consciousness. Against the so-called 'laboratory poets' he championed the 'occasional poem'; in 1960 famously proclaiming himself wedded to reality and sceptical about ideas (XIV, pp. 26–32). Yet when Grass sent his poetry into the political foray in 1967 with the collection *Cross-Examined* and preached realistic compromise, he was accused of misunderstanding the intellectual agenda of the radical left. Grass was perhaps most in tune with the general mood in his unadorned poetry of the everyday in the 1970s and 1980s, though it is also difficult to argue that his voice is distinctive enough to stand out. He is certainly some way from the highly intellectual or experimental poetry setting the agenda today. In short, as a poet, Grass remains without a school, but also without imitators, without an obvious following.

The edition of selected poems and drawings of 'half a century', *Lyrische Beute* (*Lyric Booty*) of 2004, which carries the stamp of Grass's own editorial authority, says a good deal about how Grass sees himself or would like to be seen. Like the autobiography of two years later, it stands as a calculated self-invention. It betrays a conscious decision to edit out the private jokes, the most obviously slight poems or the baldly political work. Those poems most written to the moment are excluded; *Novemberland*, for example, in its entirety.[10] While it certainly reveals aspirations towards the monumental, it also does not obscure the traces of vulnerability that perhaps make for some of Grass's best work. It concludes with a relatively generous selection of the epigrammatic, subdued and ironic late vignettes and a pointed reflection on old age, which brings Grass into line with a number of distinguished poets such as Volker Braun, Michael Krüger, or Peter Rühmkorf. *Lyric Booty* is also interesting for what is says about Grass's own understanding of the relationship between his poetry and his work as an artist. Both genres are given equal weight in the edition, reflecting both the intense connection that Grass feels between these two modes, but also, arguably, a return to his beginnings: from collection to recollection. This operates in other spheres too and although much of the exuberance has gone, the wry, restrained lyricism of his late poems is in its own way just as distinctive. What can be said without doubt is that poetry has a vital place in Grass's work; whether Grass will come one day to have a central place in an account of modern German poetry is less certain.

Notes

1. Unlike his prose works, Grass's poetry has not been systematically translated. Even the translation of the titles of some collections has not been standardised. In this chapter I shall draw on the bilingual edition of Grass's *Selected Poems 1956–1993*, translated by Michael Hamburger (London: Faber & Faber, 1999) (*SP*). For other poems cited, reference will be given to the German edition, Günter Grass, *Sämtliche Gedichte 1956–2007* (Munich and Göttingen: DTV and Steidl, 2007) (*SG*), and translations will be my own.

2. Quoted in Volker Neuhaus, *Günter Grass* (Stuttgart: Metzler, 1992), p. 207. Like the poems, many of the literary essays and almost all of the interviews are yet to be translated. Where possible I shall reference the 1997 Steidl edition of Grass's works edited by Volker Neuhaus and Daniela Hermes, by volume and page number in parenthesis in the text, and translations will be my own.

3. 'Über Novemberland': Günter Grass im Gespräch mit Harro Zimmermann', 24 January 1993: www.radiobremen.de/online/grass/interviews/novemberland.shtml.

4. *Gespräche mit Günter Grass*, ed. by Klaus Stallbaum, *Werkausgabe in zehn Bänden*, ed. by Volker Neuhaus (Darmstadt und Neuwied: Luchterhand, 1987), vol. X, pp. 170–1.

5. Compare other special editions with etchings and lithographs from this period: *Mariazuehren* (*Inmarypraise*, 1974), *Liebe Geprüft* (*Love Tested*, 1974), *Mit Sophie in die Pilze gegangen* (*Gone Mushrooming with Sophie*, 1976), *Als vom Butt nur die Gräte waren* (*When Bones Were All That Was Left of the Flounder*, 1977).

6. Quoted in Julian Preece, *The Life and Work of Günter Grass: Literature, History, Politics* (Basingstoke, New York: Palgrave, 2001); Heinz Ludwig Arnold (ed.), *Günter Grass* (Munich: Text + Kritik, 1988), p. 71.

7. Günter Grass, *Vier Jahrzehnte. Ein Werkstattbericht*, ed. by Fritze Margull (Göttingen: Steidl, 1991), p. 47.

8. Stallbaum (ed.), *Gespräche mit Günter Grass*, p. 183.

9. Günter Grass, 'Zwischen den Stühlen: Rede anläßlich der Verleihung des Fritz-Bauer-Preises', in Grass, *Steine wälzen. Essays und Reden 1997–2007* (Göttingen: Steidl, 2007), pp. 34–7, at p. 36.

10. Günter Grass, *Lyrische Beute. Gedichte und Zeichnungen aus fünfzig Jahren* (Göttingen: Steidl, 2004).

12

RICHARD ERICH SCHADE

Günter Grass and art[1]

Looking back to his childhood in his memoir *Peeling the Onion* (2006), Günter Grass told of the niche in his parent's apartment reserved for him: 'There a shelf held modeling clay, poster paints and a sketch pad'.[2] He further observed 'I lived through pictures . . .' (O, p. 6), explaining that he collected coupons dispensed in cigarette packs with which he acquired reproductions of master paintings by Dürer, Botticelli and the like, pictures he mounted in albums provided by the tobacco company. His mother quizzed him on the images and the child proved himself adept in being able to distinguish one painter, one style from another. The pastime sharpened his boyhood imagination.

Grass went on to relate how this early interest in art history was accompanied by the ability to sketch and paint, an inborn skill he considered to have been inherited from an uncle (O, p. 50). These talents came into play as a sixteen-year-old paramilitary recruit, when he was ordered to decorate the unit's mess hall with paintings (O, pp. 81–2). After induction into active duty, he was interviewed for leadership training. He regaled his amazed interlocutor with his knowledge of art history and was promptly turned down for the special assignment (O, pp. 115–16) – such interests were hardly deemed crucial to final victory (*Endsieg*).

Subsequent to the defeat of the Nazi state in May 1945 and with his eventual release from an American prisoner-of-war camp, Grass moved on in search of work and his family, finally settling in the Rhineland. It was in peacetime Düsseldorf where he was able to make good on his passion for artistic representation. Indeed, the title of the memoir's chapter, 'The Third Hunger', expressed his compulsion: 'My hunger for art, however, the need to make an image for myself of everything standing still or in motion and thus of every object that casts a shadow and even of the invisible . . . this desire to conquer all images was insatiable, accompanying my conscious self by day and my dreams by night . . .' (O, p. 248).

On the suggestion of a professor at Düsseldorf's famed art academy, Grass first took up training as a stonemason. He repaired the façades of bombed-out office buildings, crafted headstones and chiselled inscriptions honouring the dead. This work as an artisan coupled with a portfolio of portrait sketches gained him entry to the academy (1948–52). The pages of the memoir name sculptors and painters whose works influenced Grass. Most importantly, however, his creativity was moulded by Otto Pankok (1893–1966), a graphic artist and confirmed pacifist (O, pp. 309–11).[3] It was Pankok who served Grass as the model for Professor Kuchen in The Tin Drum, the exponent of an Expressionist aesthetics: ' "Art is accusation, expression, passion. Art is a fight to the finish between black charcoal and white paper" . . . The coal-breathing professor gave his disciples a short briefing: What he wanted was expression, always expression, pitch-black, desperate expression.'[4] Both in the novel and in the memoir Grass implicitly rejected a classicistic aesthetic as tainted by the ideology of Nazism. Like Oskar Matzerath, the novel's protagonist, Grass opted instead for engaged art open to the depiction of gypsies and stunted humans: 'Coveted by painters and sculptors alike, he [Oskar] was ideal for emotionally charged, symbolic representation. Small and hunch-backed, he embodied the madness of the past era and the era just beginning. And because he was both, he could also be the converse of it all. Meeting him was like standing before a concave mirror: in his presence everyone took on a new shape' (O, pp. 311–12).

Here, Grass's memoir becomes very much a narrative 'portrait of the artist as a young man', a characteristic that defines the text throughout. During a vacation from his studies, young Grass hitchhiked to Italy where he sought out 'the originals [i.e. artworks] . . . that thanks to the colored cigarette cards had made me the art addicted youth I was' (O, p. 321). He, like so many Germans during the immediate postwar years, felt himself to be free as a bird, while also acknowledging that he was, like artist predecessors, in search of that legendary 'land where lemon trees bloom'. And Grass sketched everything he encountered – persons and places (O, pp. 325–6). His hunger for art and experience was truly insatiable, as further documented by his activities on a later hitchhiking trip to Paris: 'The paper byproducts preserved from my tour of France include a sketchbook plus a pile of medium-size drawings on which gull feathers and a bamboo reed have produced an all but unbroken line forming the heads of men and women who were close enough to sketch for sufficiently long intervals in cafés, on park benches, in the Métro . . .' (O, p. 338).

Grass's memoir treats the years 1939 to 1959, from the outbreak of the war to the publication of The Tin Drum when he was aged thirty-two.

It was the culminating achievement of his formative years. In the realm of representational art, however, he was still finding his way. In 1953, he moved from Düsseldorf to Berlin to train under Karl Hartung (1908–1967),[5] a sculptor renowned for abstraction influenced by the likes of Jean Arp (1887–1966), Constantin Brancusi (1876–1957) and Henry Moore (1898–1986) (O, pp. 356–9). Grass felt himself especially drawn to the seeming monumentality of Hartung's small sculptures and he created bronzes much in the spirit of his mentor (O, p. 378).[6] In Berlin, he also followed the vociferous debates on art theory between Karl Hofer (1878–1955) and Will Grohmann (1887–1968): 'Offended and hence angry, Hofer defended representational art, art determined by the human form, against the absolute priority of non-representational art' (O, p. 376) The controversy of abstraction versus representation directly affected the young Grass. He had figural drawings turned down for a juried exhibition in Berlin, and in the memoir he asserted that his thinking and reputation as a sculptor, graphic artist and painter had since been informed by those theoretical debates: 'From then on I kept my distance from all dogmatic constrictions, maligned all popes . . . and made my peace with the risk of having to resist the *Zeitgeist* as an outsider. Which had its consequences: the only way my work as an artist could gain exposure was in one-man shows, steering clear of fashion. It has remained on the fringe to this day' (O, pp. 377–8).

Art and literature

As a stand-alone artist, then, Grass judged himself to have been on the fringe in 1959 and since that time, while, as the author of the international bestseller, he knew himself to be very much at the centre of the literary universe. And from the start the interactive dynamic between art and literature has always informed his creativity: 'Am I a writer or graphic artist?', he asked himself in a brief essay. His answer was that 'drawing and writing cross-fertilise one another'.[7] This observation was grounded on the author's practice of writing out the first draft of his novels in longhand. The manuscripts themselves were often shot-through with drawings, images directly derived from the text being composed. Furthermore, when he tired of writing, he took a break to sculpt or sketch, working with his hands even as his mind worked with words later to be committed to paper. For Grass, one medium is but an extension of the other, for handwriting is in essence a *graphic* medium of communication:

> 'Look', the drawing says, how few words I need'. 'Listen', says the poem, 'what is between the lines'. And because with me writing continues drawing,

because narrative syntax may be derived from drawn structures, the question 'are you first a writer or a graphic artist?' has never concerned me. Considered from the standpoint of words or drawing: values of gray tint, position, darken and make our realities transparent. Paper alone is white. It must be stained, enlivened by hard or broken contours or covered with words, which always tell the truth anew and each time in another way. A graphic artist who writes is someone who does not switch ink. (Z, pp. 790–1)

What Grass considered to be an artificial distinction between the arts is suspended, is here cancelled out. The disciplines are not mutually exclusive. Artistic representation is equivalent in importance to literary creativity, an obvious truism to him, but one all too often not understood by scholars who are given either solely to an iconoclastic analysis of literary statement or to an exclusionary privileging of the artistic image.

Grass has always been proactive in promoting awareness of his representational art. The *Werkverzeichnis der Radierungen* (1979/80, *Catalogue of Etchings*) not only reproduced 146 prints but also listed the seventy-three exhibitions of the graphic works from 1955 to 1980. Numerous other exhibits and catalogues were to follow, most importantly, *In Kupfer, auf Stein* (*In Copper and Stone*), a catalogue of etchings and lithographs produced from 1972 to 1985. Interspersed among the prints were photographs of Grass at work in his studio and an appendix augmented the *Werkverzeichnis*-listing of exhibits by updating it to a total of 139 shows between 1955 and 1986. These statistical details are relevant, for even as he was publishing literary works and hard at work as a public intellectual, the catalogues documented a robust artistic productivity and an international public presence in galleries and museums. All previous catalogues of Grass's graphic art were superseded in 2007 by Hilke Ohsoling's edition *Catalogue Raisonné: Die Radierungen* (*Catalogue Raisoné: The Etchings*) and *Catalogue Raisonné: Die Lithographien* (*Catalogue Raisonné: The Lithographs*).

To this day, the promotion of Grass's image as an artist-writer continues unabated. The 2007 exhibition catalogue, *Günter Grass. Schriftsteller und Bildkünstler* (*Günter Grass: Writer and Representational Artist*), is a case in point. Five brief essays on his literary production are augmented by a sampling of Grass's prints, paintings and sculptures, all works exhibited in a gallery of the Günter Grass-Haus in commemoration of his eightieth birthday. Since its founding in 2002, the museum located in Lübeck has billed itself as a 'forum for literature and representational art' (www. Günter-Grass-Haus.de), a designation linking just those arts so very crucial to Grass's self-concept in a most public venue.

Grass, the artist-writer

In 1963, Grass was elected to membership of the Academy of Arts, Germany's premier cultural arts institution founded in Berlin in 1696. He became the president of its West Berlin section from 1983 to 1986, and in 1991 (a year after German unification) he sold his manuscripts and other papers to the academy. To mark the establishment of the resulting Günter-Grass-Archiv he published *Vier Jahrzehnte. Ein Werkstattbericht* (Four Decades: An Account from the Workshop) in 1991. Biographers have dutifully noted the fact, while offering but a perfunctory description of the large, coffee-table volume. Subsequent to the award of the Nobel Prize for Literature in 1999, Grass updated the text to include another decade and his publisher produced an edition in 2001 for the International Day of the Book (April 23) with the revised title *Fünf Jahrzehnte. Ein Werkstattbericht* (*Five Decades: An Account from the Workshop*). This slim imprint was subsequently republished under the same title in a more richly illustrated folio format updated to 2004. True to form, the dust-jacket depicted a bespectacled Grass, peering out from behind a multi-branched and extremely spiny cactus, one eyebrow raised in apparent scepticism. The image is a variant of the lithograph published in the 2001 printing of the *Werkstattbericht*, but here its dominant position on the cover of the folio suggested to the viewer and potential reader that Grass is a prickly presence at best. A glance at the contents of the 2004 volume indicates that both those interested in art and literary scholars have much to gain by a consideration of the book, for it was Grass's intention to define himself here and once and for all as the artist-writer he has always been.

The 2004 edition of the *Werkstattbericht* presents a variegated panopticon of Grass's life in 471 pages. The spread is framed by a greatly enlarged snapshot of Grass in Düsseldorf in 1948 and closes with the full-page photograph of him and his wife Ute in 2004.[8] The former depicts the young stonemason, mallet and chisel in hand, standing on a scaffold and next to a partially demolished stone column. The pose and demeanour, dark work-clothes and proletarian-style cap, mark him as a man involved with the trade central to Germany's postwar recovery. This carefully constructed image of the twenty-year-old contrasts markedly with the later photograph of the pleasantly satisfied seventy-seven-year-old and his wife at rest. It is an altogether fitting pose for the end of the *Werkstattbericht*, a volume featuring some eighty photographs of him interspersed throughout the book. Grass gradually ages and is pictured in all manner of surroundings, public and private. He is shown surrounded by his family, writing, typing, reading, drawing in his studio, sketching and painting out of doors, engraving plates for printing, sculpting clay, consulting with his publisher about book design, engaged in political discussion, performing on stage and speaking in public. Grass ages, to be sure, but the advancing years are linked to a steady stream of accomplishments, indeed, the photographs depict his entire life as a dynamic work in progress.

The photographs of Grass comprise a pictorial biography and the reproductions of his paintings, finished drawings and quick sketches, of prints, pottery and sculpture constitute a gallery, a retrospective exhibition catalogue of sorts. Deft sketches made on the 1951 tour to Italy suggest a carefree spirit on the road in the exotic environment (W, pp. 1–15). They capture the birdlike freedom of which he was to later write in *Peeling the Onion*. Similarly, the spontaneous sketches made in France might themselves serve to illustrate the description of his observations in the memoir (W, pp. 18–24). Here, art is very much in the service of autobiography, the images paint a portrait of the artist as a young man.

The chronological organisation of the *Werkstattbericht* results perforce in the display of artworks pertaining to specific publications. All manner of hens, both sculptures and drawings, for example, are interspersed among reproductions of manuscript pages for his poetry anthology *The Merits of Windfowl* (1956). And the layout of the *Werkstattbericht* reinforces the statement made in the accompanying text: 'While drawing and writing had gone their own ways in previous years, now both disciplines could realise themselves for the first time. They lived from the same ink [sie lebten von einer Tinte]' (W, p. 47). This pattern of presentation, the visual conflation of images and texts, repeats itself time and again throughout the folio volume. The medium becomes very much the message.

Grass's drawings, sketches, prints, and sculptures are reproduced so as to document the particularly inter-medial process of creation. Nowhere does this come more to the forefront than in the display of images for the dust-jackets of the various publications. The studies for the covers of his early theatre pieces (W, p. 62), for *The Tin Drum* (W, pp. 80–1), for various poetry anthologies (W, p. 82, pp. 94–5), for the novella *Cat and Mouse* (W, pp. 108–9) and for the novel *Dog Years* (W, p. 112), for the play *The Plebeians Rehearse the Uprising* (W, pp. 116–7), for *Too Far Afield* (W, p. 368) and *Crabwalk* (W, p. 428) reveal an emphasis on Grass's artistic process. For example, should the protagonist Mahlke alone or just a smug cat be privileged on the cover of *Cat and Mouse*? He and the publisher opted for the latter illustration. Should the sketch of a malevolent skulking dog or the human hand formed as a profile of the canine's head be selected for the dust-jacket of *Dog Years*? He and the publisher opted for the latter image. Much like the several drafts for literary texts, the various studies for the cover art aid in the interpretation of his literary intentionality.

The three studies for the cover art of the drama on the 1953 workers' revolt in Berlin, *The Plebeians Rehearse the Uprising* (1965), reveal the author's pronounced political intentionality (W, pp. 116–19). One sketch depicts a throng of workers, arms locked in solidarity, surging across the page towards the viewer. A banner reads 'NORMEN RUNTER' ('Down with Work Quotas'), the central demand of the East Berlin workers during the uprising of 17 June 1953 against the East German communist authorities. In a second study, the marchers, dominated by an oppressive cityscape, advance down the page in concerted political action. In the third sketch, the viewer is faced down by a brutal Soviet tank, by the self-same instrument of anti-revolutionary totalitarianism that suppressed the revolt, a political event with real meaning for Grass's literary programme: 'The events in Berlin of '53 came to the fore. The idea for a play on a German tragedy, *The Plebeians Rehearse the Uprising*, developed, one derived from the text of my speech on Shakespeare's *Coriolanus* and Bert Brecht's treatment *Coriolan*. A play, by the way, which early on defined the contradictions of the West German–East German process of unification since November 1989, contradictions that have yet to be laid to rest' (W, p. 117). The text of the *Werkstattbericht* enunciates the political thrust of Grass's intentions as a literary artist, but admits to the fact that the drama's dust-jacket lacked the requisite punch. For reasons of Cold War realities in 1965 Berlin – only four years after the erection of the Berlin Wall – none of the three sketches discussed above were adopted by the publisher. Instead, Grass's pleasantly appealing drawing of a number of flyers bearing the numeral 17 in red simply reminded the viewers and readers of the storied date in June 1953. The artist-author's palpable disappointment regarding the quality of the print – 'The book cover ended up being bland and meaningless' (W, p. 117) – validates the view that Grass considered it to be inadequate to convey his actual literary and political agenda.

Grass's truly active engagement with politics dates back to Willy Brandt's first campaign for the office of chancellor in 1965. He tirelessly crisscrossed West Germany and created the famous poster of a rooster boisterously cawing out ES – PE – DE, the phonetic initials of the Social Democratic Party (*Sozialdemokratische Partei Deutschlands*). The significance Grass ascribes to this phase of his career manifests itself in a photograph of him signing his poster and of him engaged in public discussion on the campaign trail. The images are followed by a reproduction of a journal entry in manuscript. The hurried hand of the scrawl lends authenticity to his profile as a politically engaged artist on the go. And the four studies for the SPD-rooster attest to the fact that significant care was rendered to art in the service of election-year politics (W, p. 129). Significantly, the pattern of presentation is repeated in the *Werkstattbericht*. A manuscript diary entry from the second Brandt campaign, textual commentary, a photograph of Grass sketching a self-portrait replete with a snail-shell in his eye-socket (*W*, pp. 138–40), all accompany the statement that it was these events that informed the text *From the Diary of a Snail* (*W*, p. 141), a semi-autobiograpical text detailing Grass's campaigning activities on behalf of Brandt, published in 1973. The sequence of the inter-medial narrative – photographs, manuscripts, drawings – portrays Grass as a *homo politicus*. The pages of his pencil sketches of snails creeping through various landscapes and along roads at their customary pace (*W*, pp. 144–5) speaks to Grass's wish to emphasise the notion of 'stasis in progress' ('Stillstand im Fortschritt'), a concept that became the central idea informing *From the Diary of a Snail*. 'Stasis in progress. Hesitation, halt between steps. Thought about thought, until the only remaining certainty is doubt. Knowledge that engenders disgust. All this is applicable to us.'[9] For Grass, the concept was linked specifically to the notion of melancholy as represented by the *Melencolia* (*Melancholia*) master engraving by Albrecht Dürer: 'Frankly, my manuscript . . . has been weighed down by . . . the work of art on which it is based . . . I was unable to dismiss Dürer's motif from my mind' (*S*, pp. 291–2). Grass's appendix to the text, in fact, is entitled 'On Stasis in Progress. Variations on Albrecht Dürer's engraving *Melencolia I*' (*S*, pp. 286–310). The campaign diary as a whole defined the modern socio-political condition, that is, the stubbornly slow pace of true social progress, and Grass's carefully selected cover-art of a snail traversing a woman's face, his idiosyncratic political iconography, represented 'stasis in progress'.

The astonishing array of art-work in the *Werkstattbericht*, documenting Grass's interests and accomplishments during the 1970s and 80s, also featured numerous self-portraits. On one print, his face emerged from the side of the speaking flounder (*W*, p. 158), the protagonist of that compendious historiographic narrative, *The Flounder* (1977). His severe visage is an analogue to the head of the fish – his eyes and voice view and speak of world history. The fish is his mouthpiece and vice versa and it is, thus, hardly coincidental that the fourth chapter of the novel portrays the interaction of seventeenth-century German poets and a locally renowned painter in Grass's city of birth, Danzig. In the chapter, the flounder-protagonist, writers and an artist replicate Grass's multivalent imagination. Years later, Grass depicted himself eyeing a rat (*W*, p. 288) on a manuscript page for the novel *The Rat* (1986), and in another print he and the rodent perched on his shoulder interact warily (*W*, p. 289). The uneasy tension between creator and created is palpable, it speaks of the inter-medial nature of the project at hand. Grass writes: 'The first manuscript version of the novel *The Rat* was written in a notebook shot-through with drawings. The more technology offers handy personal computers and similar work-saving instruments, the more old fashioned I become, relying on ink and pen' (W, p. 275). The engraved and sketched self-portraits give explicit visual definition to the artist-writer Grass. Indeed, *The Meeting in Telgte* (1979), a novella set in seventeenth-century Germany, explored multivalent options for literary expression, a notion visualised by the striking dust-jacket image of a hand grasping a quill (W, p. 223). The decidedly 'old-fashioned' writing instrument, while strictly speaking not a self-portrait of Grass, implicitly depicts the triumph of his artistic energy.

The mid-1980s saw a shift in Grass's artistry from a dominance of etching to red-chalk drawings (*Rötelzeichnungen*), messy black-brown ink washes (*Tuschezeichnungen*) and lithographs. The washes were especially appropriate to *Show your Tongue* (1988), a literary and visual diary of his sojourn in India. He experienced and depicted the reeking squalor of the slums (W, pp. 299–308, pp. 313–18): 'Calcutta stayed with me for a long time. In my new studio . . . I drew with stinking octopus ink . . . This natural black bleeding to sepia was just right for the scenes of Calcutta, also for the written words which were derived from the drawings' (W, p. 319). Subsequently, the hard-hitting lithographic images of the dying forests and bleak landscapes of Communist East Germany's industrial strip-mining (W, pp. 322–38) gave expression to Grass's severe anger about, and explicit criticism of, Germany's socio-political environment during the years surrounding unification in 1989/90. The text of *Dead Wood* (1990), with its cover image of a scene from the man-made destruction of the nation's once darkly romantic forests, linked environmental disaster to political dissolution: '*Dead Wood* was conceived of parallel to the fall of the East German state and the start of its co-option by the Federal Republic, also known as Reunification. It was a process of clearcutting in two senses that manifested itself in the images of the latter part of the book: concise aphoristic texts augmented by citations from the government's status reports on the forests' (W, p. 323). Grass then went on to link Calcutta with Germany: 'Just as I was face to face with the realities of Calcutta, now – lost in dead wood – I was unable to stop bearing witness while drawing' (W, p. 325). Art, text and Grass's political agenda coalesced here meaningfully, a trend that continued in the text, lithographs and charcoal drawings attending his controversial novel *Too Far Afield* (1995), an imaginative critique of German unification that met with withering criticism (W, pp. 356–69).

As an escape from the slings and arrows of controversy, Grass sought solace in painting. Beginning in the mid-1990s, he turned from the sombre shades of grey, black and brown to shimmering colour: 'Water colours demand the interplay of hesitant waiting and quick decisive coloration. Wet on wet' (W, p. 373). The variegated folio-sized images of *Found Things for Non-Readers* (1997), conjoined paint and poem. The words of each epigrammatic text, so-called *Aquadichte* – a title combining allusion to *Gedicht* (poem) and *(wasser) dicht* (water)tight – were painted with the same brush as used to illustrate the found object. In synaesthetic interaction, colourfully painted words float, dive, and play themselves off against the image thematised by the poem's text (W, pp. 379–87).

The intermedial harmony achieved in the anthology of colourful poems became the defining characteristic of *My Century* (1999), Grass's idiosyncratic review in prose of the twentieth century. Each chapter corresponded to a year, 1900 to 1999, and each was accompanied by an illustration in watercolour. 'What was there first, the texts or the watercolors?' was the question put to him in an interview: 'Often the watercolors. There was an interaction between writing and painting . . . These new watercolors are emblematic, they compress a story.'[10] The paintings personalise each text and reinforce the textual message visually, a creative process from inception to completion implicitly documented in the pages of the *Werkstattbericht* (W, pp. 390–401).

As if to dramatise this linkage of the arts, variations of several dust-jacket illustrations reappear as watercolours in *My Century*. These include the strident drummer of *The Tin Drum* in chapter 1959 (MC, p. 239)[11] and the flounder in chapters 1975 to 1977; in the latter case, the image of the fish became progressively larger, until the painting of the flounder alone fills the facing folio-sized pages (MC, p. 305, p. 308, pp. 312–13). And each chapter's painting includes the numerals of the year in question, imparting chronological continuity to the disjointed narrative. The multiplicity of topics, however, allows for very little thematic consistency in the watercolours. There is a fascination with the depiction of headgear, from military helmets to inline skating gear. Crowd scenes from Communist and Nazi rallies to the present-day abound, but individuals are also depicted, including the Communist agitator Karl Liebknecht and Chancellor Willy Brandt, but neither Hitler nor Chancellor Helmut Kohl. Technological devices such as the zeppelin, battlefield scenes, dead trees, mushrooms, angry-looking bovines, a rubber duck, and cloned sheep all march vividly in review across the interior pages of the book in a serendipitous sweep of apparently culinary ornamentation.

The ordering principle to the text is offered by the painted numerals, but Grass also intersperses facing-page watercolours of a tangled mass of numbers at irregular intervals throughout the interior of the volume. Their placement subdivides the flow of the overall narrative, causing the reader to pause, look and ponder, and suggesting a visual periodisation of the century. Additionally, each painting of the tangled numerals is characterised by a dominant colour (for example, a Nazi brown watercolour for the years encompassing the Third Reich, chapters 1933–1945). As such, the visual medium structures the micro-historical episodes into coherent macro-historical units: from the Second Empire (1900–1918), to the Weimar Republic (1919–1932), Hitler's dictatorship (1933–1945), and the Cold War Germanies (1946–1990), and, finally, to the unified Germany at the century's close. The function of the watercolours is to impart meaning and a certain order to Grass's thematically diffuse literary take on 'his century'.

The new century saw unabated literary and artistic activity on Grass's part. An updated *Werkstattbericht*, covering five decades of his work, was published in 2001 (to be followed in 2004 by the edition cited in this chapter). It closed with the all-too telling words: 'just as at the writer's desk, now at the potter's wheel. My eye directed only at sculptural processes. And no demands to write any more, even if one subject matter does place demands on the other – as ideas come knocking, are ignored and yet time and again insistently making their presence known in my workshop – hoping for a sixth decade . . .' (*W*, p. 411). And indeed, by a second printing in 2004, the hopes had been realised. Sculptures are depicted (pp. 410, 413, 434, 436, 439) as well as the plans, manuscripts and typescripts of the novella *Crabwalk* (2002). Grass's dedication at the opening of this work, 'in memoriam', says it all, for the bestselling fictional work documents the sinking of a ship filled with several thousand German civilian refugees and a much smaller number of military personnel in January of 1945. The dust-jacket, a lithograph printed in a red tone, presents two crabs – or was it a time-lapse of a single crustacean scuttling across the cover, back to front? The image turns out not to be the representation of an actual sea creature but is rather the metaphor for the text's narrative flow. The narrator, a survivor of the catastrophe at sea, born at the moment the ship sinks, explores the horrific historical events even as he seeks to uncover and understand his own son's ideologically radicalised and ultimately criminal obsession with the same issues. He is in a quandary: 'But I'm still not sure how to go about this: should I do as I was taught and unpack one life at a time, in order, or do I have to sneak up on time in a crabwalk, seeming to go backward but actually scuttling sideways, and thereby working my way forward fairly rapidly?'.[12] The father's search for truths, past and present, occurs obliquely at best: 'Now let me leave the ship where it was relatively safe . . . and crabwalk forward to return to my private misery' (*CW*, p. 91). And he continually interrupts the story to characterise this technique: 'But we haven't reached that point [in the story] yet. Again I have to do a little crabwalk in order to move forward . . .' (*CW*, p. 112) The narrator scuttles back and forth chronologically, very much like the crab – or crabs – depicted on the novella's dust-jacket.

This artistic visualisation of the literary enterprise is analogous to the function of the images created for Grass's memoir *Peeling the Onion* (2006). Not only does the red-toned lithograph of the vegetable grace the dust-jacket, but the artist also develops the image's full potential. Each chapter opens with a graphic representation of an onion, with the very first emitting fumes of discernible letters later to be described in the memoir's text: 'When pestered with questions, memory is like an onion that wishes to be peeled so we can read what is laid bare letter by letter. It is seldom unambiguous and often in mirror writing or otherwise disguised' (*O*, p. 3). The onion serves Grass as a metaphor for memory, that most crucial mental capacity for the author of an autobiography. Indeed, so central is the image of peeling back the layers of time and personal meaning that the German text opens with an untranslatable phonetic wordplay. The title of the chapter thus reads 'Die Häute unter der Haut', that is, 'Skins beneath the Skin' (*O*, p. 1), a heading immediately followed by the sentence 'Ob heute oder vor Jahren, lockend bleibt die Versuchung, sich in dritter Person zu verkappen' ('Today, as in years past, the temptation to camouflage oneself in the third person remains great', *O*, p. 1). The German adverb 'heute' (today) plays on the plural noun 'Häute' (skins). As such, the opening sentence suggests to the reader that the author must seek to explore the temporal surfaces of his third-person self beneath the outer appearance of his current physical being. As the reader encounters the eleven lithographic illustrations in the bound book, he or she peels back the layered pages of the author's life and times. As such, the physical object printed by the memoir's publisher is analogous to the metaphorical onion of which Grass writes and is comparable to Grass's drawing on the cover. Each subsequent print depicts the ever more peeled vegetable, until at the last nothing more than random shreds remain scattered about. The visual dynamic is one of a *de*structive peeling back of layers, even as the reader's experience with the text *con*structs the story of Grass's life.

The exploration of Günter Grass, the artist-writer, has come full circle. From boyhood to old age, he has truly 'lived through pictures'. His rejoinder to the furore about his Waffen SS revelations in the memoir was to publish in 2007 the poems and lithographs contained in the anthology *Dummer August*. (The title 'Stupid August(e)' refers to the month in 2006 when the story broke on Grass's wartime service in the notorious Waffen SS but also to the collection's cover illustration depicting Grass wearing a dunce's cap – he is an *August*, the German word for clown.) The anthology validates the notion that Grass turns to graphic art and literary statement to define his position. The poem 'At the Pillory', accompanied by the image of a kitchen knife, one halved onion and two whole onions, makes his rejoinder explicit. He calls the bluff of his critics:

> At the Pillory
>   It occurred after the onion,
>   layer after layer,
>   had become helpful to me.
>   'Look, now he stands there skinned',
>   many call out,
>   who themselves don't want to take up an onion,
>   because they fear that they will discover something,
> no — worse! — nothing
>   which would distinguish them.[13]

Grass challenges his critics to pick up the abandoned kitchen knife and cut the whole onion in half, revealing the truth about themselves. Now as in the past, the kinds and usages of his artwork have varied, yet an absolute reliance on the powerful interplay between visual image and literary work has remained a constant, defining his creative intellect as an artist-writer.

Notes

1. Research for this article was facilitated by a research fellowship granted by the Charles Phelps Taft Research Center, University of Cincinnati.
2. Günter Grass, *Peeling the Onion*, trans. by Michael H. Heim (New York: Harcourt, 2007), p. 20. Subsequent references appear in the text as O with the page number in brackets.
3. See Grass, 'Otto Pankok', Günter Grass, *Werkausgabe in zehn Bänden*, vol. IX (Darmstadt: Luchterhand, 1987), pp. 797–8.
4. Günter Grass, *The Tin Drum*, trans. by Ralph Manheim (New York: Pantheon Books, 1962), pp. 462–3.
5. See Grass, 'Genau hingucken. Zum Tod des Bildhauers Karl Hartung', Grass, *Werkausgabe*, vol. IX, pp. 256–8.
6. See Günter Grass, *Gebrannte Erde* (Göttingen: Steidl, 2002), pp. 9–12, 16–19, 22–3.
7. Günter Grass, 'Bin ich nun Schreiber oder Zeichner?', Grass, *Werkausgabe*, vol. IX, pp. 789–91, at p. 789. Subsequent references appear in the text as Z with the page number in brackets.
8. Günter Grass, *Fünf Jahrzehnte. Ein Werkstattbericht* (Göttingen: Steidl, 2004). Subsequent references appear in the text as W with the page number in brackets.
9. Günter Grass, *From the Diary of a Snail*, trans. by Ralph Manheim (New York: Harcourt, 1973), p. 299. Subsequent references appear in the text as S with the page number in brackets.

10. Interview in the magazine *Focus*, cited in Richard E. Schade, 'Günter Grass's *Mein Jahrhundert*: Histories, Paintings, and Performances', *Monatshefte* 96 (2004), 409–21, at p. 409.

11. Günter Grass, *My Century*, trans. by Michael Henry Heim (New York: Harcourt, 1999). Since this translation does not incorporate Grass's watercolour illustrations, page references here are to Günter Grass, *Mein Jahrhundert* (Göttingen: Steidl, 1999). References appear in the text as *MC* with the page number in brackets.

12. Günter Grass, *Crabwalk*, trans. by Krishna Winston (New York: Harcourt, 2003), p. 3. Subsequent references appear in the text as *CW* with the page number in brackets.

13. Günter Grass, *Dummer August* (Göttingen: Steidl, 2007), p. 13. The translation of the poem is mine.

13

DAVID BARNETT

Günter Grass as dramatist

When Günter Grass was awarded the prestigious Büchner prize in 1965 it was for both his prose and his poetry. He had written five of his seven full-length plays by then, and all four of his one-acters, yet they were not recognised by the awards committee. The plays have not proved especially popular in theatres; however, they may have become more stageable in the light of contemporary directing practices. This chapter will consider the problems Grass sets the theatre in his dramatic work by identifying recurring patterns in the form of the plays. I shall examine selected texts in order to suggest new readings that challenge a more conventional pigeon-holing of Grass's drama and assess Grass's stature as a playwright.

It is fair to say that Grass wrote his plays in two phases, the first from 1954 to 1958; and the second from 1963 to 1968. The first has generally been termed 'absurd' or 'poetic'; the second 'political'. The watershed between the two was the writing of *The Tin Drum* (1959). However, as with so many borders nowadays, breaches may be detected: there is a surprising constancy in certain of Grass's dramaturgical practices which defy the easy model of two phases, and these can be identified in the playwright's first foray into the dramatic genre, the short sketch *Rocking Back and Forth* (1954).

While Grass has never discussed the aesthetics of his plays in any great depth, he does present a series of dramaturgical features that was to inform the rest of the work, however unconsciously, in the form of this short play. *Rocking* is subtitled 'A Prologue in the Theatre', the same term Goethe uses for metatheatrical reflection at the beginning of his *Faust I*, yet in Grass's case, the prologue actually covers almost all his dramatic output. The playlet is set in a theatre on a bare stage. At its centre is Conelli, a clown who is seated on a rocking horse which he will never dismount. Conelli's days at the circus are numbered because the owners no longer consider him funny. Enter a dramaturge, an actor and a playwright, who seek to unlock Conelli's potential for the theatre before the people from the cinema and television get their hands on him. They try to impose a tragic role on the clown and contemplate his comic possibilities; they see him as a potential Everyman and as Everyman's mortal enemy, Death. At each turn, Conelli defies their ruses and proves himself immalleable. The theatre-makers try to introduce conflict in various forms: the actor attempts an improvisation with Conelli but the clown refuses to be drawn. The others bring on his daughter and her boyfriend, whom Conelli despises, but they fail to induce the tension they seek. By the end of the short play, Conelli agrees to his own death but fears he will be too late for his own funeral, given that he is still riding his rocking horse.

One may extrapolate several features of Grass's theatre from *Rocking*. Perhaps the most important is that the stage no longer has to offer material that is inherently 'dramatic'. Conelli, the subject matter for the theatre-makers, actively resists any attempt to corral him into the conflicts and tensions that are the staples of a dramatic plot. He tells no story and initiates no action, if we understand action in the theatre as something that brings about a change of state. In part, this position has a certain ancestry in modern drama. Very little happens, for example, in Chekhov's plays, yet it is the depth of the characters' emotional worlds that provide the focus of interest. In playwright Samuel Beckett's work, who is mentioned by name in *Rocking*, language, a cocktail of humour and despair, and the contemplation of an empty universe serve as surrogates for the missing action. Grass seems to be approaching a far more radical position, however, in that he asks what happens when something that actively eschews conventional dramatic categories is put on stage.

Another notable feature in *Rocking* is the absence of character psychology. There is no indication as to why the theatre-makers want the eminently undramatic Conelli for the theatre nor why he refuses to engage with them. The appearance of the daughter and her boyfriend, magically summoned by the theatre-makers, is similarly unexplained. In addition, Grass's treatment of time runs counter to its more conventional function in drama. Time is always in short supply in drama because without its constraints there would be no conflict and no tension. A less ordered and non-linear model of time is to be found in the structures of a dream. Dreams also contain a variety of contradictions which happily coexist with each other because the contradictory elements are not bound together under the pressure of time. The same is true in *Rocking*: while time is indubitably passing, it does not have the same effect as in other dramas. What the spectator experiences is a condition, which is re-rehearsed in differing permutations; there is nothing that drives the play through time. The single conflict that does arise takes place on a meta-level, between the play and the audience, debating whether this is a drama at all. There is also a suspicion of language that runs through the play, focused on Conelli's repeated overuse of the word 'pleasant'. It is never quite certain what he means by the word, whether he is being facetious, ironic or sincere. The slipperiness of language figures early in Grass's dramatic work and recurs regularly thereafter.

On a more material note, *Rocking* treats the theatre itself as a cornucopia. While the theatre-makers can spirit Conelli's daughter and her boyfriend onto the stage, they can also demand large props, which appear at will. When the actor attempts the failed improvisation with Conelli, he calls for both a double-bed to be brought on and, more extravagantly, for a grand piano to be lowered from the flies. This part of Grass's writing locates him within the institution of the West German theatre, where funding, effectively up until the fall of the Berlin Wall in 1989, was generous and plentiful. One finds a series of elaborate sets and complex effects in most of Grass's early plays, which are clearly written to be staged within a well-funded theatre system.

Interestingly, Grass chose to omit *Rocking* from his collection of work for the stage, *Theaterspiele (Plays for the Stage)*, in 1970. One can only speculate on the reasons for the decision, but one possibility is that the piece exposes a problem that will run through Grass's theatrical work as a whole: the disjunction between a play's intellectual aims and its dramatic execution. That is, the work may interest us as readers but not necessarily as spectators. *Rocking* is nonetheless a useful lens through which to view the rest of the plays; it sets out much of what is to be found in both the 'absurd' and the 'political' phases of Grass's work as a playwright, yet, as one would expect, the dramas are not formulaic and, naturally, do not incorporate *Rocking*'s ideas all the time, as will become clear in the following analyses.

Grass's first full-length play, *Hochwasser* (1955) is usually translated as *Flood*, although a more useful rendition would be *High Tide*, as the catastrophic waters that threaten to overwhelm the characters' house recede in the second of the two acts. While one of the central characters is indeed called Noah, the German for the biblical flood is 'Sintflut', a word Grass consciously rejects. This titular starting point already engages the reader with issues of the absurd. The move from divine intervention to the rhythms of nature would suggest that Grass is seeking to present the moral vacuum of a godless world, yet a closer examination reveals something more social and historical.

The play is set in a house which we view in section: there are steps down to a cellar, a small room and a flat roof. The house is inhabited by both a human family and two rats, the latter a motif that will recur later in Grass's fiction. The family struggles to deal with the watery catastrophe while the rats add a commentary of sorts on the scenes from their vantage point on the roof. There are certainly absurd features to the play: Noah is, for no given reason, a collector of inkwells and candelabras, and his daughter Jutta seems to be a classically existentialist character in that she thirsts for sensation away from conventional morality. She is party to the forceful expulsion of her fiancé Henn by her brother's friend Kongo who then sleeps with her, although she treats the affair with indifference. She is also given the play's curtain line when she declares that she wishes that the rains would return, presumably for the excitement and danger they bring. There are also 'absurd' stage directions: Jutta's brother, Leo, and Kongo arrive not through a door but are discovered in a crate Noah believed had housed his possessions. An 'investigator', who appears towards the end of the play and who is charged with cataloguing the damage done by the water, climbs out of a broken grandfather clock as if he had been there all the time.

On the other hand, however, Noah's sister-in-law offsets the inkwells with her collection of photo albums, suggesting a meaningful link with the past. There are also contemporary connections with history: Leo and Kongo enter in uniform-like clothing and we learn that Kongo had taken Leo off to the Rhineland, the area of Germany that Hitler re-militarised in 1936 in direct contravention of the Treaty of Versailles. One of the rats also tells of how its family was murdered by a doctor in medical experiments, a resonant allusion to the atrocities of Dr Mengele. With these details from the recent German past in mind, the flood waters become more allegorical, and begin to stand for the catastrophe of history itself. Such a reading is augmented by the rats' commentary on learning that the waters are receding: they speculate that their human neighbours will carry on as if nothing had happened.

The play is thus a curious mixture of absurd and historical elements. The presence of history, however, calls the absurd into question and opens up a dialogue between a violent past and an indifferent present. The plight of the blind humans is symbolically suggested by one of the final stage directions: Leo and Kongo depart with the broken grandfather clock en route to the North Pole. The clock is of no use, it can no longer measure time, and the two young men depart and take it to a barren place without seasons. Thus, while the characters present the veneer of an action, they also relativise its value.

The Wicked Cooks (1956/7) is a five-act play that revolves around the eponymous cooks and their attempts to convince a character known to them as 'the Count' to divulge his recipe for a soup. The soup, it seems, was produced by the Count on a whim when he was invited to cook it by the restaurant's owner. As with *Flood*, the play has its fair share of absurd motifs. In the first act, the cooks are summoned by the head chef, Petri, who blasts out tones through an overlarge trumpet. No explanation is given for the procedure. The cooks appear one by one and make entrances that are perhaps even more unexpected than those in *Flood*: Grün arrives in a giant egg and Vasco is dug out of a man-size pile of salt which arises from the stage floor at the trumpet's behest. Each act features a different attempt to gain the recipe involving cajoling, the threat of violence and even the procuring of a lover for the Count. By the final act, the Count reveals that there never was a recipe, it was more a matter of instinct and experience. The plot, then, seems to have been a quest for something that never arrives, a variation of Beckett's *Waiting for Godot* (1952). By the conclusion of the play no one is any wiser and all efforts made have been in vain. The absence of absolute values is reinforced by the second and third acts in which Vasco's aunt, Therese, is on her deathbed and is then reported by her nurse, Martha, to have died (an announcement which elicits laughter from the rest of the cooks). Therese is a devout Catholic and her death serves to represent the death of a theological truth.

There are, however, several facets of the play that resist a simple absurdist understanding of its form and content. *The Wicked Cooks* is a dense symbolic matrix that is continually alluding to other ideas in the manner of an allegory. The repeated references to cooks, soups, spoons, whiteness (of the cook's aprons and hats mainly), and the act of stirring suggest that these culinary terms, not to mention the recipe itself, have a significance beyond their literal meaning. Clearly if this is the case, the absurd world is redeemed because absurdity is merely a surface manifestation of a deeper logic. There are additional features of the play that support this view. Language, rather than presenting itself as a meaningless shell that reflects the insignificance of existence, is, at certain points, actually powerful and dynamic.

The text draws attention to the act of nomination at several junctures. The *dramatis personae* signals this from the outset in that Herbert Schymanski is 'known as' the Count, that is, his prestige is the product of those who are naming him. Later, in act one, Martha, Therese's nurse, enters '*in the uniform of a nurse*'; it is a costume and does not necessarily denote her profession. In the fifth act, when the Count/Schymanski takes Martha as a lover, she is changed and is no longer a nurse. Vasco is amazed at the transformation, and Schymanski calls her Ruth rather than Martha. Vasco, too, is a nickname, which locates the cook as a discoverer of distant spices; Martha prefers to call him Stephan when they are alone. The soup itself has no name and is referred to as the November Soup, the Soup of the Phoenix and the Grey Eminence. What this set of examples shows is that language is not reliable, as alternative terms can refer to the same object and change it, and that there can be multiple connotations within one term. 'November soup', for example, refers in German to a thick, foggy day but might also, in the play more broadly, allude to the Russian revolution of 1917 (which took place in November according to the Gregorian calendar), or to the odd regularity with which key events in German history seem to occur in November, and particularly on the 9 November (e.g. the Proclamation of the Weimar Republic on 9 November 1918; Hitler's failed attempt to take over the government on 9 November 1923; the pogrom against the Jews across Germany on 9 November 1938; the opening of the Berlin Wall on 9 November 1989) – Grass would later return again to the bizarre centrality of this month in German history in his collection of poems *Novemberland* (2001). The world of *The Wicked Cooks*, then, is one of flux, not an absurd stability in which nothing can be said to change. The targeted use of language engenders changes of state and this is highlighted in several passages involving Vasco. For example, on hearing that his aunt Therese is dying at the end of the first act, he wonders whether he should suspend his 'cook' status by taking off his hat for five minutes. Once he has removed his headgear, he meditates on what the word 'wicked' might mean and whether he stops being wicked once the hat is off. The interaction between language and its object is rendered problematic in this play. While French playwright Eugène Ionesco is happy to reduce all language to meaninglessness in *The Bald Soprano* (1950), Grass is exploring the possibilities of nomination and the effects it can have on the characters and their relationships.

When examining two of Grass's apparently 'absurdist' plays, one finds a more uncomfortable dialogue with the term. While the plays feature absurd motifs and ideas, they are always offset by questions of history and significance. Indeed political questions are raised about how humans interact with disaster and how language is used, who sanctions its usage, and how it affects the social order. However, when one turns to the post-*Tin Drum* plays, in which politics is apparently the focus, the very notion of 'the political' invites further consideration.

Grass's first play of the second phase, *Goldie Mouth* (1963), is a reworked version of the playlet found in the 'Hundredth Publicly Discussed Materniad' in the novel *Dog Years* (1963). The dramatic episode features the anti-hero of the novel, Walter Matern, in a talkshow answering questions about his past (and is presented in dramatic form in the novel itself). The host and members of the audience interrogate their unwilling guest about his past, especially on what he did or did not do during the Third Reich. To assist them, the host's sidekick, Walli S., who is also Matern's niece, wears a pair of 'miracle glasses', which allow her magically to see Matern's past when the questioners believe Matern to be lying.

This fantastical device is part of an unreal atmosphere in which Matern is the apparent victim of a group of people who already know his biography and who use the public forum as a way of humiliating him.

The form of the talkshow allows for an almost classical confrontation between the protagonist, the chorus and the chorus leader. Certain sections are written in rhymed verse and delivered by more than one speaker, and have the effect of heightening the group dynamics that continually buffet Matern. The agonistic appearance, however, belies the lack of conflict that is actually being played out: Matern's attempts at creating contradiction lead nowhere, as he is always compelled to serve up the truth by a knowing audience. On the face of it, this is a stimulating political form: the short play is divided into twenty-two scenes that stop the flow of what could be considered a single act. Such interruptions create thinking space for an audience to process what has gone before. While the opening scenes provide novel action, this starts to repeat itself as the play proceeds, allowing spectators to process the ever-recurring pattern of accusatory question, denial and admission. The audience is thus being asked to question the value of such a show and the aims of Matern's interrogators. The group's dynamics are of interest, as is the notion of a surveillance society in which information is deliberately stored for use at politically tactical junctures. The audience, in other words, is being asked to fill in gaps that are not provided on stage, turning the spectators into a curious and activated part of the theatrical event. One of the gaps that they are not, however, able to fill is the status of Matern.

Matern is something of a question mark, and while one may speculate about the social context of such ritual humiliation, his lack of context generates an ambiguity that undermines the fabric of the piece. Is he a critique of a German failure to come to terms with the past, or is he a put-upon innocent caught up in events beyond his control? The lack of evident answers undermines the political frame of the sinister talkshow. Matern's responses are never linked to a political context and he appears to be a sovereign individual, defending his semblance of individuality in vain against a rapacious communal grilling: the scene resembles a Stalinist show trial. As a result, the play echoes the theme of the struggling individual against a vindictive collective, the basis for much apolitical theatre which insists on the ability of the individual to follow his or her 'nature', a category that resists the social.

Grass's only major national and international hit was his *The Plebeians Rehearse the Uprising* (1965/6). The play was always going to be controversial in that it featured modern German theatre's most important figure, Bertolt Brecht, characterised as 'the Boss'. The play is set in a theatre in the

German Democratic Republic (GDR) on 17 June 1953, the day on which workers downed tools and protested against their working conditions. Over four acts we observe the attempts of a group of stonemasons to persuade the Boss to endorse their action and thus flex his symbolic power as a politically engaged artist. The Boss equivocates for the most part of three acts before he is persuaded to act by a hairdresser. However, no sooner has he decided to follow the hairdresser to the radio station than the tanks roll through the streets and he returns to his theatre. So, once again, there is a lack of action, subject matter that resists the mechanisms of dramatic tension, and a series of potential points of conflict which are continually neutralised by the central character.

There is little doubt that the Boss is based on Brecht. He is rehearsing his unfinished adaptation of *Coriolanus* when the stonemasons enter and he is given Brecht's biographical data and quotations from Brecht's poems. The uprising, too, has authentic details and there are figures in the play, such as Volumnia and Kosanke, who represent Brecht's wife Helene Weigel and the regime's official poet Kurt Bartel (aka Kuba) respectively, and they are easy to identify. Grass has contended that the allegorical nature of the play shifts the focus away from a personal attack on Brecht to the wider issues of the artist's role in society and history, that the play is a model rather than an accurate depiction of the GDR. In addition, Grass uses the device of the play-within-a-play as a way of asking the audience to consider layers of theatricality: are, for instance, the primary characters (as opposed to the secondary ones in *Coriolanus*) following scripts like their embedded counterparts? If so, who is providing the text and to what ends? Grass also maintains that he is interested in the characters' contradictions, much in the way the real Brecht was, which makes the characters models of behaviours rather than realistic representations. Grass also subtitles the play 'ein deutsches Trauerspiel' (a German tragedy). A 'Trauerspiel' is literally a 'mourning play' and thus casts its net wider than the more individualised 'Tragödie' (tragedy). Grass is seeking to inculcate all the characters in a specifically German problem and again the desire to move beyond the specific into the general is evident.

In many ways, the play is interesting as a model. One observes the various attitudes the characters adopt towards the masons' various gambits, and this is a position well rooted in Brechtian dramaturgy. Yet a closer investigation reveals that notions of an essential self obscure those of Brecht's ever-changing, unfixed notion of the self in constant dialogue with its social contexts. The character of Volumnia, for example, encourages the masons and names their action a 'people's uprising', yet once the tanks arrive she fears for the revolving stage the company has been promised. She is criticised by the Boss for being a chameleon, that is, she changes her views to match her circumstances; she does not change herself as in Brecht's theatre. Grass's understanding of a character's contradictions is not as radical as Brecht's, and this can be seen more importantly in the figure of the Boss himself.

For the most part, the Boss is a fairly satirical representation. His views on theatre are parodied and he is revealed as a hypocrite when he ridicules a conservative speech justifying the existing social order in *Coriolanus* before prompting his dramaturge to deliver the selfsame text to defend them both from a lynch mob of proletarians. Even his good advice to the masons in the first act about the tasks they must complete in order to organise a successful uprising misrecognises the workers' grievances. So, we might wish to view the Boss from the outside as a model of incorrect behaviour, Brecht's 'negative example'. However, the Boss's character tends to follow Aristotle's definition of the tragic hero in his *Poetics*: the hero makes a mistake (*harmatia*) which comes to light when a reversal of fortune occurs (*peripeteia*) which induces a recognition of the error (*anagnorisis*) and this is often followed by suffering (*pathos*). The Boss goes through all these stages. His mistake is that he fails to side with the workers and entertains alternative ideas instead. Once the tanks come, he recognises that he was wrong: in a speech in the final act he acknowledges that he was laughing at the workers when he should have been supporting them. The Boss's final speech, itself a quotation from one of Brecht's own *Buckow Elegies* – the set of poems Brecht composed during the year of the uprising – is laden with guilt and misery. The one divergence here is that Aristotle maintains that we identify with the tragic hero throughout the play in order to see ourselves in him or her and be purged of the passions that brought about the *harmatia*. The Boss, as discussed above, is usually at some distance from the spectator since he is presented satirically. However, there are several examples from post-Athenian tragedy (Marlowe's *Edward II* and Shakespeare's *Richard III*, or even Arthur Miller's *Death of a Salesman*, for example) in which sympathy and later empathy develop over time, and it would seem that the Boss's short-lived commitment to the uprising, not to mention his unjust treatment at the hands of the lynch mob, serve as points of contact between the protagonist and the audience.

Thus, Grass's 'political' play is in fact rather more conservative than it appears. The changeable individual of Brechtian theatre, in constant dialogue with society, is replaced by Grass's Aristotelian model of the inevitably doomed tragic hero. In this light, one might cast doubt on Grass's 'Trauerspiel' and consider it a 'Tragödie'. This would be in keeping with Grass's views of the character of Coriolanus (who is often associated with the Boss in the play) in a speech given in 1964. Here, Grass reproaches Brecht for turning Coriolanus away from 'his own passion'[1] and locating his *harmatia* in an inability to understand history and society.

There is a similarly unpoliticised 'human' take on contemporary politics in Grass's final play both of his 'political' phase and as a dramatist altogether. *Max: A Play* (the translation of the German original *Davor* – '*Before*' – from 1968) uses student protests against the Vietnam War as its central subject matter and features two teachers, Starusch and Seiffert, two seventeen-year-old pupils, Scherbaum and Lewald, a Dentist, and Scherbaum's never-seen dog, Max. The play is a dramatisation of the second part of Grass's novel *Local Anaesthetic* (1969), in which Scherbaum announces to Starusch that he plans to burn his dog in public protest before the bourgeois ladies who eat cakes on the terrace of the Kempinski hotel in what was then West Berlin.

Grass insists on the artificiality of his stage in this play: there is an open space in which all the action takes place. The venues of the play – the dentist's consulting room, Starusch's abode, the school, etc. – melt into each other and there is also a fluidity of time. Characters move from one place to the other without realistic justification, and characters comment on scenes in the play's past that are simultaneously taking place in the performed present. Grass also expressly forbids additional material, such as film projections, cabaret sketches or crowd scenes, and I shall return to this direction below.

Max is a play of ideas. As in *The Plebeians* there is the possibility of action but by the final scene Scherbaum relents, spares his dog, and becomes the editor of the school newspaper, as Starusch had counselled from the beginning. Again, the object of the drama resists the dramatic process, and thus the audience is presented with thirteen scenes, all of which contain sub-scenes, focused on the issue of Scherbaum's threatened act of outrage. The different characters represent a range of political perspectives: Starusch is a liberal reformer, the Dentist is a dialectician, and Lewald is a left-wing radical. The play is something of a talk shop, not unlike the plays I have already discussed. The liberal agenda wins the day and so the play is more a set of permutations: ideas are set beside each other and tweaked over the course of the performance. The mélange of thoughts and the fluidity of time and space implicit to *Max*'s dramaturgy echo one of the Dentist's lines: 'Already in the Before begins the After'[2] (from which the German title of the play is taken). The line should be read in conjunction with one of Starusch's speeches given a page or so earlier: 'Foretaste overlaps with aftertaste. You taste it all at the same time and it contradicts itself'.[3] This is Grass's understanding of dialectics in the play: that reality is contradictory, something reflected in the play's treatment of time and space on a bare stage. Yet these dialectics are politically meaningless without a sense of historical context. If one understands political theatre in Brecht's sense, dialectics is a dynamic process that brings about change, but this is missing in *Max*. Grass actively prevents the addition of social context, as outlined in the stage directions mentioned above, in order to isolate the characters and to give them autonomy. The lack of mutability is stressed throughout when Starusch the teacher compares himself with Scherbaum the pupil and reflects on how similar they were at seventeen, and his female counterpart Seiffert does the same when considering Lewald. Radicalism is a 'natural' phase, not a political position. The blurring of time and space merely underlines this view: scenes and possible actions emerge and retreat, and this is all a part of the chaotic and contradictory nature of reality, but by the end of the play very little has changed in the 'natural' order of things.

The political in Grass's 'political' phase is thus as problematic as the absurd is in his 'absurd' phase. Both simple attributions hide more complex mechanisms and, as we have seen, even the phase model may be unpicked by the common dramaturgical features spanning both phases and first located in the early playlet *Rocking Back and Forth*. But what is to be said of Grass's dramatic *oeuvre* as a whole? It has certainly been unpopular with critics and audiences alike, and even the explosive material of *The Plebeians* has hardly made the play a staple of the international stage. The problem with *Rocking* returns to haunt almost all the rest of Grass's dramatic output: when summarised the plays can appear interesting but onstage they are leaden, opaque and overly repetitive. The lack of action, the obscurity of the metaphors (especially in the earlier plays – consider the intricate complex of cookery-related terms in *The Wicked Cooks*) and the sheer length of the dramas (which could easily be cut) have frustrated theatre-goers from the first full-length production onward. Grass has moved from one phase to the other, yet his dramaturgy has not been modified to suit a different subject matter. Perhaps his desire to become a political commentator in the theatre stems from the success of the Danzig Trilogy, yet he was unable to transform the politics of a novelistic form into a theatrical one. We may have to concede that while Grass achieved great things in his prose, he was unable to translate his ideas onto the stage. In this respect, he finds himself in good company, alongside James Joyce, Graham Greene and Muriel Spark, to name but three. Grass himself turned his back on the theatre after *Max*, announcing in 1979 that he was unhappy with recent developments in German theatre. He criticised the West German phenomenon of 'Regietheater' (literally 'a theatre of direction', as opposed to one of writing) in which the director of a play was free to do what he or she wanted with a text, relegating the playwright to little more than a scrivener in Grass's opinion.

Yet it is perhaps this very type of theatre, little known in the English-speaking world, that offers hope for the disgruntled writer. For the most part, the plays are unperformable as they stand. They are weighty, they are lengthy, and they tend to exclude an active engagement from the audience due to their density and/or their repetitive structures. However, they approach what has been called a postdramatic theatre by Hans-Thies Lehmann.[4] The postdramatic is concerned with neither action nor character; on the contrary it is fascinated by conditions, by states, by language. 'Text bearers' deliver rather than represent text, and the audience is invited to enter a different kind of theatre in which experience of uninflected text holds in check more conventional processes that articulate a dramatic interpretation. A more stylised staging is also possible: while the German première of *The Plebeians* tried to recreate Brecht's Berliner Ensemble, the first production in the US showed no interest in the Boss as Brecht and instead followed Grass's hope that the Boss would stand in for a model of the politically engaged artist. Staged in the style of the Chinese Opera, the production focused on the play's themes rather than its characters and offered a refreshing view of the text away from the tendentious treatment of its central character. Alternatively, Brecht's stagecraft itself could prove useful for a play like *The Wicked Cooks* (and indeed the plays of the 'political' phase). Brecht believed in locating character in its own social contexts and in showing these contexts through the actor's body in what he termed *Gestus*. Psychology defers to society in that characters do not exist as sovereign individuals but as subjects defined by their relationships to other characters and to other contexts. Thus Martha, for example, could be shown as different people when she is first a nurse and later the Count's lover. Starusch could expose his liberal views as a product of his biography – they emerge in reaction to his youth spent in the Third Reich. Such strategies run counter to Grass's own instructions, and yet it might well be that it is the theatre's means, and not those of the playwright, that could offer the plays a second chance on the contemporary stage.

Notes

1. Günter Grass, 'Prehistory and Post-History of *Coriolanus* from Livy and Plutarch via Shakespeare to Brecht and Myself', in Günter Grass, *The Plebeians Rehearse The Uprising. A German Tragedy*', trans. by Ralph Manheim (London: Penguin, 1972), pp. 7–35, at p. 15.

2. The line is curiously missing in the English version and the translation is thus mine. It appears in German in Günter Grass, *Davor*, in Günter Grass, *Theaterspiele*, *Werkausgabe*, vol. 2, edited by Dieter Stolz (Göttingen: Steidl, 1997), pp. 425–94, at p. 489.

3. This line does appear in the translation. See Günter Grass, *Max: A Play*, trans. by A. Leslie Willson and Ralph Manheim (New York: Harvest, 1972). However, I have chosen a more literal rendering: 'contradicts itself' over the published 'cancels itself out' (p. 114).

4. See Hans-Thies Lehmann, *Postdramatic Theatre*, trans. by Karen Jürs-Munby (London: Routledge, 2006).

14

ROGER HILLMAN

Film adaptations of Günter Grass's prose work

Grass's output documents not just a history of the German language, its restitution and reinvigoration in *The Tin Drum* (1959) after its corruption by National Socialism, but also a history of film. Though recent scholarship has partially salvaged the 1950s as a decade not limited to escapist *Heimat* films, that is, films playing in 'innocent' country settings and characterised by their sentimental tone and simplistic morality, the Nazi years created a major hiatus between the glories of Weimar cinema and the beginnings of the New German Cinema around the mid-1960s. The 1970s then saw a number of film adaptations of literary texts, the two most famous being Rainer Werner Fassbinder's film version of nineteenth-century novelist Theodor Fontane's *Effi Briest* and Volker Schlöndorff's *The Tin Drum*. The issue is still more complex today, when leading figures in German literature and film (Emine Sevgi Özdamar and Fatih Akin, respectively) come from ethnically mixed Turkish-German backgrounds. This chapter cannot do justice to the broader issue of film adaptations of literature, which in Germany have long been caught up in debates surrounding 'high' and 'low' art. But the case of Grass is very different to that of another frequently filmed author, Thomas Mann. The challenge posed to film by Mann's works resides in their verbal irony, particularly in the abstract nouns and Classical allusions. By contrast, Grass's larger works sprawl across linguistic canvases that are equally intricate, but which also combine levels of reality and time (for example, the context of magical realism, as discussed elsewhere in this volume) that stretch concrete images in realistic film traditions.

In this chapter, I briefly analyse adaptations of Grass's *Cat and Mouse*, *The Rat* and *The Call of the Toad*, before offering a detailed exploration of perhaps the most successful, and certainly the best known, film version of Grass's literary works, that is, Schlöndorff's adaptation of *The Tin Drum*.

Cat and Mouse

When this novella appeared in 1961, it was part of an evolving Danzig Trilogy, and ultimately of a still more panoramic Danzig Quintet (see Katharina Hall's chapter in this book). Its economical concentration of material facilitated the first film version of a Grass prosework, Hans-Jürgen Pohland's of 1967. Pohland had been one of the signatories of the Oberhausen Manifesto of 1962, which generated momentum for the New German Cinema, and his film does address some of the challenges posed by narrative perspectives in Grass's work. These arose primarily from the iridescent play with memory, and its repression, as the reluctant narrator Pilenz evoked and was engulfed by childhood events recalled from an adult vantage point. His confessional mode, not just as stylistic 'voice' but with full religious overtones, progressively pursued him right through to the final sentence of the novella: 'But you didn't show up. You didn't surface' ('Aber Du wolltest nicht auftauchen'). The enigmatic object of his peers' adulation, Mahlke is the figure most demanding reappraisal in the light of Grass's 2006 autobiographical revelations concerning his service in the Waffen SS. In this ending, Mahlke's non-resurrection is still attributed to his willpower. And Grass characteristically reinvests an everyday verb with its original meaning, prepared for by the imagery permeating the work.

Pohland's film starts with the school assembly scene of the novella's final page, and then reconstructs events leading to it, so that the effect of the concluding sentence, almost a theological sentence imposed on the narrator, is lost. The extended flashback is initially backed by jazzy music accompanying a passionless voice-over, whose content we shall return to. Twenty years after the Second World War, the narrator returns to Gdańsk. But Pohland adopts a kind of chronological split-screen approach, with Pilenz ever the adult, even when seen in group tableaux with his teenage peers. This is a visually arresting combination of the two time levels co-present for so much of Grass's narrative, with all their transpositions, superimpositions, and haunting quality. In a medium as concrete as film it may have been the better choice than continuous flashbacks within a core narrative. But the alienation effect of an interactive peer group with one member significantly older is potentially disorienting, rather than enriching, and the time levels clash rather than fuse. The sense is that just as Mahlke could not grow old, however desperately Pilenz hopes otherwise, Pilenz cannot (could never?) be young. A potentially interesting slant thus points well beyond the novella.

This holds especially for the central episode with which the novella had begun, the cat's attack on the defenceless Mahlke. This is repeated with variations in regard to who was guilty of exposing Mahlke's Adam's apple to the cat's claws. In the film, the perpetrator is always Pilenz, and always a Pilenz who is adult in appearance. The interaction progresses, with early stages in turn varying the novella's perspective. When Mahlke surfaces with the screwdriver there is commentary from a number of the boys, shot individually and as a group, and then a cut to Pilenz (ever the adult), watching from a distance at the end of the boat. This makes him into a director of his memories rather than one of the boys. Such theatricality is extended in one of the film's more enterprising inventions. To signal flash-backs rather than re-enactments of events on the wreck, figures which look like props appear. The first time they have human heads but plaster torsos, at other times they are completely doll-like figures. The speech by the second Knights' Cross hero is given to an auditorium inhabited only by a naturalistic Mahlke, and the other boys, who are portrayed as mannequins, a cross between stage props and bandaged corpses.

A still more prominent feature of *The Tin Drum*, Grass's linguistic virtuosity remains tied to a literary text (which does not rule out filmic possibilities, but does constrain them). Two examples among many are the fluctuation between talking about Mahlke and addressing him directly within the one paragraph, and the obsessive catalogues, cumulative lists of details recalled (partially fabricated?) in evoking Mahlke and their days together. A paragraph in chapter eleven of the novella relates to the way they continue to be left in Mahlke's wake during wartime training, part of the story omitted in the film:

> What with the accuracy of the quotation and the awesome secrecy of the place, I might almost have got religion in the course of time. And then this gloomy conscience of mine wouldn't be driving me to do underpaid social work in a settlement house. I wouldn't spend my time trying to discover early Communism in Nazareth or late Christianity in Ukrainian kolkhozes. I should at least be delivered from those all-night discussions with Father Alban, from trying to determine, in the course of endless investigations, to what extent blasphemy can take the place of prayer. I should be able to believe, to believe something, no matter what, perhaps even to believe in the resurrection of the flesh. But one day after I had been chopping kindling in the battalion kitchen, I took out the axe and hacked Mahlke's favourite sequence out of the board and eradicated your name.[1]

The passage is typical in progressing from the evasive subjunctive ('might'; 'wouldn't'; 'should') to the inescapable (by this stage of the story) indicative mood ('I took out the axe'). It also tellingly contextualises helpless attempts to emerge from Mahlke's shadow. In the novella these render more credible Pilenz's foot on the can opener, a key act of betrayal. Fewer such examples in the film make this aspect more puzzling.

On the other hand, the film does excel in places with montage, one of film's strengths as a medium. About a quarter of an hour in, the following sequence convincingly condenses earlier stages of Mahlke's development, while also suggestively evoking (more explicitly than in the novella) the historical macrocosm beyond the boys' schooling: The scene, a beach. Pilenz is obscured by a smiling boy with a triangular hat (Oskar!), whose drum-rolls usher in intertitles: 'the rise of Mahlke' in old German script ('Mahlkes Aufstieg'), as if this were the start of a newsreel. Cut to Mahlke, who belly-flops on the sand (on the soundtrack, 'Oskar' continues to drum); simultan-eously, we see the courtyard drill (and a bigger band sound) of massed standard-bearing youths as well as Mahlke doing awkward chin-ups; we also see a Nazi rally complete with swastikas and a front-on shot (seemingly on the beach) of Mahlke on parallel bars as well as an instructor walking along a pier with a kind of fishing line attached to Mahlke, who swims in a harness (as the martial music continues). This effectively prepares for Mahlke's diving for mementos from the wreck, isolated relics from the immediate past, as the other boys lounge on the deck, in all senses embody-ing stranded youth.

Such promise is unfortunately balanced by the opening 'passionless voice-over', referred to above. For over establishing shots, it imparts this infor-mation to the viewer:

> Twenty years after the War, a German travels to the city of his youth, to Danzig. And he sees this city, now called Gdańsk, as it is today. Wherever he goes, the adult man, Pilenz, is confronted by the memory of his schoolfriend Mahlke, for whose tragic fate he shares the burden of guilt. The present melts into the past. Just as no one recalling their childhood puts on children's clothes, neither does Pilenz stand among his classmates as someone their age, but instead he enters the circle of youths from those days as an adult man. (My translation).

This puts all too little trust in the narrator, and in film as a medium. It does justify the visually challenging constellation of one middle-aged member standing out from the group, but at the cost of making all too explicit the ambiguous guilt haunting Pilenz and the fluctuations between time levels. The 'clothes' metaphor certainly emphasises the performative aspects of memory, rather than establishing a binary 'then-now' spectrum. But some years on from Resnais' *Hiroshima mon amour* (1959) and alongside Alexander Kluge's *Yesterday Girl* (*Abschied von gestern*) (1966), Pohland's lack of faith in the power of images and the discernment of the viewer is disappointing, and a clear indication of the fledgling stage of the New German Cinema.

The Rat

Grass's multi-stranded novel of 1986 thematises film production directly. This yields more insights into the interrelationship between film and novel than does Martin Buchhorn's 1997 adaptation for television of motifs of this novel. The multiple strands in the novel mean that it lacks cohesion. The danger in the film, which substantially reduces the range of thematic threads, is rather a problem of coherence, since so much of the novel's effect builds on the cross-stitching of its threads. The intervening decade had of course qualified the actuality of Grass's allusions to Orwell's *1984*, had defused the acute threat of the Pershing missile issue for its apocalyptic tone, and had perhaps dulled in consciousness and freshness the ecological debate contemporaneous with the novel. The art forger Malskat is absent from the film, as a pendant to the discredited statesmen Adenauer and Ulbricht (the first Chancellor of the Federal Republic and first Prime Minister of the German Democratic Republic, respectively). So too is the novel's elaborate parallel between the world of the Grimm brothers and German fairytales, and current threats to the forest, which in the book appear as an assault on the cultural heart of a (divided) people.

The film's simplification of motifs is further impoverished by the exclusion of the poems interspersed throughout the novel, crucial for its arguments and further expanding its bursting formal boundaries. It also declines the invitation to intertextuality that Grass surely holds out when the threat of the hybrid 'pig-rats' emanates from the harbour of Visby (some versions of Murnau's silent classic *Nosferatu* were set in Wisborg, the fortress in Visby). The reduction of subject matter, technically required for a film of ninety minutes, seems to rely on a millennial thrust intrinsic to its subject matter, and the relatively new toy in German cinema of digital effects. The tin-drummer Oskar, who in the novel *The Rat* has already lost his original anarchic zest, is simply puzzling in the film, and the dialogue between the captain of the ship *Ilsebill* and the flounder shrinks to an arbitrary self-reference.

In the novel, there is an implicit discourse about the narrative possibilities of prose and film at this apocalyptic stage of human history. The return in the novel to the silent era, even to a colour silent film is designed as a protest against technological advance.[2] Silent film captions double as newspaper headlines for a speechless world of survivors (*R*, p. 343). The self-reflexiveness (of the novel, not the film) even extends to mention of the author of a film version of Oskar's exploits, and to a characterisation (*R*, p. 360) that has to be Volker Schlöndorff, the director of the film version of *The Tin Drum* (to be discussed later in this chapter). The layers of reference would probably be beyond any film of ninety minutes; they remain sketchy at best in this one.

The Call of the Toad

Robert Gliński's film premièred in both Poland and Germany in September 2005. The lead roles of art historian Aleksander and conservator Aleksandra are played by Matthias Habich and Krystyna Janda, the former finding a script far more congenial to his talents than *The Rat*. In fact this is an altogether more satisfying film, and an adaptation which finds it easier to render more of the literary text. Its central love story is credible and engaging, without forsaking the social edge of the novel. This is retained in the couple's grapplings with a past once shared by their forebears in Danzig/Gdańsk, and rather less so, in a shared present/future that has been restored in post-Wall Europe. The Lithuanian axis of Aleksandra's child-hood is perhaps too thinly delineated, being less familiar narrative territory than, for instance, the continuity suggested in the film version of *The Rat* between marching Nazi soldiers and the lure of the Pied Piper of Hamelin.

The past figures in a number of flashback sequences or segues. One example of the latter comes when Aleksander looks out of Aleksandra's window, and sees down at street level himself as a boy; this figure then enters the house opposite, sits down at the meal table, and ostentatiously switches on a propaganda broadcast from the radio, which his mother had just silenced. A more daring example is a parodic sketch of German tourists, to a soundtrack of the Scherzo ('joke') movement of Beethoven's Ninth Symphony, succeeded by black and white scenes of the fall of the Berlin Wall, now accompanied by the final choral movement, originally the 'Ode to Joy', for which a famous Leonard Bernstein performance on New Year's Eve 1989 had replaced 'Freude' (joy) with 'Freiheit' (freedom). The latter is witnessed on television by the salt of the earth figure Erna Brakup, and commentated by the Cassandra-like Toad's Call.

The satirical tone (echoed in the soundtrack) is no more than suggestive at a historical level. It is sustained more convincingly when it portrays the parochial mentality of those supposedly enlightened, as in the first burial at the cemetery intended by Alexander and Alexandra to bridge nations and heal historical wounds. As in the novel, the Toad's final Call leads to a fatal car accident as a dramatic resolution of the lovers' insoluble problems, with the extra resonance of their burial outside the 'Mauer' (wall; alluding to the Berlin 'Wall') of an unnamed town. This does accord them a peaceful resting site in European ground that is not part of the German/Polish/Lithuanian triangle. But both the novel's and the film's accents make this seem a sleight of hand rather than an affirmation of possibilities emerging in the new Europe. Positive possibilities have in any case been absent, with the schematic depictions of the couple's uncomprehending and unfeeling children.

The Tin Drum

Schlöndorff's film premièred in 1979; in 1980 it won Germany's first Oscar award in the category of 'best foreign language film' (see Figures 2 and 3). This was undoubtedly also a cumulative acknowledgment of the international resonance of the New German Cinema in the 1970s, though the director's already evident penchant for literary classics as script models had little in common with other prominent directors of the movement (with Fassbinder's *Fontane – Effi Briest* and Herzog's adaptation of Büchner's *Woyzeck* as the exceptions proving the rule). Among films based on novels this is a rare example of a script to which the author of the novel has contributed, in this case some twenty years later. Both novel and film have assumed the status of classics, as in the following example of dual intertextuality. Tykwer's *Run Lola Run* (1998) has a scene in which Lola's scream gathers in intensity as the spin of the croupier's wheel decides her fate. The shattered glass occasioned by her upper registers undoubtedly evokes Schlöndorff's film, as part of Tykwer's panoramic roving across German film history. But it also evokes the novel behind

Figure 2. Oskar drumming in Volker Schlöndorff's adaptation of *The Tin Drum*
© The Kobal Collection.

Figure 3. The rostrum scene in Volker Schlöndorff's adaptation of *The Tin Drum*
© The Kobal Collection.

Schlöndorff's film, *Berlin Alexanderplatz* (1929) by Alfred Döblin, a conjunction with an author acknowledged by Grass to be his mentor. In each of the three sections, Lola bumps into a lady, triggering rapidly edited projections of the latter's future, with extravagantly divergent variations. It is a technique straight out of the arsenal of Döblin, whose narrator is similarly capable of predicting the future of secondary figures, as an emphatic performance of authorial power.

Novel into film issues

For all its linguistic virtuosity, its blend of literary traditions (picaresque novel, novel of education, social novel), and its Rabelaisian plenitude, *The Tin Drum* is frequently filmic. Grass's affinity to British-Indian author Salman Rushdie is further evidenced here. The film's opening chase across Kaschubian fields, with its 'stick-figure' fugitives, has a strong sense of silent film comedy capers.

The final third of the novel is omitted from the film, a move that harnesses its sprawling quality. In forsaking Danzig for the Federal Republic, the novel also leaves behind its greatest strength, though the Onion Cellar scene surely remains the most telling icon of the immediate postwar years, pre-empting the Mitscherlichs' title *The Inability to Mourn: Principles of Collective Behaviour.* The film's process of condensation also affects some of the most distinctive features of the novel. Not only is a wealth of details inevitably omitted, but a sense of themes with variations is forgone, of repetition and the accumulation of catalogues, including contrafactual alternatives, or others in the subjunctive mood. The reverse phenomenon is also in operation, a momentary eliding of key information, as with the long delay in revealing the name 'Danzig'. The novel's verbal accumulation can in turn reflect the plot, as with the tangled family tree of Oskar, or the orgasmic process of cataloguing the effects of sherbet (much sparser in the film) in Oskar's sexual initiation with Marie. When such verbal games are added to further mannerisms of narrating, there is clearly an important core of the novel that defies rendition in film, a virtuosity relating to language that is written or spoken (or sung, the many incantations), rather than visual. If Grass did not invent words like 'zersingen' or 'entglasen' (literally meaning 'to sing to bits' and 'to divest of glass'), he did stake unique claims for the modifying power of German prefixes. Wonderful verbal satires (e.g. the last two sentences of the chapter 'Smash a Little Window-Pane', and the last sentence of 'Rasputin and the Alphabet'), untranslatable into visual equivalents, iridesce throughout the novel. Literary satires ('Just wait, soon you too will be drumming')[3] are not filmable because the context of words is missing.[4] The novel abounds with references to the sense of smell, transcending the domains both of novel and film, and (until Tykwer's 2006 film of Patrick Süskind's 1985 novel *Perfume*) rarely essayed in film beyond isolated sequences. Whereas when Pilenz smears his typewriter with onions in *Cat and Mouse*, it functions as an evocation of what is hidden in the wings of wartime, and as defence against their unspeakable olfactory horrors.

Schlöndorff's film does work with synecdoche, a figure of speech in which an individual case illustrates a much broader phenomenon. The memorable death scene of Sigmund Markus serves as a personalised version of the abstraction 'Crystal Night'. But elsewhere Oskar's perspective dominates as individually surreal, less anchored in geography and history than Grass's narrative. For all Oskar's amorality, a strong sense of European history (for example, witch-hunts, *TD*, p. 165) emerges from the novel, as does a background to Danzig, for instance as a Hanseatic town alongside Lübeck.

This can combine with language mannerisms, as in the overview of Danzig history (*TD*, pp. 363–6) replete with mocking diminutives and puns.[5] Local colour also emerges, with brief views of current affairs, within and beyond the Second World War (e.g. *TD*, p. 271). This contrasts all the more strikingly with the sequence 'Inspection of Concrete, or Barbaric, Mystical, Bored', whose absurdist theatre reflects an absurdist stage of the War (the final, desperate resistance to the turned tide of D-Day). Variation of the novel's prose through dialogue typographically set out like a play signals a shift in register, whereas a film always scripts dialogue in this form, and so the theatrical quality no longer stands out. The poem 'On the Atlantic Wall' is a further shift in genre. Surreal material such as the nuns' ascent to heaven (omitted in the final cut of the film, an edit suggested by Grass) exhibits a general tendency for fantastic events of fiction to be laced with a feeling for the changing tide of warfare; this is Grass's brand of magical realism. Secondary figures proliferate at this stage of the novel, difficult in a film centred on an individual, rather than a collective hero. Elided in the film, almost of necessity, are the *Ostarbeiterinnen*, female slave labourers from occupied Eastern territories, as Slavs deemed to be racially inferior. Their contextualisation within the reality behind the fiction is barbed: as a 'sub-normal' human, Oskar's life (the novel suggests) would indeed have been endangered under the Nazis.

Reversing the anchor point of the novel-film relationship, the following features of the final cut are symptomatic. The mobility of the camera and the potential of camera angles are of course ideal for the picaresque perspective so crucial for this narrative. They reinforce the notion of a child whose years progressively belie the three-year-old stage at which he has arrested his own growth. Scenes such as the cards game, in which Jan's toe explores Anna's welcoming thighs, are lent humour but also a certain credibility by Oskar's perspective, his natural domain being the world beneath the table. The quality of actor David Bennent's voice in the many voice-overs reinforces this, inasmuch as its distinctive timbre remains in its high register, as a vocal instrument that will never break despite Oskar's chronological advance through teenage years. The silent film quality in the opening sequence is perpetuated by the editing. Iris shots, in which the screen frame either contracts to or opens out from a small circle (the iris of the eye), match the elaboration of Oskar's genealogy with an archaic film style. In the opening scenes there is thus a strong sense of equivalences, of a film striving to tell a story in images and sound with an eye to the history of its own medium, rather than slavishly adhering to a written text.

That in turn contributes to a brand of humour that is wisely faithful to the spirit rather than the letter of the novel. When Jan is not called up, the melodramatic reactions of joy are akin to the opening scenes of Verhoeven's *Nasty Girl* (1990), with its similarly off-centre tone. Oskar's grandfather failed to surface after diving off a raft, setting in motion a similar process of myth-making to that surrounding another diver who never surfaced, Mahlke. While omitting to develop some figures altogether (Herbert Truczinski and the 'Niobe' chapter), the film sustains extended sequences such as the eels' scene by the beach through to the death of Agnes, or the 'Polish Post Office'. Beyond their innate dramatic strength, these are crucial to the plot, or rather Oskar's skewed version of the plot. With a mix of amorphous guilt and inflated self-importance he attributes the death of both putative fathers and of his mother to himself, indirectly. But in compressing its materials, the film in places seems episodic, especially towards the end. It also forgoes devices which, in the novel, rein in the storyline strands, namely the framing device of Oskar's institutionalisation, and references to his nurse, Bruno. The lack of this frame undoubtedly affects our perception of David Bennent's performance, and our assessment of key plot elements such as Oskar's claimed complicity in the death of his parents. It does avoid repeated flashbacks, but at the price of one layer of complexity in the character of Oskar and the narrative perspective.

Grass ultimately endorsed Schlöndorff's film, and the director was consistently aware that the final product had to be his film rather than an impossible attempt to document the novel on the screen. But for all its brilliance, the film is vulnerable to the following critique, as summarised in Schlöndorff's account of Grass's reaction at an early stage of its realisation: 'He misses the irrational inroads of time, the linkages where everything clashes and collapses in a blend of tragedy and comedy. On the one hand he demands more gritty realism, on the other, more courage in approaching what's unreal. Fantasy as a part of reality, Oscar's reality.'[6] But that alchemy would challenge any filmmaker, especially perhaps any German filmmaker. Grass seems to envision a Döblin of the screen, perhaps in the direction of Guillermo del Toro's *Pan's Labyrinth* (2006), with its mix of childhood fantasy as self-defence against the encroachment of history's cruelties.

Detailed analysis of the Rostrum scene suggests possibilities for how to approach others in the film. One of the most successful transfers to film, not least because of the latter's acoustic dimension, is the chapter 'The Rostrum'. It is preceded by the circus performance by Bebra and his troupe. The soothing sounds he extracts from rubbing the rims of partly-filled glasses provide the antidote (in sense, and musicality) to Oskar's relationship to glass, as well as to the raucous tones of the succeeding scene. Oskar and Bebra engage in earnest discussion, the scene closing with Bebra's repetition of his earlier injunction: 'They ("the others") are coming.' Within

Schlöndorff's film, the 'others' can be farcical rather than sinister, with the viewer left to draw on a reservoir of knowledge going well beyond the frame of images presented. A degree of absurdity attaches to Matzerath as he smartens up for the rally. When the shot frames his leg, extended for his boot to be strapped, the gesture is like a Nazi salute from the trunk instead of the shoulder. His invitation to Maria and Jan to keep the stew simmering further renders him ridiculous, our last view of them having been at their lovers' tryst.

Immediately ahead of Matzerath's preparations, the duo of Beethoven's image and Hitler's photo atop the piano has been disturbed by the arrival of a radio, the Nazis' most powerful propaganda channel. It in fact supplants Beethoven, not just in screen space, but as cultural heritage. The scene cuts to Matzerath's mild disapproval of Jan's opting for the Poles in his choice of newspaper. But Matzerath is anything but a demagogue, and Jan's patriotism is both low-key, and secondary to his erotic attraction to Agnes. When the Germans, and later the Russians, take Danzig, the same sense prevails of being dwarfed by history, with Jan a passive recruit to the frontline, and Matzerath vainly trying to conceal his compromising traces. The way characters are swept up by events is communicated by the rhythm and choreography of the film, supplemented by its more episodic quality. The characters remain *Mitläufer*, or fellow-travellers, in a politically neutral sense. This distances them from the novel's ground bass of a more specific social and historical anchoring.

Oskar turns on the radio broadcast. A sound bridge takes us from a close-up of the radio to the speaker, the Nazi functionary Löbsack, dominating a sepia image of the rally. His would-be fanatical countenance undercuts his bracing rhetoric, just as the historical patina of the images is clearly contrived. The brief sequence sustains its mock 'documentation', until a general waving of standards is accompanied by an echo chamber effect that distorts the cheers. These are voices without sonic profile; resonating emptily, they bounce back upon themselves within a closed circuit. Further undermined by this sound design, Löbsack's voice continues as the film returns to colour. Oskar makes his way to the rally, accompanied as ever by his drum, and the camera follows his path through the fence and into the arena, further eclipsing any magnificence attaching to Löbsack's impassioned but out-of-frame tones. Instead, we see a snapshot of history from below, both world history in the making (though beyond the ken of this festive crowd, and at this stage probably of the orator), and the most domestic version of history imaginable, as Oskar passes a child squatting on a potty. With Löbsack still present in voice only, a voice evacuated of any substance, the camera tracks from behind the stands, at the level of the assembled crowd's feet.

A cross-hatching of woodwork reinforces the uncertain location of the voice's source. Finally Oskar takes up position directly beneath the rostrum, his position protected against views in, but affording him a view out through a tiny hole in the wood. (He is positioned like a tank driver, about to launch his offensive.)

Oskar's perspective is an inspired marriage of film technique and literary history. He is the picaro incarnate, his view from below about to be matched by the register of the tones his drum emits. He sees through the legs of the assembled crowd; he sees through the real, apolitical desires of the crowd gathered in the open. Matching the novel, the film continually switches from first to third person perspective, that is, from point-of-view shots from Oskar's perspective, to shots depicting Oskar and his immediate environment. When, from Oskar's point of view, we see Löbsack towering above on the platform, everything has already led us to divest the latter of any majesty or power, though that would be the standard sense of such a shot in conventional film language. Oskar's perspective, in all senses, is subversive. And once alien tones emerge from the true seat of power in this scene, sonic mayhem ensues. The strained earnestness of the massed boys yields to puzzlement, but their training ensures that they follow Oskar's lead into anarchic musical territory, the original march yielding to ragtime, riffs, and worse. The cacophony unleashed by Oskar's drum transmits to the march steps of the dignitaries making their way towards Löbsack, through the midst of the supposedly reverential crowd. Already directed by Schlöndorff to be jaunty rather than robot-like, these steps retrace their path briefly in close-up, and their preordained rhythm is routed. The camera in turn cuts loose, and positions itself to the side of the dignitaries and then in an aerial perspective. Similar techniques employed by Hitler's favoured filmmaker Leni Riefenstahl had created a panoramic containment of an immaculately directed piece of theatre; here they signal the event spiralling out of control.

The debunking of Riefenstahl's (in)famous *Triumph of the Will* (1935) is all but complete. The gestures of the 1934 Nazi Party rally in Nuremberg depicted in Riefenstahl's film are present, but gutted; Riefenstahl's aesthetics attach to representations of any such rally, but they too are undermined, above all by the liberated soundtrack. (A very different match between Riefenstahl images and arresting music obtains in the scene of Alex's 'cure' in Stanley Kubrick's 1971 *Clockwork Orange*.) No longer martial, the instruments seemingly follow the lead of the two girls who interlink their hands in a waltz pose and home in on the Blue Danube waltz. This mobilises the crowd in unforeseen directions, creating a unified mass, but not the one intended by the Nazi organisers. For all the lightness of touch, Schlöndorff's late-1970s audience is aware that the march/jazz/waltz sequence frames music deemed decadent by Nazi cultural politics. And while never reducible to a transparent symbol, Oskar's capacity to induce the massed musical forces to follow the beat of a very different drum says much about the bigger power play at this early stage of its formation.

A storm descends, perhaps with overtones of a similar scene towards the end of Heinrich Mann's *Der Untertan* (*Man of Straw*, 1918), and all but Löbsack seek shelter. Oskar prevails, not as some alternative to the rally and all it foreshadows, but simply as its undoing, consistent with his amoral stance throughout both film and novel. Löbsack rotates his hand, frozen in a Nazi salute, for his palm to register the rain, returning his body from the symbolic realm to the human. He then strikes a still more hapless figure as he skates across the mud, throws his arms around in frustration, and remains in the distance or at best mid-frame, a miserable reduction of his original imperious appearance. Order is restored by a recurring device in the film, a tableau of the skyline of Danzig, as the last bars of the merry music fade.

Spilling beyond this scene, the repetition of the Danzig skyline in long or extreme long shot calls for comment. No longer an establishing shot, it operates as a linking device across scenes, an ongoing constant, but an ambiguous one to the audience of Schlöndorff's contemporaries. Within two years of Grass's novel appearing, Cold War boundaries solidified with the Berlin Wall. The last section of the novel, omitted in the film, started exploring the western side (only) of the new European equation, without politicising it, and Grass's stance on the acknowledgment of Germany's de facto postwar boundaries is well known. But even the semantic change from 'Danzig' to 'Gdańsk', mentioned at the start of Pohland's *Cat and Mouse*, goes beyond the last frame of Schlöndorff's film. Danzig then remains the setting of Oskar's unnaturally extended childhood years, lending the film a note of mythology, and of involuntary nostalgia.

Music

From the section above, the importance of the soundtrack should be clear (see E. C. Hamilton's article on this subject, listed in the Guide to further reading at the end of this volume). Novels are confined to words about music, but music is present in films as a channel of information interacting with the images. Where its presence has to be signalled in a novel by naming or description, the effect of music in film (other than in scenes like 'The Rostrum', where its performance takes centre stage) is generally less foregrounded, but all the more powerful for that reason. And percussive music is of course central to this story with its key image, the tin drum. The sound emitted by percussion instruments corresponds to Oskar's own positioning on the fringe of the adult world of society. It is not music in the usual sense of melody or harmony, but as rhythm and pulse, something at once more primitive and more visceral, less aesthetic and less rational. The drum is tailor-made for Oskar's perspective; its potential for military connotations has just been examined. In the film, Oskar's eloquence is conveyed by his eyes; apart from his voice-overs he says little in dialogue. The registers of his expressiveness remain at opposite extremes beyond discourse (and beyond the range of the piano, centrepiece of the bourgeois salon); either the vocal pitch that shatters glass, or the bass pulse of the drum.

That alone profiles the use of music on the soundtrack. It ranges from martial drum rhythms over the opening credits to music box-type music to accompany the innocence, ultimately lost, of Sigismund Markus's toyshop. An elegiac melody in the lower strings recurs (as when Oskar and both his 'fathers' drive away from Agnes's funeral), sometimes (as in the potato fields sequence) overlaid with a jangling, synthesiser-type sound (a Jew's harp). There are also borrowings from the more melodramatic end of the canon. Agnes and Jan give a lusty rendition of a melody from the *Gypsy Baron*, almost swooning at the refrain extolling love. A domestic dispute follows on from her consumption of eels. In what is surely an ironic comment on the 'hunting' scene just witnessed by the shore, she expresses her rage by thumping out the Huntsmen's Chorus from Carl Maria von Weber's Romantic opera *Der Freischütz* (*The Marksman*), accompanying her own hysterical voice at the piano. These examples from opera/operetta combine an intact musical tradition prior to the Nazi takeover of 'the most German art', with an outlet for heightened emotions in a bourgeois parlour. The technique is similar, the tone different, when Neapolitan music overlays Oskar's idyll with Roswitha, and then seems to mock him after her death. World War II actress and singer, heart-throb Zarah Leander, who was also part of Mahlke's record collection in *Cat and Mouse*, croons in the background to his comforting of Lina Greff. And a Chopin-esque mazurka weaves through the 'Polish Post Office' sequence, breaking off on a stark discord, which combines senses of unresolved protest and of a pianist slumped across the keyboard, mirroring the surrendered Poles lined up before the firing squad.

Conclusion

The prose works of Grass crystallise the issues involved in film adaptation. Gaps among the examples above are telling. *Dog Years* offers some of the potential riches of *Tin Drum*, but also its problems, with the elaborate linguistic parody of philosopher Martin Heidegger defying rendition in a medium that operates primarily with concrete images. The as yet unfilmed *Crabwalk* would seem to offer far more fertile material. It also exemplifies the growing interdependence of prose works and films in referring to each other as part of reader/viewer expectations. Grass's novella not only references a 1959 film by the German-American director Frank Wisbar, which treats the sinking of the *Wilhelm Gustloff*; when Aleksandr Marinesko's birthplace is given as Odessa, the natural source of documentation evoked is Sergei Eisenstein's film classic *Battleship Potemkin*. Increasingly, transnational issues in approaching national identity are paralleled by mutual cross-fertilisation among artforms.

Music may be potentially the most fertile base for exploring film adaptations, because it automatically gets beyond the unproductive issue of fidelity or otherwise to a written model. Of the Grass adaptations explored, *The Tin Drum* is the only one widely known, not just in the English-speaking world, and its richness owes much to a soundtrack that evokes both mood and cultural resonances.

Notes

1. Günter Grass, *Cat and Mouse*, transl. by Ralph Manheim (London: Penguin, 1966), pp. 84–5.
2. Günter Grass, *The Rat* (New York: Harcourt, 1987), p. 92. Subsequent references appear in the text as *R* with the page number in brackets.
3. Günter Grass, *The Tin Drum*, transl. by Ralph Manheim (New York: Knopf, 1993), p. 290. Subsequent references appear in the text as *TD* with the page number in brackets.
4. Nor is this easily rendered in translation – the German 'Warte nur, balde trommelst auch du' parodies quintessential lines from the Goethe poem *Über allen Wipfeln ist Ruh*.
5. A single example will indicate their verbal specificity: 'Napoleons General . . . Rapp . . . an den mussten die Danziger . . . 20 Millionen Franken berappen'. The name 'Rapp' reappears in the verb, making his agency even more instrumental: 'Napoleon's general was called Rapp [. . .] the people of Danzig had to rap out twenty million francs to him'. (*TD*, p. 365).
6. Volker Schlöndorff, *Die Blechtrommel: Tagebuch einer Verfilmung* (Darmstadt und Neuwied, Luchterhand, 1979), p. 49. My translation.

15

STUART PARKES

Günter Grass and his contemporaries in East and West

Writing in the German daily newspaper *Süddeutsche Zeitung* in August 2006 at the time of the controversy over Günter Grass's membership of the Waffen SS, the sociologist Heinz Bude launched a hymn of praise to those he called the 'schoolboy soldiers'. By this term he meant the people born between 1926 and 1929, who, like Grass, went more or less straight from school into the final stages of the Second World War. Referring not just to writers and intellectuals but also to the recently elected 'German Pope' Joseph Ratzinger, he maintained that they continue to form 'the foundation of the Republic', as well as providing 'the material for our collective self-concern'. The reason Bude gives for this predominant role is the opportunity offered by their date of birth. Given the social and political changes they have experienced, they have been able to observe 'how patterns of behaviour were exchanged and points of identification shifted', something that has not been possible for subsequent generations (*Süddeutsche Zeitung*, 17 August 2006). Others, too, reflected at the time of the Grass debate on the important role played by people born in the second half of the Weimar Republic. Extending the years in question to include 1930, Eckhard Fuhr, in an article for the daily *Die Welt* (28 August 2006), came up with fifteen influential names, mainly writers and intellectuals, whilst also suggesting that this list is far from complete. He also used, admittedly within quotation marks, the term frequently employed for the people in question: 'the anti-aircraft auxiliary [*Flakhelfer*] generation' (the term refers to the kind of military service into which these seventeen- and eighteen-year olds were first conscripted).

It has in fact become common practice to differentiate German society in terms of generations. The sociologist Helmut Schelsky spoke in the 1950s of the 'sceptical generation', whilst the student movement of the late 1960s led to the coinage '68er', who over the past two decades have been contrasted with the '89er' – a younger generation for which the formative experience was the fall of the Berlin Wall in 1989 – and even the 'Generation Golf', characterised, it is claimed, by a less overriding concern with all things political, and obsessed, instead, with consumerism (hence the name 'Golf' after the Volkswagen Golf car). Despite the popularity of this generation-based view of society, it is still necessary to consider if date of birth remains a more significant factor in the biographies of the people in question than, for example, gender, social class or, given the postwar division of Germany, citizenship of two ideologically opposed states. Fuhr's list contains two names primarily associated with the literature of the GDR (the German Democratic Republic, or former East Germany), Christa Wolf and Heiner Müller, a literature, which, for a time in the 1970s and early 1980s, was frequently seen as distinct from that of the Federal Republic. Some degree of caution is therefore required, even if the significance of generation is not to be denied. As the political scientists Martin and Sylvia Greiffenhagen point out, differences of views between parents and children have often been much more marked in Germany than in other European countries, something that has to be explained by the rapid social changes Bude speaks of in relation to Grass and his contemporaries.[1] In the case of West German writers of this generation, an added factor that arguably bound them together was the literary and political socialisation they experienced in the Group 47, the loose consortium of West German writers which emerged in the immediate postwar period. Although this body only met once or twice a year, it exerted a considerable influence by bringing together physically most of the writers, who made a name for themselves in the 1950s and 1960s and, like Grass, Martin Walser and Hans Magnus Enzensberger (all born between 1927 and 1929), are often still the first names to spring to mind in relation to contemporary German literature and are equally a watchword for writers' involvement in political debate.

Even if one accepts the importance of generation in relation to Grass and his contemporaries, the question of their achievements remains open. Not surprisingly, Grass's confessions in 2006 provoked a number of hostile reactions. Writing in the *Süddeutsche Zeitung*, younger writers Eva Menasse and Michael Kumpfmüller entitled their polemic, in which they spoke of the need for writers and intellectuals to concentrate on contemporary issues such as the Middle East rather than the German past, 'against the intellectual gerontocracy', a choice which, leaving aside any accusation of 'ageism', at least assumes the importance of generations (17 August 2006). In what is in part a response to Bude, conservative publicist Ulrich Greiner asked in *Die Zeit* 'where the intellectual benefit for the nation was to be found' in all the outpourings of Grass and his colleagues on such topics as National Socialism (24 August 2006). The editor of the high-brow periodical *Merkur*, Karl Heinz Bohrer attempted to get to the heart of the matter.

Noting that many children of anti-Nazi families have remained silent about the past, he suggests that many of those who have spoken come from nationalist or even Nazi backgrounds. What is more, he detects the same strident tones in their admissions of guilt as those found at the time in declarations of faith in Nazism and its leaders. However, it has to be noted that Bohrer's critique goes beyond the person of Grass and even his contemporaries to include, for example, the 1968 generation.[2]

The role of Günter Grass in the literary and wider intellectual life of the Federal Republic is a major subject of this volume. This essay, whilst inevitably referring to Grass, will concentrate on his contemporaries in an attempt to determine how far it is possible to speak of a 'generation Grass' and, given the criticisms referred to above, to decide whether its influence has been benign or otherwise. A brief glance at the works of Grass and his contemporaries quickly reveals a number of common themes related to the times they have experienced. These include childhood and adolescence under National Socialist rule, German identity, particularly in the aftermath of National Socialism, the division of the country and the nature of the societies created in the new postwar Germany. If the example of childhood and adolescence is taken, then it was Grass, who arguably led the way with his 'Danzig Trilogy'. Especially in *Cat and Mouse*, he is at pains to show the role of an unhealthy Prussian-German tradition in fostering National Socialism. A similar idea is present in Siegfried Lenz's 1968 novel *German Lesson*, where the narrative consists of a (very extended) essay on the joys of doing one's duty imposed as a punishment on borstal boy Siggi Jepsen. Jepsen recalls how his father, a village policeman, unthinkingly did his 'duty', supervising the ban imposed by the Nazis on the painter Nansen, a figure clearly based on the German Expressionist Emil Nolde. Acceptance of the traditional Prussian virtue of 'doing one's duty' leads to slavish subservience to an evil ideology. By contrast, in the much later *Ein springender Brunnen* (A Springing Fountain, 1998), Martin Walser stresses the economic factors that led Germans to accept National Socialism. The first section of this clearly autobiographical novel is centred on the decision of the young protagonist's innkeeper mother to join the Nazi party. Her motive in doing so is to secure the trade of local Nazis and thus stabilise the family business. Yet another emphasis is provided by Christa Wolf's 1976 novel *Patterns of Childhood*. In this novel, the main character Nelly Jordan, who seems to be at least partly based on Wolf herself, returns to the town of her birth, which is now part of Poland. She is forced to confront the reality of her childhood under National Socialism, not least the enthusiasm of her fellow townspeople for the new rulers. In its insistence on such factors, the novel was on its appearance a challenge to the crude GDR historiography, which sought to lay the blame for Nazism at the door of a few capitalists, all of whom were subsequently conveniently located in the Federal Republic. The setting underlines the role of the former eastern territories in the work of the writers in question. Like Grass, Lenz was born in this area, his novel *The Heritage* of 1978 dealing with life there and attempts to preserve its memory in the postwar period. The deliberate burning down of the local history museum by its curator at the end of the novel can be seen as a criticism of the official policy in the Federal Republic of presenting those expelled from the east one-sidedly as victims of communist injustice.

On other issues, the varying stances adopted by the individual writers in question have been less a matter of different emphases than of the adoption of opposed views. One example is provided by the question of German unification. With the notable exception of Günter de Bruyn, most GDR writers of the generation in question, for example Hermann Kant (unsurprisingly given his role over the years as a cultural functionary close to the Party) and the mercurial Heiner Müller, did not welcome the prospect. Among GDR writers, Christa Wolf undoubtedly came closest to Grass in her rejection of unification. On the one hand, she aspired to a renewed GDR as a 'socialist alternative' to the Federal Republic, as it was formulated in the manifesto 'For our country' of 28 November 1989, of which she was a co-signatory. On the other, like Grass, she expressed fear that the unification process could raise spectres from the German past. In a December 1989 interview with a Dutch journalist, she said of current political developments: 'The nationalistic sounds and xenophobia which are now manifesting themselves are capable of driving me to despair, we know all about these sounds.'[3] By contrast, Martin Walser stood at the opposite end of the spectrum to Grass and Wolf. Throughout the 1980s, he had expressed his frustrations over the continuing division of Germany. Hence it was entirely logical that he should welcome the achievement of unity. The contrast with Grass was great enough for the radio station Norddeutscher Rundfunk to broadcast debates between the two men in 1995 and 1999. In these they disagree on such matters as the achievements of Helmut Kohl and whether unification should have led to more radical constitutional change. Somewhere between the positions of Grass and Walser was that adopted by fellow writer Hans Magnus Enzensberger. Although he welcomed the end of division, unlike his contemporaries he did not see it as a major historical event, be it for good or ill, that had to be seen in ideological or philosophical terms. His claim was that the Germans were not concerned about 'the intellectual space of the nation' or 'the idea of Socialism', but about pragmatic issues such as jobs and housing.[4] This was in turn a sign of political maturity on the part of the majority, who in Enzensberger's view were not likely to lapse into the excesses feared by Grass and Wolf.

Given the differences of opinion over such a significant issue, it seems difficult to speak of lasting generational unity in the area of political issues. Nevertheless, these varied contributions to the debate at the time of unification emphasise one important factor that links many of the writers under discussion here: their role as public intellectuals. It is of course Grass himself, who is most associated with such a role. Nevertheless, he was not the first to give voice to the idea of the intellectual as someone who might make a constructive contribution to society. The year 1961 saw the publication of a volume entitled *Ich lebe in der Bundesrepublik* (I live in the Federal Republic), a choice of words which implied that the contributors, incidentally from a variety of age groups, were identifying with the Federal Republic, rather than keeping their distance from a state which many had initially viewed with scepticism. In this context one of the most significant essays is that by Martin Walser with the title 'Sketch for a Reproach'. Rather than criticising the state or the government, Walser turns his fire on writers and intellectuals including himself, as the opening comment shows: '. . . we, however, sit around in Europe, generally leaning back in elegant armchairs'. In addition to the invocation of the material privileges enjoyed by intellectuals, the punctuation suggests a never-ending ritual that leads nowhere. The exact nature of Walser's critique becomes clear towards the end of the essay: 'What embarrassment we would be caused by a state, a society which invited us to co-operate!'. He then concludes by suggesting that the democracy of the Federal Republic needs any help intellectuals might be able to offer.[5]

It is this kind of sentiment that lies behind much of the volume, even if some contributors, not least Hans Magnus Enzensberger, appear to embrace the idea somewhat reluctantly. His essay 'Cursing under Palm Trees', which initially takes the form of a highly critical letter written in Rome, concludes with a postscript from Frankfurt, which says that a critical view from abroad cannot be maintained permanently. As for Walser, he began to follow his own advice by compiling a volume entitled *Die Alternative oder Brauchen wir eine neue Regierung?* (The alternative or do we need a new government?, 1961) in support of the Social Democratic Party (SPD) for the forthcoming federal elections. Although many of the essays are critical of the party, which by this time had abandoned many traditional socialist positions, the willingness of writers to support a mainstream party and participate in the democratic process did represent a turning point. Moreover, many of the writers associated with the 'generation Grass' did contribute: in addition to Walser, Grass himself, as well as Enzensberger and Lenz.

Any kind of political consensus did not, however, last long. By the second half of the decade, a wide gap had appeared between those, such as Grass, who continued along the path entered upon in the early 1960s and those who now saw this way as leading to failure. In 1967 Enzensberger spoke of the 'demise of a literature, of which the aspiration since 1945 has been to balance out, with its puny powers, the construction failures of the Federal Republic by criticism from within and through direct intervention in the mechanism of opinion formation and parliamentary elections.'[6] Enzensberger's espousal of revolutionary politics, for example at the time of May 1968 in Paris, unsurprisingly met with the disapproval of Grass. Shortly after the end of the Prague Spring, Grass attacked the New Left for its rejection of the Czechs' attempts, on the basis of compromise rather than ideology, to create democratic socialism, quoting Enzensberger's lukewarm attitude. He adds sarcastically: 'The Prague attempt at reform turned out to be feeble and unattractive, when measured against the aspirations of Hans Magnus Enzensberger.'[7] Martin Walser, who had long since broken with the SPD, took something of a middle position between Grass's pragmatism and the revolutionary élan that famously led Enzensberger to prefer Cuba to the United States. When the weekly news magazine *Der Spiegel* asked, following Enzensberger's apparent espousal of revolutionary politics in the essay quoted above, whether revolution was required in the Federal Republic, Walser replied: 'Who really wants evolution, must indulge in revolution.'[8] As he goes on to make clear, any revolution might take centuries to achieve. Despite the different kind of language, this does not seem too far removed from Grass's vision of progress coming at a snail's pace.

It is not proposed here to describe in minute, and possibly tortuous, detail the evolution of the political ideas of the writers in question, but rather to look at their attitudes to their roles in political debate. If Grass has continued unabashed to be the 'committed writer' par excellence, his contemporaries appear to have been more questioning. In the case of Enzensberger, it is instructive to look at the titles of some of his collections of essays, for example *Palaver* and *Zickzack*, and equally those of essays such as 'The End of Consistency', published in the collection *Politische Brosamen* (Political Bread Crumbs, 1982). It is these that provide ammunition to those who are happy to describe him as a 'chameleon' or some other such term. Whilst there are clear examples of inconsistencies in his work, it is possibly more accurate to speak of experimentation with ideas: specially, the adoption of extreme stances to try out arguments. One of his recent works, a rare example of a sortie into prose fiction on his part, provides a good example of that. *Josefine und ich* (Josefine and I, 2006) recounts the relationship that develops between the narrator and a former singer after he has rescued the much older woman from a street attack. When he subsequently embarks on a programme of regular visits, much of the time is spent in debating, which is marked by the contrast between the progressive liberal views of the narrator, in many ways a model citizen of the Federal Republic, and his interlocutor's extreme standpoints. The young economist is confronted with such statements as 'I have always been amazed that there are people who believe that the economy works rationally', whilst his idealism, expressed, for example, in his belief in public support for the arts evokes the response that culture is for the minority and: 'So-called normal people prefer noise and pleasure.' However extreme her views might be, on a number of occasions, there is reason to associate Josefine with positions adopted elsewhere by Enzensberger. One example is her comments on tyrants such as the Iraqi dictator Saddam Hussein:

> Humanity will never lack gangsters like that Iraqi bastard, she said. Nobody seems to blame them for ruining whole nations, at least not at the beginning of their careers. On the contrary, people cheer them.

She then goes on to talk in the same breath of Hitler, who, she claims, still fascinates the Germans, although he was really 'a monumental bore'.[9] The link between Hitler and Saddam was made by Enzensberger at the time of the First Gulf War in the essay 'Hitler's Emulator',[10] whilst the havoc wreaked by extremists is the subject of the more recent long essay *Schreckens Männer* (The Radical Loser), which stresses the way extremists, in this case Islamic fundamentalists, inevitably wreak havoc.[11]

What can be set against this? There is first of all the intertext contained in the name. Kafka's Josefine, it is implied, is something of a fraud; the same may be said of her namesake. Certainly, following her death and despite much research, the narrator finds very little evidence of the glittering career she seems to have claimed. However, as he says himself, this may not be the point. He is happy to have known such an unsentimental person. Here, too, it is possible to see a link with Enzensberger himself. His willingness to put forward unconventional ideas and his refusal to be tied down could be said to show a similar lack of sentimentality. In a 1995 interview in *Die Zeit* he spoke of this attitude in the following colourful terms: 'I don't wish to be the cloth for people to polish the world with' (4 February 1995). Many years earlier, in a polemic exchange with dramatist Peter Weiss at the time of the Vietnam War, he concluded his argument by saying: 'I am not an idealist. I prefer arguments to confessions of faith. I prefer doubts to emotions . . . I don't need views of the world which are free of contradictions. In cases of doubt reality decides.'[12] In a similar vein, his probably most anthologised poem 'Ins lesebuch für die oberstufe' (For the sixth-former's anthology), begins with the imprecation to read timetables rather than odes, because they are exact (from the collection *Gedichte* (Poems), 1962) It is in this area that some similarities with Grass emerge, specifically the rejection of ideology. Grass, regarding himself as a child of the Enlightenment, has always rejected abstract theories, something that can easily be linked to his generation's exposure to Nazism. Whereas this experience has led him to consistent pragmatism and a rejection of political extremism, Enzensberger, as has been shown, has preferred to try out a variety of positions, some of which may admittedly not have been too far from extremism. Moreover, as the quotation from the 1995 interview shows, he is reluctant to be regarded as an opinion former.

If links between Enzensberger and Walser are sought, then there are two areas that come into question: the desire to provoke and the questioning of the role of the intellectuals. Many of the points raised above in connection with Enzensberger, not least his choice of titles, imply provocation, whilst Walser's career has been marked by a series of what might be called scandals. The most recent and arguably most intense was the furore provoked by his 2002 work *Tod eines Kritikers* (Death of a Critic), which was read in some quarters as an anti-Semitic attack on Marcel Reich-Ranicki.[13] Moreover, Reich-Ranicki himself had described Walser many years earlier, in his collection of essays on *Deutsche Literatur in West und Ost* (German literature in East and West, 1963) as a 'provocateur'. Such a categorisation should not of course be accepted at face value; nevertheless, Walser's comment in the magazine *Bunte* before the publication of *Tod eines Kritikers* – 'Even the title is scandalous' (21 February 2002) – does suggest that he had some inkling of possible reactions and that his subsequent expressions of surprise were somewhat disingenuous.

As for the question of intellectuals, it is not difficult to find disparaging comments about intellectuals in the works of both Enzensberger and Walser; for example, Enzensberger's comments on unification referred to above include a swipe at both politicians and intellectuals, who have great difficulties in accepting the new political maturity of the people. In the case of Walser, questioning of aspects of intellectual life has frequently been a feature of his work. In the 1966 novel *The Unicorn*, much of the narrative is devoted to a satire of intellectual milieus. The narrator, Anselm Kristlein, having changed from being a salesman to a writer, is a frequent participant in panel discussions, which he realises are little more than a ritual, both in terms of the language used and the standpoints adopted. There seems little doubt that the narrative here is based on Walser's own experiences in the early 1960s when he emerged as a public intellectual. The author's doubts about this role are also expressed in the 1968 essay 'Commitment as a Compulsory Subject for Writers', written, however, at the time when he was a strong campaigner against the American presence in Vietnam. Indeed,

Walser has always been faced with the dilemma of trying to reconcile his frequently expressed distaste for much that passes for intellectual debate with his own wish to contribute to such debate. The two sides of the coin are visible in the controversial speech he made on being awarded the 'Peace Prize of the German Book Trade' in 1998. The title *Erfahrungen beim Verfassen einer Sonntagsrede* (Experiences while drafting a Sunday speech) is itself, through the word 'Sonntagsrede', a questioning of such public appearances, as the term implies a kind of discourse for the time when serious business is not being enacted.[13] This apparent scepticism is also reinforced by the way the title implies it is a speech about a speech or about speeches in general. However, by using the occasion not just to reflect on what is expected on such occasions but also to criticise what he sees as the prevailing intellectual discourse, specifically in relation to the Nazi past, he also puts forward his own viewpoint that the Federal Republic should increasingly be regarded as a 'normal' country.

Since unification, Walser has increasingly railed against the world of 'opinion', criticising the superficiality of the mass media and attacking intellectual discourse. These comments from a 2000 essay, which reflect his increasing emphasis on his right to individuality: 'I do not have to represent anything. I have nobody to enlighten except myself', seem at loggerheads with Grass's public role, based on enlightenment and what he sees as the principles of the Enlightenment. Whilst Walser shows respect for the latter, he now sees the term as having been misappropriated by leftist intellectuals for 'buying into the *zeitgeist*'.[14] There is no reason to think Walser is specifically thinking of Grass at this point. Despite their differences on such issues as unification, at a personal level the two have been quick to leap to each other's defence: Grass rejecting the accusations of anti-Semitism made against Walser and Walser defending Grass's belated admission of his Waffen SS membership. Nevertheless, an intellectual gap has developed, encapsulated in Grass's criticism of Walser's championing of individuality based on personal feeling at the expense of historical consciousness, as shown in the title of an interview in which Grass criticises his colleague over his attitude to unification: 'Viel Gefühl, wenig Bewußtsein' (Plenty of feeling, too little awareness, 1990).

In contrast to Grass, Enzensberger and Walser, Lenz would appear to have largely withdrawn from the role of public intellectual. As early as 1973, in a speech to the recently formed West German Writers Association he expressed doubts about the socio-political role of writers, suggesting that their efforts to change society had achieved little. His solution at that time was for them to relinquish their role as outsiders. In fact, with Grass, he had already accompanied Chancellor Brandt to Poland in 1970 for the signing of the Warsaw Treaty and, ten years later, again with Grass, he took part in a pre-election discussion with Chancellor Schmidt. More recently, however, it is in his novels that he has taken up political issues. His 2003 work *Fundbüro* (Lost property office), for instance, concludes with the utopian vision of a whole district rising up to put a group of xenophobic louts to flight. Insofar as the novel also contains criticism of a protagonist who seeks only to occupy a peripheral position in society, Lenz can be said to have remained true to the ideal of commitment, even if his voice is generally absent from topical debates.

Given the lack of a public sphere in the GDR, it was also largely through their fictional writing that GDR writers of Grass's generation expressed their ideas on politics and society. Admittedly, there were occasional semi-public exchanges, whilst they could show their loyalty or otherwise by participation in official institutions, Günter de Bruyn, for example, withdrawing from the executive of the GDR Writers' Union in 1978. When there were debates, at the time of the East German authorities' expulsion of singer-songwriter Wolf Biermann, for example, in 1976 and the meetings about nuclear arms between East and West German writers in the early 1980s, not everything permeated through the controlled mass media, with the transcripts of the debates on nuclear arms in particular not being made available to the general public. It is then to their fictional works that one must look to determine the existence or not of any shared attitudes among the writers of the generation in question here. In general terms, it is possible to speak of a parallel development to that in the Federal Republic: by the 1960s a degree of identification with the state was followed by the adoption of a greater variety of stances in subsequent decades. To the extent that they were into their thirties at the time of the building of the Berlin Wall, East German writers of Grass's generation can be said to have made a conscious decision to stay in the GDR. Christa Wolf's *The Divided Sky* of 1963 is in fact the story of one woman's decision to remain in the GDR, whilst Hermann Kant's *Die Aula* (The Great Hall) of 1965 shows approvingly how people with little school education could, in the early years of the GDR, make good this deficiency through the system of 'worker and peasant faculties' and go on to occupy important positions in society. By the 1980s, more critical voices were to be heard. Günter de Bruyn's ironically entitled *Neue Herrlichkeit* (New Splendour) of 1984 presents such a critical picture of the GDR's elite, in particular the spoiled son of a functionary, that it is hard to believe that it was published in the country. If at the opposite extreme, Hermann Kant's *Die Summe* (The Sum) of 1987 reflects unchanging identification, particularly in its favourable juxtaposition of the GDR with the Federal Republic, Christa Wolf's criticism of certain aspects of GDR society, despite her continuing loyalty, is arguably more to the fore in a work such as *Kassandra* of 1983, which was not well received by the GDR's cultural old guard, than in her earlier works.

One other writer of this generation, Heiner Müller (born, like Wolf, in 1929) is difficult to fit into any generalised view of GDR literature. In 1961 he was expelled from the Writers' Union, whereupon, over the next three decades, he established himself as a leading dramatist in the Federal Republic and beyond. Unlike his older colleague Stefan Heym, whose situation was in many ways similar, he did not suffer judicial persecution, but even enjoyed permission to travel freely between the two German states. This may have had to do with his collaboration with the Stasi, the extent of which still remains somewhat unclear. He certainly did not suffer the same opprobrium as Christa Wolf, whose cooperation was minimal, despite the scepticism he showed towards unification. In the light of this and his criticisms of capitalism, he certainly cannot be classified as entirely disloyal to the GDR.

At the time of unification GDR literature was the subject of much criticism in what became known as the 'German-German literature conflict', with Christa Wolf (in)famously being dubbed as the 'state poet' of the GDR by conservative West German critics such as Ulrich Greiner and Frank Schirrmacher. Since this term implied uncritical identification with the state, it was clearly incorrect, although it could have been applied to her colleague Hermann Kant. It might be more accurate to speak of Wolf and some others of her generation as the 'poets of the people' of the GDR, who, like they, once the Wall was built, largely identified with their state, albeit critically. This is not to say that the situations of the two groups were the same; GDR citizens had no choice, as long as the Soviet Union wished to maintain the GDR. They were making the best of a bad job. By contrast, from the late 1970s, many critical writers had the chance to leave the GDR. Those under discussion here did not do so. Nevertheless, ironically, their criticisms of their state can be said to have contributed to the rebellious mood that developed in the 1980s and found expression in the demonstrations of 1989.

In this area of the relationship between poets and people, it would also be possible to speak in similar terms of the Grass generation in the Federal Republic. It too contributed, by some of the activities referred to above, to growing identification with the Federal Republic by helping to create a public sphere increasingly marked by democratic debate. It is true that writers of an older generation had given themselves such a mission; it is only necessary to think of Hans Werner Richter, both as co-editor of the postwar periodical *Der Ruf* and as convenor of the Group 47. That he did not achieve as much as, for example, Grass has to do with his moderate talent as a writer, but also arguably with the time. Grass, Walser and contemporaries came to the fore when the Federal Republic, having reached economic maturity, was ready for cultural maturity. Their potential influence was increased not just by their literary talents, but also by the way they were in many ways representative of those of a similar age, who increasingly played a role in the development of the country. None belonged, for example, to traditional social elites, the influence of which had been reduced by Nazism, but came from lower middle-class backgrounds, that is to say the social class that was increasingly to the fore. As noted above, Grass and Lenz had been displaced by the changes to Germany's frontiers after 1945, a fate shared by many of their fellow citizens. If their choice of subjects reflected their backgrounds and experiences, their concerns were shared by many others with similar biographies. Nazism and its legacy are only one such subject; the struggles of Walser's protagonists to make their way under changed economic circumstances can also be said to have been representative. Finally, if this generation contributed to the creation of the Federal Republic's public sphere, it also knew how to remain in the limelight, hence the frustration of Menasse and Kumpfmüller referred to at the beginning of this chapter.

There remains the question posed by Greiner of 'intellectual benefit', a term somewhat difficult to deal with in a context where benefit cannot be quantified, unlike when it is used in such expressions as cost benefit analysis. Nevertheless, that the Federal Republic is an open society, which, unlike Turkey and arguably Austria, not to mention those countries with a troubled colonial history, has faced up to its past, and that the Grass generation has contributed to this, can be said to come into this category of 'intellectual benefit'. Space has not permitted much discussion here of aesthetic achievement, the other area which would seem to come into this particular equation. Unsurprisingly, given the length of their careers, most of the authors under discussion here have written works of varied quality. Nevertheless, there can be no doubting their overall achievements. It is only necessary to remove from any history of post-1945 German literature the names most referred to here and ask, in the words of one of Christa Wolf's titles plus question mark, 'Was bleibt?' (What is left?) to have an idea of their massive achievements.

Postscript

This chapter began with a reference to the debate following Günter Grass's admission of membership in the Waffen SS. A similar debate erupted a year later when the issue was whether Walser, Lenz and the cabaret artist Dieter

Hildebrandt had knowingly enrolled as members of the Nazi party. Given the denials of those concerned and the disagreements among historians about whether it was possible for someone to be made a member without their knowledge, the allegations remained unproven. However, once again the importance of the experiences of the generation under discussion here was evident. Its importance for the subjects themselves emerged in a joint interview by Grass and Walser in *Die Zeit*, which used as its title, admittedly somewhat out of context, but presumably with his approval, Walser's comment: 'Wer ein Jahr jünger ist, hat keine Ahnung' (People just a year younger than us don't have a clue, 14 June 2007). As for outside observers, those under attack could take comfort from words in, of all places, *Die Welt*, part of the conservative Springer group of publications which had for so long been the ideological enemy of the Group 47 and the generally left-wing writers associated with it. Writing for the 1 July 2007 edition under the heading 'Generation Flakhelfer' (the anti-aircraft auxiliary generation), Sven Felix Kellerhof states: 'What is beyond question is that the possible membership of the Nazi party of Lenz, Walser and Hildebrandt in no way puts their life-time achievements into question.'[15] The use of the phrase 'life-time achievements' represents an admission from an unlikely quarter of the importance of those concerned.

Notes

1. Martin Greiffenhagen and Sylvia Greiffenhagen, *Ein schwieriges Vaterland. Zur politischen Kultur im vereinigten Deutschland* (Munich and Leipzig: List, 1993), esp. p. 441.

2. Karl Heinz Bohrer, 'Politisches Sprechen ohne Scham', *die tageszeitung*, 4 November 2006, p. 22. This is a shortened version of the original essay, which appeared in *Merkur* in November 2006.

3. Christa Wolf, 'Schreiben im Zeitbezug', in Wolf, *Im Dialog* (Frankfurt am Main, Luchterhand, 1990), pp. 131–57, at p. 135. See also 'Für unser Land', ibid., pp. 170–1.

4. Hans Magnus Enzensberger, 'Gangarten. Ein Nachtrag zur Utopie' in Enzensberger, *Zickzack* (Frankfurt am Main: Suhrkamp, 1997), pp. 64–78, at p. 77.

5. Martin Walser, 'Skizze zu einem Vorwurf', in Wolfgang Weyrauch (ed.), *Ich lebe in der Bundesrepublik* (Munich: List, 1961), pp. 110–14, at p. 110 and p. 114.

6. Hans Magnus Enzensberger, 'Klare Entscheidungen und trübe Aussichten', in Klaus Wagenach *et al.* (eds), *Vaterland, Muttersprache* (Berlin: Wagenbach, 1979), pp. 254–7, at p. 256.

7. Günter Grass, 'Die Prager Lektion', in Günter Grass, *Über das Selbstverständliche* (Munich: Deutscher Taschenbuch Verlag, 1969), pp. 181–5, at p. 183.

8. Quoted in *Vaterland, Muttersprache*, p. 260.

9. Hans Magnus Enzensberger, *Josefine und ich* (Frankfurt am Main: Suhrkamp, 2006), pp. 56, 44 and 91.

10. Hans Magnus Enzensberger, 'Hitlers Wiedergänger', in Klaus Bittermann (ed.), *Liebesgrüße aus Bagdad* (Berlin: Tiamat, 1991), pp. 44–52.

11. Hans Magnus Enzensberger, *Schreckens Männer* (Frankfurt am Main: Suhrkamp, 2006). Extracts in English in *signandsight* as 'The Radical Loser', http://print.signandsight.com/features/493.html, accessed 19 December 2007.

12. Peter Weiss and Hans Magnus Enzensberger, 'Eine Kontroverse', *Kursbuch 6* (1966), pp. 165–76, at p. 176.

13. See Stuart Parkes, '*Tod eines Kritikers*. Text and Context', in Stuart Parkes and Fritz Wefelmeyer (eds.), *Seelenarbeit an Deutschland. Martin Walser in Perspective* (Amsterdam, New York: Rodopi, 2004), pp. 447–68.

14. Martin Walser, 'Über das Selbstgespräch', in Martin Walser, *Ich vertraue. Querfeldein* (Frankfurt am Main: Suhrkamp, 2000), pp. 125–50, at p. 128 and p. 129.

15. Sven Felix Kellerhof, 'Generation Flakhelfer. Gab es Kollektivaufnahmen in die NSDAP?', *Die Welt*, www.welt.de/kultur/article989523 (accessed 17 December 2007).

GUIDE TO FURTHER READING

The suggested reading below is for the most part in English and is not exhaustive.

Abbott, S. H. 'Günter Grass' *Hundejahre*: A Realistic Novel about Myth', *Germanic Quarterly*, 55:2 (1982), 212–20

Adler, H. 'Günter Grass: Novemberland', in H. Adler and J. Hermand (eds.), *Günter Grass: Ästhetik des Engagements* (New York: Peter Lang, 1996), pp. 93–109

Arnds, P. *Representation, Subversion, and Eugenics in Günter Grass's The Tin Drum* (London: Boydell & Brewer, 2004)

Bauer Pickar, G. (ed.). *Adventures of a Flounder: Critical Essays on Günter Grass's Der Butt* (Munich: Wilhelm Fink, 1982)

Beard, R. 'The Art of Self-Construction: Günter Grass's Use of Camus and Orwell in "Headbirths or The Germans Are Dying Out"', *Comparative Critical Studies*, 1 (2004), 323–36

Beyersdorf, H. E. 'The Narrator as Artful Deceiver: Aspects of Narrative Perspective in *Die Blechtrommel*', *Germanic Review*, 55 (1980), 129–38

Bowers, M. A., *Magic(al) Realism* (London and New York: Routledge, 2004)

Brady, P. V., T. D. McFarland and J. J. White (eds.). *Günter Grass's 'Der Butt': Sexual Politics and the Myth of Male History* (Oxford University Press, 1989)

Braun, R. *Constructing Authorship in the Work of Günter Grass* (Oxford University Press, 2008)

Brockmann, S. *Literature and German Reunification* (Cambridge University Press, 1999)

'Cultural Critique in the Two Unifications of Germany', in R. Speirs and J. Breuilly (eds.), *Germany's Two Unifications: Anticipations, Experiences, Responses* (Basingstoke: Palgrave Macmillan, 2005), 62–75

Bruce, J. C. 'The Motif of Failure and the Act of Narrating in Günter Grass's *Ortlich betäubt*', *Modern Fiction Studies*, 17 (1971), 45–60

Brunssen, F. *Das Absurde in Günter Grass' Literatur der achtziger Jahre* (Würzburg: Würzburger Wissenschaftliche Schriften, 1997)

'Günter Grass and the Cold War', *Journal of Contemporary European Studies*, 15:3 (2007), 149–62

'Speak Out! – Günter Grass as an International Intellectual', *Debatte: Journal of Contemporary Central and Eastern Europe*, 15:3 (2007), 321–42

Bullivant, K. (ed.). *The Future of German Literature* (Oxford and Providence, RI: Berg, 1994)

Burns, R. and W. van der Will. *Protest and Democracy in West Germany: Extra-Parliamentary Opposition and the Democratic Agenda* (New York: St. Martin's Press, 1988)

'Intellectuals as Cultural Agenda-Setters in The Federal Republic', *International Journal of Cultural Policy*, 12:3 (2006), 294–322

Butler, G. P. '*The Call of the Toad* and the Szczepan Phenomenon', *German Life and Letters*, 47:1 (1994), 94–103

Cory, M. 'Sisyphus and the Snail: Metaphors for the Political Process in Günter Grass' *Aus dem Tagebuch einer Schnecke* and *Kopfgeburten oder Die Deutschen sterben aus*', *German Studies Review*, 6 (1983), 519–33

Coury, D. 'Transformational Considerations in the Filmic Adaptation of Günter Grass' *Die Blechtrommel*', *New German Review: A Journal of Germanic Studies*, 8 (1992), 74–84.

Cunliffe, W. G. 'Grass and the Denial of Drama', in A. Leslie Willson (ed.), *A Günter Grass Symposium* (Austin, TX and London: University of Texas Press, 1973), pp. 60–70

Günter Grass (New York: Twayne, 1980)

Danow, D. K. *The Spirit of Carnival: Magical Realism and the Grotesque* (Lexington, KY: University Press of Kentucky, 1995)

Dittberner, H. 'Das Gedicht als Werkstück. Ein Essay zur Lyrik des Günter Grass', in H. L. Arnold (ed.), *Günter Grass. Text + Kritik* (Munich: edition text + kritik, 1988), pp. 19–26

Durzak, M. (ed.). *Zu Günter Grass: Geschichte auf dem poetischen Prüfstand* (Stuttgart: Klett, 1985)

Frisch, M. *Sketchbook 1966–1971*, trans. by Geoffrey Skelton (New York: Harcourt Brace Jovanovich, Inc, 1974), pp. 253–60

Garde, B. ' "Die Frauengasse ist eine Gasse, durch die man lebenslang geht." Frauen in den Romanen von Günter Grass', in H. L. Arnold (ed.), *Günter Grass, Text + Kritik* (Munich: edition text + kritik, 1988), pp. 101–7

Grass, G. *Ateliers des metamorphoses. Entretiens avec Nicole Casanova* (Paris: Belfond, 1979)

Selected Poems 1956–1993, trans. by Michael Hamburger (London: Faber, 1999)

Grass, G. and Helen Wolff, *Briefe 1959–1994*, ed. D. Hermes (Göttingen: Steidl, 2003

Hall, K. *Günter Grass's 'Danzig Quintet': Explorations in the Memory and History of the Nazi Era from Die Blechtrommel to Im Krebsgang* (Oxford: Peter Lang, 2007)

'Günter Grass's 'Danzig Quintet', *Alltagsgeschichte*, and the historiography of National Socialism', in R. Braun and F. Brunssen (eds.), *Changing the Nation: Günter Grass in International Perspective* (Würzburg: Königshausen & Neumann, 2008)

Hamburger, M. 'Moralist and Jester: The Poetry of Günter Grass', in A. L. Willson (ed.), *A Günter Grass Symposium* (Austin, TX and London: University of Texas Press, 1971), pp. 71–86

After the Second Flood: Essays in Modern German Literature (New York: St Martin's Press, 1986)

Hamilton, E. C. 'Deafening Sound and Troubling Silence in Volker Schlöndorff's *Die Blechtrommel*', in Nora M. Alter et al. (eds.), *Sound Matters: Essays on*

The Acoustics of Modern German Culture, (New York: Berghahn, 2004), pp. 130–41

Head, D. 'Volker Schlöndorff's *Die Blechtrommel* and the "Literaturverfilmung" Debate', *German Life and Letters*, 36:4 (1983), 347–67

Hermes, D (ed.). *Die Deutschen und ihre Dichter: Günter Grass* (Göttingen: Steidl, 1995)

Hickethier, K. 'Der Film nach der Literatur ist Film. Volker Schlöndorffs *Die Blechtrommel* (1979) nach dem Roman von Günter Grass (1959)', in Franz-Josef Albersmeier et al. (eds.), *Literaturverfilmungen* (Frankfurt am Main: Suhrkamp, 1989), pp. 183–98

Hille-Sandvoss, A. *Überlegungen zur Bildlichkeit im Werk von Günter Grass* (Stuttgart: Akademischer Verlag, 1987)

Hilliard, K. F. 'Showing, Telling and Believing: Günter Grass's *Katz und Maus* and Narratology', *The Modern Language Review*, 96:2 (2001), 420–36

Hoffmeister, W. 'Dach, Distel und die Dichter: Günter Grass' Das Treffen in Telgte', *Zeitschrift für deutsche Philologie*, 100 (1981), 274–87

Hollington, M. *Günter Grass: The Writer in a Pluralist Society* (London: Marion Boyars, 1980)

Hughes, J. '"The Tin Drum": Volker Schlöndorff's "Dream of Childhood"', *Film Quarterly*, 34:3 (1981), 2–10

Hummel, C. 'Gegen rhetorische Ohnmacht: die Rezeption politischer Lyrik von Günter Grass aus den 6oer Jahren', *Wirkendes Wort*, 50:1 (2000), 48–66

Hutchinson, P. 'Politics and Playfulness in Günter Grass's Sonnet Cycle *Novemberland*', *German Quarterly*, 78:2 (2005), 224–39

Jürgensen, M. *Über Günter Grass. Untersuchungen zur sprachlichen Rollenfunktion* (Bern and Munich: Francke Verlag, 1974)

Kane, M. 'In the Firing Line: Günter Grass and his Critics in the 1990s', in M. Kane (ed.), *Legacies and Identity: East and West German Literary Responses to Unification* (Oxford: Peter Lang, 2002), pp. 181–97

Keele, A. F. *Understanding Günter Grass* (Columbia, SC: University of South Carolina Press, 1988)

Kniesche, T. *Die Genealogie der Post-Apocalypse: Günter Grass' Die Rättin* (Vienna: Passagen Verlag, 1991)

Krolow, K. 'Günter Grass in seinen Gedichten', in M. Jürgensen (ed.), *Grass: Kritik — Thesen – Analysen*, Queensland Studies in German Language and Literature IV (Bern and Munich: Franke Verlag, 1973), pp. 11–20

Lawson, R. H. *Günter Grass* (New York: Frederick Ungar Publishing Co., 1985)

Leeder, K. 'Günter Grass's Lateness: Reading Grass with Adorno and Said', in F. Brunssen and R. Beard (eds.), *Changing the Nation: Günter Grass in International Perspective* (Würzburg: Königshausen & Neumann, 2008)

Mason, A. L. *The Skeptical Muse: A Study of Günter Grass's Conception of the Artist* (Bern: Peter Lang, 1974)

'The Artist and Politics in Günter Grass's *Aus dem Tagebuch einer Schnecke*', *The Germanic Review*, 51 (1976), 105–20

Mayer, C. 'Von "Unterbrechungen" und "Engführungen". Lyrik und Prosa in "Butt" und "Rättin"', in H. L. Arnold (ed.), *Günter Grass. Text und Kritik, Zeitschrift für Literatur*, 1988 (originally 1971), pp. 86–94

Mayer, S. 'Günter Grass in Calcutta: Der intertextuelle Diskurs in "Zunge Zeigen"',
in G. Labroisse and D. von Steckenburg (eds.), *Günter Grass; Ein europäischer
Autor?* Amsterdamer Beiträge zur neueren Germanistik 35 (Amsterdam,
Atlanta: Rodopi, 1992), pp. 151–61

Meier, A. 'Eine "irenische Provokation": *Novemberland* von Günter Grass und der
'Niedergang der politischen Kultur', *Zeitschrift für deutsche Philologie*,
120 (2001), 252–84

Mews, S. (ed.). *The Fisherman and His Wife: Gunter Grass's The Flounder in
Critical Perspective* (New York: AMS Press, 1983)

Miles, K. *Günter Grass Studies* (London: Vision Press, 1975)

Moeller, R. 'Sinking Ships, the Lost *Heimat* and Broken Taboos: Günter Grass and
the Politics of Memory in Contemporary Germany', *Contemporary European
History*, 12:2 (2003), 147–81

Neuhaus, V. 'Das Chaos hoffnungslos leben . . . Zu Günter Grass' lyrischem Werk',
in M. Durzak (ed.), *Zu Günter Grass: Geschichte auf dem poetischen
Prüfstand*, LGW-Interpretationen 68 (Stuttgart: Ernst Klett Verlag, 1985),
pp. 20–45

Günter Grass (Stuttgart: Metzler, 1992)

Schreiben gegen die verstreichende Zeit. Zu Leben und Werk von Günter Grass
(Munich: Deutscher Taschenbuch Verlag, 1997)

Niven, B. *Facing the Nazi Past* (London: New York, Routledge, 2001)

O'Neill, P. *Critical Essays on Günter Grass* (Columbia, SC: University of South
Carolina Press, 1988)

Günter Grass Revisited (New York: Twayne Publishers, 1999)

Parkes, S. *Writers and Politics in West Germany* (London: Palgrave Macmillan,
1986)

Parkinson Zamora, L. and W. B. Faris (eds.). *Magical Realism: Theory, History,
Community* (Durham, NC and London: Duke University Press, 1995)

Paver, C. 'Lois Lane, Donald Duck and Joan Baez: Popular Culture and Protest
Culture in Günter Grass's *Örtlich Betäubt*', *German Life and Letters*,
50 (1997), 53–64

'Jesus in the Market Place: Ethical Capitalism in Günter Grass's *Unkenrufe*', in A.
Williams, S. Parkes and J. Preece (eds.), *Literature, Markets and Media in
Germany and Austria Today* (Bern: Peter Lang, 2000), pp. 71–84

Petrescu, C. 'The Narrative of Apocalypse: Mathias Horx' *Es geht voran. Ein
Ernstfall Roman* and Günter Grass's *Die Rättin*', *New German Review*,
15/16 (1999–2001), 53–82

Petz, B. 'Günter Grass since the *Wende*: German and International', in A. Williams,
S. Parkes and J. Preece (eds.), *German-Language Literature Today:
International and Popular?* (Oxford: Peter Lang, 2000), pp. 67–84

Preece, J. 'Sexual-Textual Politics: The Transparency of the Male Narrative in "Der
Butt" by Günter Grass', *The Modern Language Review*, 90:4. (1995), 955–66

'Seven Theses on "Der Fall Fonty"', in C. Flanagan and S. Taberner (eds.), *1949/
1989: Cultural Perspectives on Division and Unity in East and West*
(Amsterdam: Rodopi, 2000), pp. 215–30

The Life and Work of Günter Grass: Literature, History, Politics (Basingstoke:
Palgrave, 2004)

Reddick, J. *The 'Danzig Trilogy' of Günter Grass: A Study of The Tin Drum, Cat and Mouse and Dog Years* (London: Secker and Warburg, 1975)

Reed, D. *The Novel and the Nazi Past* (New York and Frankfurt: Lang, 1985)

Reich-Ranicki, M. *Günter Grass. Aufsätze* (Zürich: Ammann, 1992)

Reid, J. H. *Writing without Taboos: The New East German Literature* (Oxford and Providence, RI: Berg, 1990)

Rushdie, S. 'Günter Grass', in *Imaginary Homelands. Essays and Criticism 1981–1991* (Harmondsworth: Penguin, 1991), pp. 273–82.

Ryan, J. 'Resistance and Resignation: A Reinterpretation of Günter Grass' *Katz und Maus*', *Germanic Review*, 52 (1977), 148–65

  'Beyond *The Flounder*: Narrative Dialectic in *The Meeting at Telgte*, in S. Mews (ed.), *The Fisherman and His Wife: Gunter Grass's The Flounder in Critical Perspective* (New York: AMS Press, 1983), pp. 39–53

Schade, R. E. 'Günter Grass's *Mein Jahrhundert*: Histories, Paintings, and Performance', *Monatshefte*, 96:3 (2004), 409–21

Shafi, M. '"*Gezz will ich ma erzähln*": Narrative and History in Günter Grass's *Mein Jahrhundert*', *Gegenwartsliteratur: Ein germanistisches Jahrbuch*, 1 (2002), 39–62

  Vom privaten Motivkomplex zum poetischen Weltentwurf. Konstanten und Entwicklungen im literarischen Werk von Günter Grass (1955–1986) (Würzburg: Königshausen & Neumann, 1994)

Stolz, D. 'Nomen est omen: *Ein weites Feld* by Günter Grass', in A. Williams, S. Parkes and J. Preece (eds.), *Whose Story? — Continuities in Contemporary German-Language Literature* (Bern: Peter Lang, 1998), pp. 149–66

Taberner, S. 'Feigning the Anaesthetization of Literary Inventiveness: Günter Grass's *Örtlich Betäubt* and the Public Responsibility of the Politically Engaged Author', *Forum for Modern Language Studies*, 34:1 (1997), 69–81

  Distorted Reflections: The Public and Private Faces of the Author in the Work of Uwe Johnson, Günter Grass and Martin Walser, 1965–1975 (Amsterdam and Atlanta, GA: Rodopi, 1998)

  '"Sowas läuft nur im Dritten Programm": Winning Over the Audience for Political Engagement in Günter Grass's *Kopfgeburten oder Die Deutschen sterben aus*', *Monatshefte*, 91:1 (1999), 84–100

  '"Normalization" and the New German Consensus on the Nazi Past: Günter Grass's *Im Krebsgang* and the "Problem" of German Wartime Suffering', *Oxford German Studies*, 31 (2002), 161–86

Vondung, K. *The Apocalypse in Germany*, trans. by Stephan D. Ricks (Columbia, MO: University of Missouri Press, 2000)

Vormweg, H. *Günter Grass. Mit Selbstzeugnissen und Bilddokumenten* (Hamburg: Rowohlt, 1986)

Voznesenskig, A. 'Der Dichter Günter Grass', in D. Hermes and V. Neuhaus (eds.), *Günter Grass im Ausland: Texte, Daten, Bilder zur Rezeption* (Frankfurt am Main, Luchterhand, 1990), pp. 148–54

Weber, A. *Günter Grass's Use of Baroque Literature* (Leeds: Maney, 1995)

Wertheimer, J. (ed.). *Günter Grass: Wort und Bild* (Tübingen: Konkursbuchverlag, 1999)

Wirth, A. 'Günter Grass and the Dilemma of the Documentary Drama', in A. Leslie Willson (ed.), *A Günter Grass Symposium* (Austin, TX and London: University of Texas Press, 1973), pp. 18–31

Wißkirchen, H. *Günter Grass: Schriftsteller und Bildkünstler* (Lübeck: Grass-Haus, 2007)

Zimmermann, H. *Günter Grass unter den Deutschen: Chronik eines Verhältnisses* (Göttingen: Steidl, 2006)

INDEX

Cambridge Companions to . . .

AUTHORS

TOPICS